PERIODS

for Leon,
who "grew me"
and makes everything possible

PERIODS

From Menarche to Menopause

Sharon Golub

SAGE PUBLICATIONS
International Educational and Professional Publisher
Newbury Park   London   New Delhi

For information address:

SAGE Publications, Inc.
2455 Teller Road
Newbury Park, California 91320

SAGE Publications Ltd.
6 Bonhill Street
London EC2A 4PU
United Kingdom

SAGE Publications India Pvt. Ltd.
M-32 Market
Greater Kailash I
New Delhi 110 048 India

Printed in the United States of America

Library of Congress Cataloging-in-Publication Data

Golub, Sharon.
    Periods : from menarche to menopause / Sharon Golub.
        p. cm.
    Includes bibliographical references and index.
    ISBN 0-8039-4205-2 (cl.) — ISBN 0-8039-4206-0 (pbk.)
    1. Menstruation. 2. Menstruation—Psychological aspects.
    I. Title.
    [DNLM: 1. Menstruation. WP 550 G629pj]
    QP263.G65   1992
    612.6'62—dc20

                                                        91-46821

92 93 94 95 10 9 8 7 6 5 4 3 2 1

Sage Production Editor: Astrid Virding

Contents

Acknowledgments

I would like to express my gratitude to the National Library of Medicine for its support of my work on this book through a Special Scientific Project Grant NLM-EP (1 K10 LM 00072-01), and to the College of New Rochelle for a sabbatical leave that enabled me to complete the project.

Special thanks are due to many people:

To Alice Dan, Leon Golub, Rosemary Reiss, and Barbara Sommer for their thoughtful and helpful reviews of part or all of the manuscript and for their moral support as well.

To the students and patients who have asked interesting questions and described their experiences with menstruation.

To Judy Abplanalp, Joan Chrisler, Mary Anna Friederich, Sheryle Gallant, Leslie Gise, Madeleine Goodman, Elissa Koff, Fredi Kronenberg, Phyllis Mansfield, Anne Petersen, Nancy Reame, Jill Rierdan, Esther Rome, Kathy Ulman, Rhoda Unger, Ann Voda, Nancy Woods, and the other members of the Society for Menstrual Cycle Research, as well as the many other colleagues who generously shared their research findings, opinions, and advice.

To friends and family who offered support and encouragement when things moved slowly and I thought the book would never be done—especially to my mother, Ray Bramson, my sister, Bunny Feigenbaum, and to my dear friends Evie Bielenson, Patia Burns, Eileen

Canty, Joan Carson, Vicki Condro, Rudy Eckhardt, Rita Freedman, Gloria Goldstein, Joyce Hauser, Hollie Hurrell, Kathleen Jones, Gloria Kahn, John Lukens, Jackie Plumez, Ona Robinson, Linie Steckler, and Russel Taylor (who provided an earlier version of the title and haunted me regularly).

To the men in my life who nurture me: my husband and best friend, to whom this book is dedicated; and my sons, Lawrence and David, who, to their surprise, found that their women friends are quite interested in books about menstruation.

To the College of New Rochelle Library Staff, past and present: Mark Haber, Lynne Karen, Rosemary Lewis, Charlotte Moslander, Pat Rader, Jim Schleifer, and Fred Smith. And to Steve Bradley for bringing his creativity and computer graphics skills to some of the figures. They are helpful, wonderful people, individually and collectively.

Foreword

Twenty-five years ago, before the latest wave of the women's movement began, a book like *Periods* could not have been written, for most of the information simply did not exist. One of the lesser-known effects of that social movement for women's equality was the legitimation of women's experience as a suitable topic for research—and the resulting expansion of our knowledge about menstruation has been extremely rapid. No other available volume presents such a systematic overview of this remarkable increase in information about women's experiences with the menstrual cycle.

Several aspects of this new knowledge deserve particular recognition. The earliest feminist critics of the older medical literature on menstruation emphasized that the menstrual cycle had been pathologized and that we needed to have information about the *normal* characteristics of this universal female experience. Based on stereotypes, women were assumed to be less capable during menstruation, or too upset to cope premenstrually, or at the mercy of their "raging hormones" during the menopausal transition. Now we have good research debunking these myths, and Dr. Golub presents a particularly well-balanced perspective on areas that are still controversial, such as premenstrual syndrome and postmenopausal hormone replacement therapy.

Another set of insights from the new research concerns the social psychology of menstruation—the ways in which old, distorted views of menstrual function can continue to influence women's lives. Making widely available the information contained in *Periods* would be an important first step in countering these inaccuracies and in creating a social understanding of menstrual phenomena that supports women, whatever their diverse experiences. Although menstruation has traditionally been difficult to talk about in "polite society," it has occupied a central place in social definitions of women's bodies. Of course, it is next to impossible to change ideas that cannot be talked about, so breaking these taboos is likely to have a healthy effect on the social context for women.

Finally, the importance of the menstrual cycle to women's sense of themselves—who they are, how they function, how they are related to the rest of the cosmos—needs to be acknowledged. Such an admission is still not politically wise, for women are still disadvantaged in contemporary society by being different from men. Nevertheless, we can envision a world in which admitting that we experience monthly changes will not be used against us, but will be seen as a healthy sensitivity and a way to maximize our effectiveness. The knowledge contained in this book can help bring about such a world.

—ALICE J. DAN
Center for Research on Women and Gender
The University of Illinois at Chicago

Preface

There has been a remarkable increase in knowledge about menstrual-cycle phenomena over the past 20 years. In large part this is the result of the women's movement and research by women (and men) who are studying normal aspects of women's bodies, trying to separate stereotypes from reality.

In writing this book my aim was to look at old and new ideas about the menstrual cycle and attempt to evaluate just what the influence of menstruation on women's lives really is. Myths and folktales abound. Religious practices dating back over the centuries are still with us. Menstrual huts in which menstruating women are isolated exist even today in certain cultures. Some communities perpetuate attempts to keep the menstruating woman from touching grapes or tools for fear of her spoiling them. And there are still taboos about avoiding sexual intercourse with a woman at "that time of the month" lest the male be made unclean by his contact with her.

Modern-day advertisers in the United States often play to our anxieties and create new ones as well. Ads tell women to take care, not to have an accident, in other words, "Beware of the blood!" Psychological studies have found that both women and men have negative attitudes about menstruation, but whether these bad feelings are related to menstrual discomfort or to cultural taboos is still being explored. It is interesting that literature, the great translator of human experience, had practically ignored menstruation altogether until relatively recently. However, we have begun to see books that directly address the way in which women experience menstruation, among them: Toni Morrison, *The Bluest Eye*; Alix Kates Shulman, *Memoirs of a Prom Queen*; Judy Blume, *Are You There God? It's Me, Margaret*; Marilyn French, *The Women's Room*; Maxine Kumin, *Why Can't We Live Together Like Civilized Human Beings*; Barbara Raskin, *Hot Flashes*; and Alice Walker, *The Color Purple*.

A great deal is known about the biology of the cycle: the anatomy of the reproductive system, the hormonal changes, and the complex feedback system that exists between the brain and the body regulating menstruation. This seems to be the area professionals are most comfortable with, and it is the least controversial.

Yet, when we move on to clinical and psychosocial research, there is far less agreement about what we do and do not know. Much of the earlier clinical research was seriously flawed. For example, in some studies subjects were not randomly selected, and they were often gynecological or psychiatric patients. Authors often generalized findings from these groups to all women, drawing conclusions that were obviously wrong and misleading.

Lately, with greater numbers of women entering the work force, among them more female physicians, and with many more women now actively engaged in doing research, what was once the exclusive domain of the male gynecologist has become a subject of interest and scrutiny by researchers in a wide variety of disciplines, including anthropology, sociology, psychology, and physiology, as well as nursing and medicine. A bibliography citing 1,485 references titled, *Human Performance: Women in Nontraditional Occupations and the Influence of the Menstrual Cycle*, was published by the United States Army Human Engineering Laboratory in 1980. Most of these citations refer to work published in the previous 10 years, and now there is even more new information. There have been major conferences devoted to menarche, dysmenorrhea, menopause, toxic shock syndrome, and premenstrual syndrome. The sheer quantity of this research presents a problem: It must be evaluated, synthesized, and communicated in an understandable way to the people working in all of these different fields as well as to lay people. Unfortunately, interdisciplinary communication is sorely lacking. For the most part, behavioral scientists do not understand the advances that have been made in medical science. And physicians, who tend to emphasize pathology rather than normalcy, are not aware of social scientists' studies of normal women. Thus women themselves need to know more about these findings in order to foster their own health and well-being and to counter the ever-present claims that they are physically, emotionally, and/or intellectually handicapped during menstruation.

As recently as 1982, a Latin American diplomat rose in the United Nations General Assembly and referred to British Prime Minister Margaret Thatcher's actions in the Falkland Islands as related to "the glandular system of women." Loudly and clearly, and on the basis of sound research, the myths about raging hormones and menstrual impairment must be dispelled.

In the past, research focused on pathology: menstrual pain, and premenstrual symptoms. The emphasis in most published reports, both in the professional and lay literature, has been on symptoms that impaired the abilities of women. More recent research argues against the idea that menstruation is debilitating for most women. However, the new research does not deny that many women do experience unpleasant symptoms and discomfort during the premenstrual and menstrual phases of the cycle. Indeed, much of the medical research has targeted the problem of what can be done to alleviate women's discomfort. The new focus in both the medical and behavioral science research is on what can be done for women rather than what is wrong with women. The latter approach, more common in the past, tended to use menstruation—the major difference between the sexes—as a way of man's maintaining control over women and justifying claims of male superiority. Menstrual cyclicity was sometimes used as a vehicle for keeping women in their place.

Old myths die hard, and menstruation is still considered a taboo topic by many people in our culture. Talking about menstrual periods makes some people quite uncomfortable. Witness a few of the euphemisms that are often used to describe menstruation: "The Curse," "Falling Off the Roof," "Riding the Rag." Yet the menstrual cycle is part of every woman's life for about 37 years, approximately from the ages of 13 to 50. And, with the advent of more effective methods of controlling female fertility, women are pregnant less often and hence experience menstruation more often than they have at any other time in history. Because changes in hormone levels, reproductive organs, other body systems, mood, and behavior accompany the cycle, it seems important for women and the men with whom they live to know how these cyclic changes influence their lives. My hope is that this book will lead to a greater understanding of women and the meaning of menstruation in women's lives.

1

The Meaning of Menstruation

A Cross-Cultural View

Menstrual myths, misconceptions, and taboos are universal, even today. In Alice Walker's novel *The Color Purple*, an American Black woman who is working as an African missionary writes a letter to her sister about getting her "friend" and the cramps that come along with it. She says, "I must still keep going on as if nothing is happening, or be an embarrassment to Samuel, the children, and myself. Not to mention the villagers who think women who have their friends should not even be seen" (Walker, 1982, p. 172). Thus she notes the village custom of isolating menstruating women from the rest of the community.

The contemporary female reader struggles with a modern version of the same dilemma: How to handle menstruation? Do women want "special treatment?" And are we willing to pay the price for being "different," that is, different from men? Or is it preferable to deny any effect, carry on, and pay no attention to symptoms of menstrual distress? (Of course, there is another option: If we do not accept the notion that male is normative and female is "other," we can accept our periods as a normal part of being a woman and pay attention to getting our needs met rather than feeling that there is something wrong with us when we are menstruating.)

1

Until relatively recently, separation of menstruating women from the rest of the population was a common experience, and it is still practiced in some areas of the world. In Ethiopia, for example, menstruating women are considered unclean and are sent to a special hut for a week to avoid contaminating others. When large numbers of Ethiopian Jews emigrated to Israel, they were confronted with a difficult adjustment. There were no menstrual huts, so menstruating women were forced to stay in their apartments with their families, which made everyone very uncomfortable.

Menstrual blood has been considered both magical and poisonous. Sometimes the menstruating woman has been seen as a danger to the community, which is why some communities developed avoidance customs in order to protect themselves. Menstrual taboos have been defined as "beliefs or superstitions about dangers inherent in menstruation" (Stephens, 1967). These beliefs, and the rituals that arise to accompany them, are extremely common and widespread. Many of them have been described in detail; thus Frazer (1951) writes:

> The Dieri of Central Australia believe that if a menstruating woman were to eat fish or bathe in a river, the fish would all die and the water would dry up.
>
> In Muralug, one of the Torres Straits Islands, a menstruating woman may not eat anything that lives in the sea or the fisheries will fail.
>
> In Galela, women may not enter a tobacco field or the plants will be attacked by disease.
>
> Among the Minangkabauers of Sumatra, it is believed that if a menstruating woman were to go near a rice field, the crop would be spoiled.
>
> Among some tribes in South Africa, it is thought that cattle will die if their milk is drunk by a menstruous woman. The cattle will also die if they were to walk on ground stained with menstrual blood.
>
> Other tribes believe that if a menstruating woman visits a well, the water will dry up.

Among most tribes of Indians in North America, it was the custom for menstruating women to retire from the village and live in special menstrual huts. They lived apart, eating and sleeping by themselves, and abstaining from any contact with men. One group, the Indians of the Hudson Bay Territory, required menstruating women to wear long hoods covering their heads and breasts. They were not allowed to touch any objects used by men, for their touch would defile the object and subsequently lead to the man's illness or death.

Even in a matriarchal society—such as the Minaro, a tribe of about 800 people living between India and Pakistan in the Himalayas— eating utensils are shunned if they have been used by "impure" people such as menstruating or pregnant women or women who have recently given birth (Asia's lost tribe . . . , 1984).

In a review of menstruation taboos in 64 societies, Ford found that nearly one-third would forbid menstruating women to prepare food for men. More than 20% of the societies isolated menstruating women in some sort of special shelter, and very few societies considered the menstruating woman a suitable sex partner. The most lenient societies were those that limited menstruation taboos to abstinence from sexual intercourse (Ford & Beach, 1951).

In his study of menstrual taboos, Stephens (1967) found that there was a pattern to certain menstrual customs that occurred in widely scattered areas. If menstruating women were segregated and supposed to spend their menstrual periods in a place apart, such as a menstrual hut, then they would also be forbidden to cook for their husbands; menstrual blood was believed to be dangerous to men, and sexual intercourse during menstruation was taboo.

Although Stephens studied primitive cultures, many of these customs and beliefs continued to exist among "more civilized nations." Sir James Frazer cites several in his book *The Golden Bough* (1951, p. 702):

> Amongst the civilized nations of Europe the superstitions which cluster round this mysterious aspect of woman's nature are not less extravagant than those which prevail among savages. In the oldest existing cyclopedia—the *Natural History of Pliny*—the list of dangers apprehended from menstruation is longer than any furnished by mere barbarians. According to Pliny, the touch of a menstruous woman turned wine to vinegar, blighted crops, killed seedlings, blasted gardens, brought down the fruit from trees, dimmed mirrors, blunted razors, rusted iron and brass (especially at the waning of the moon), killed bees, or at least drove them from their hives, caused mares to miscarry, and so forth. Similarly, in various parts of Europe, it is still believed that if a woman in her courses enters a brewery the beer will turn sour; if she touches beer, wine, vinegar, or milk, it will go bad; if she makes jam it will not keep; if she mounts a mare, it will

miscarry; if she touches buds they will wither; if she climbs a cherry tree, it will die. In Brunswick people think that if a menstruous woman assists in the killing of a pig, the pork will putrefy. In the Greek Island of Calymnos a woman at such times may not go to the well to draw water, nor cross a running stream, nor enter the sea. Her presence in a boat is said to raise storms.

Nevertheless, some things have changed. For example, menstruating women in an Indian village who were prohibited from preparing food a generation ago no longer experience this prohibition (Frazer, 1951).

Occasionally customs are seen that are designed to protect the menstruating woman herself. Among some old Italian communities, for example, women are seen as more vulnerable to psychological and physical disturbances when menstruating. They are told not to go out in the cold, or take cold baths, or wash their hair, or do heavy housework. They are supposed to drink wine to restore their blood and avoid sour foods. The flow of blood is to be encouraged. Thus, it is thought that sanitary napkins should not be changed too often, for clean ones are believed to stop the blood.

However, even among groups that protect women, the menstruating woman is still seen as a danger to the community. It is thought that the bread she bakes will not rise; her tomato sauce will not turn out well; flowers that she touches will wither; her gaze will dull mirrors, blunt knives, and cause pregnant animals to abort. What power!

Many of these myths and the primitive injunctions that go along with them persist. In a 1973 study of attitudes toward menstruation in Iran, researchers questioning high school girls found that 39% complained about menstruation being dirty or annoying. The girls were particularly troubled by the injunction against bathing. They said that they "hate the uncleanness" and "want to get clean" as soon as they can (Bahrami & Izadi, 1973).

A striking example of a contemporary menstrual taboo exists in Portugal. In 1982, Lawrence wrote about a town in southern Portugal that has strict community taboos relating to the curing of pork. A menstruating woman is thought to be able to cause the pork to spoil simply by looking at it. She need not intend to spoil the pork when she looks at it, but because she is menstruating this power is beyond her control. Therefore, menstruating women are excluded from the preparation of pork sausages. Women organize a team of male and female workers who will be involved in the sausage making. All female members are asked when they arrive, "Are you able to see?" If the woman is not menstruating, she answers, "I can see," and she enters. The group then gets on with the slaughtering of the pigs and the preparation of the sausages. An interesting part of the Portuguese menstrual taboo is the women's role in its maintenance. These women both accept the negative (but powerful) image of themselves and use it to control an important community custom, for it is the women who regulate the sausage making.

Some menstrual injunctions exist in contemporary American culture. Perhaps the most common is the avoidance of sexual intercourse during menstruation. About half the U.S. population believes that one should abstain. Do these people fear contamination or illness? Probably not. The likelihood is that they attribute their behavior to religious beliefs or aesthetic considerations. But does this taboo really stem from the belief that menstruating women are dirty? And do women think of themselves that way too?

The Role of Language

The myths and taboos associated with menstruation can readily be seen in the words we use to describe it. Language both reflects and shapes the way we see ourselves and the world around us. Things that are psychologically stressful, such as excretory functions, are often couched in euphemistic terms. For example, we speak of the powder room, rest room, or water closet, when we really mean the toilet. Menstruation apparently makes us uncomfortable too. Thus studies of menstrual expressions in both the United States and other countries have shown that there is a variety of terms to describe the "discharging of blood, secretions, and tissue debris from the uterus that recurs . . . at approximately monthly intervals" (*Webster's Seventh New Collegiate Dictionary*, 1972) (see Table 1.1).

A file on American menstruation folkspeech in the Folklore Archives at the University of California, Berkeley, contains 128 euphemistic expressions. Although there is some repetition in these terms, that is still a lot of words to describe one naturally occurring biological event (Ernster, 1975).

TABLE 1.1 Menstrual Expressions

Cyclicity	*References to a Visitor*
Period	I've Got My Friend
Monthlies	Aunt Tilly Is Here
That Time of the Month	George Is Visiting
Those Days	My Redheaded Friend
Old Faithful	Somebody's Visiting
The Moon	Got the Grannies
Negative References	*References to Menstrual*
The Curse	*Accoutrements*
Unwell	Riding a White Horse
Sick Time	Riding the Cotton Pony
I've Got the Misery	Plug Is In
Under the Weather	White Cylinder Week
Cramps	On the Rag
Weeping Womb	Back in the Saddle
Wrong Time of the Month	Cotton Bicycle
Monthly Troubles	
I'm Indisposed	*Sexual Unavailability*
I Fell Off the Roof	The Red Flag Is Up
The Nuisance	Too Wet to Plough
The Plague	Flying Baker
Package of Troubles	Can't Go Swimming
	Tide's In
Positive Expressions	Tide's Out
The Red Flag Is Up	Red Light
(meaning: not pregnant)	Ice-Boxed
Celebrating	Cherry in Sherry
Red Letter Day	Covering the Waterfront
Safe Again	Beno (There'll be no fun)
This Is My Day	
Mother Nature's Gift	
I've Got My Flowers	
The Benefit	
Woman's Friend	

Researchers have found that the terms reflect several broad themes. Most commonly used are those referring to cyclicity. In English we have "period," "monthlies," and "that time of the month." In other languages, such as Italian, Yiddish, Polish, and German, the reference is to some variation of "the monthly time."

Technical terms, such as "menstruation" or "menses" are more likely to be used by older women rather than teenagers, who more often say, "I've got it" or allude to a visitor or friend ("George is here" or "I've got my friend"). Other commonly used categories include references to menstrual paraphernalia. Tampons are described as "plugs" and sanitary napkins may be referred to as "cotton ponies" or "Mickey Mouse mattresses."

The old familiar term "the curse" is still with us, though it is rarely used by young women. Nor are they likely to use references to menstrual disability, such as "being sick" or "unwell," terms that were common 20 or 30 years ago.

Girls and women often view the different terms as a secret language, a way of maintaining privacy when boys are around. And women have a much wider variety of terms for menstruation than do men. Which term is used at any particular time is influenced by where the woman is, with whom, and her mood at the moment.

Among men, menstrual expressions tend to have sexual and sometimes derogatory connotations. "On the rag," for example, tends to be a male expression. It is generally learned by males from other males and is usually interpreted as describing someone who is irritable and moody. Thus some menstrual euphemisms perpetuate a view of the menstruating woman as impaired, physically and psychologically. Other terms allude to sexual unavailability, for instance, "the red flag is up," "too wet to plough," or "flying baker" (a reference to the navy signal meaning keep off). It is also interesting that females tend to learn menstrual expressions early, around the time of menarche, whereas males learn them later—in high school, college, or the armed service.

In reviewing the list of menstrual expressions, it is easy to see that most of the terms are negative. They seem to be intended to maintain secrecy or avoid embarrassment. There are very few positive expressions. Why? Why "the Curse?" One might more logically think that because menstruation represents fertility, it would be called "the Blessing." But no, it is the curse, stemming from the notion that it was inflicted upon Eve, and passed on to all women, for her sins in the Garden of Eden. This idea is then reinforced by the Bible and other religious works.

Religious Origins

The Koran refers to menstruation as an illness and says that men must not go near women until they are clean. Muslim women are not permitted to say their prayers during menstruation. The physical presence of a woman at any time defiles a Buddhist shrine. On the first day of her period a Hindu woman is considered unclean and a pariah, and throughout her period it is a sin for her to think of the gods. In Bali, a menstruating woman may not enter the temple, not even the small garden-temple courtyard in her own home.

Among the Zoroastrians there are strict rules about menstruation, which some think had a strong influence on Judaism and Christianity. A monotheistic faith, Zoroastrianism is a religion that originated in Persia in the late seventh century B.C. It is still practiced in modified form among the Ghibers of Iran and among the Parsees of India. In the creation story of the Zoroastrians, menstruation is bound up with evil, and the menstruating woman must therefore be treated very carefully. She is isolated from the rest of the community and required to stay in a place set apart for menstruants, where she must remain for as long as she is menstruating plus one day. During this time she must wear special clothing, which, if possible, should come from a woman who has given birth to a stillborn child or is otherwise polluted, for instance, by contact with a corpse, and has been purified by going through an extensive cleansing process of several months' duration. The idea here is that this clothing, though clean, is only fit for a menstruating woman or a man who is unclean. There are rules about the preparation of the menstruant's food, how much she is to eat, and how it is to be brought to her. She is not fed very much, and the person who brings the food to her must be careful not to be contaminated by physical contact with her. Thus a distance of three paces is maintained, and the food is given to the menstruant on a metal implement so that the pollution cannot be transmitted to the sacred elements: Earth, Fire, and Water. Dry dust is spread on the ground so that she will not touch it directly, and she must be separated from fire, water, and people as well. She is not allowed to look out of the hut, for her look can defile anything. Sexual intercourse with a menstruating woman is surrounded by the strongest taboo: It is one of the greatest sins. All of these rules were, of course, generated by the males of a patriarchal community who described menstruation and childbirth—uniquely female functions—as unhealthy or abnormal (Culpepper, 1974).

Among the ancient Hebrews, menstruation was also looked upon as a sickness, perhaps reflecting ancient beliefs that menstruation was the result of a wound. In the Hebrew Bible, menstrual blood is considered a form of pollution (*The Holy Scriptures*, 1955). It is "an issue" and like all "issues," or excretions, from the human body, it is considered unclean. Similarly, the menstruous woman is unclean.

> And if a woman have an issue, and her issue in her flesh be blood, she shall be put apart seven days: and whosoever toucheth her shall be unclean until the even.
>
> And every thing that she lieth upon in her separation shall be unclean; every thing also that she sitteth upon shall be unclean.
>
> And whosoever toucheth her bed shall wash his clothes, and bathe himself in water, and be unclean until the even.
>
> And whosoever toucheth any thing that she sat upon shall wash his clothes, and bathe himself in water, and be unclean until the even.
>
> And if it be on her bed, or on any thing whereon she sitteth, when he toucheth it, he shall be unclean until the even.
>
> And if any man lie with her at all, and her flowers be upon him, he shall be unclean seven days; and all the bed whereon he lieth shall be unclean. (Leviticus 15:19-24)

> And thou shalt not approach unto a woman to uncover her nakedness, as long as she is put apart for her uncleanness. (Leviticus 18:19)

The position of women in both the Old and New Testaments is based upon these rules in Leviticus. An entire section of the *Mishnah* (the collection of Jewish traditions and law, in this case those involving family purity) is primarily concerned with menstruation. A woman is supposed to take care to know when she is menstruating and to observe all the laws about menstruation, lest she transmit her uncleanness to others. The woman's responsibility includes self-examination twice a day, morning and evening, and before intercourse, using test rags to be sure that she is free from any sign of blood. Intercourse during menses, even if unintentional, was considered a serious offense.

In biblical times menstrual taboos kept women out of the temples. And even today Orthodox Jewish women are expected to observe the *niddah* laws and follow a prescribed ritual in dealing with menstruation. According to Sheila Siegel, the menstruating woman becomes *niddah* (a term meaning isolation or separation), and she is considered spiritually unclean from the onset of menstruation until the end of her period plus seven clean days (Siegel, 1985/1986). During this time she is forbidden physical contact with her husband. They must have no physical interactions; they may not sit next to each other, a third person must sit between them; and they may not sleep in the same bed, or lie in each other's beds, or undress in front of each other. The woman is not to wear rouge, in order to reduce her attractiveness to her husband. And coitus during menstruation is strictly prohibited. There is also a "no touching" injunction. Therefore, at meals, when one pours a drink for the other it is to be done with the left hand, or when the other is not present; they must not hand anything from one to the other.

Once the menstrual flow has ceased, the woman must examine herself to be sure that no blood remains in the vagina. The woman washes the genital area prior to the examination and may douche if she wishes to. She must then take a cloth, the type and size of which are specified, and insert it deeply into the vagina. Moving slowly and carefully, she presses the cloth against the wall of the vagina, in a circular, top to bottom search, to be sure that all the bleeding has completely stopped. Once she has established that her menstrual flow has ended, the woman enters the period of seven "clean" days.

To be sure that the seven clean days are stain free, the woman must wear white undergarments, sleep on white sheets, and do daily internal examinations as described above. At the end of the seven clean days the woman is ready to go to the *mikvah*, a ritual bath in which the woman totally immerses herself and says a prayer. Siegel points out that since going to *mikvah* is usually preparatory to having sexual relations, women go after sundown and do not talk about their *mikvah* visits.

Thus theoretically traditional Jewish women could spend half their adult lives in a state of ritual uncleanness. One might expect that all of this ritualization of menstruation would negatively influence women's attitudes toward it. But apparently this is not so. A recent study of college-educated women who participate in the *mikvah* ritual found that these women were no more likely than a comparable group of nonobservant Jewish women to have negative attitudes toward menstruation (Siegel, 1985/1986). Moreover, Sacks (1974), who considers herself both an Orthodox Jew and a feminist, has written in defense of *mikvah*. She says, "We do this because God commanded it." She denies that women are unclean and goes on to say, "The woman is not kept out of the synagogue, nor is she forbidden to carry out most of her activities. Only the sexual relationship is forbidden."

Datan (1986), who studied Jewish law in an attempt better to understand the menstrual taboos, concluded that the imagery of the Talmudic writers—who describe the different colors of menstrual blood with great clarity—suggests that the menstruating woman was potentially very enticing, having an appeal to be fought off only through elaborate proscriptions. Thus ritual impurity may be seen as an expression of power: sexual power.

Nevertheless, many Orthodox Jewish women have grown up with messages that can hardly be called positive. Susan Schnur (1985), writing in *The New York Times*, remembers being told that "if a menstruating woman passed between two men, one of the men would die, and that if a menstruating woman looked hard at a mirror she could make drops of blood appear on the glass." Power again, yes, but this time scary and dangerous in an aggressive way.

Christian women fared only slightly better with regard to menstruation. Although Jesus was more enlightened than some of his contemporaries, and even went so far as to share a drinking cup with a Samaritan woman who was considered unclean, his followers continued to observe the customs of their time, generally clinging to the Old Testament belief that women were unclean and imperfect as a consequence of menstruation (Delaney, Lupton, & Toth, 1988). Menstruating women were excluded from the Jewish synagogues and from communion in the early days of the Christian Church. In fact, as late as the twentieth century, Greek Orthodox women were prohibited from taking communion when they were menstruating.

A recurring question among the early clergy seemed to be whether a menstruating woman should be allowed to enter a church or receive communion. In A.D. 597 Pope Gregory the Great did eliminate the old Levitical prohibitions. Gregory said that menstruation was both a mark of sin—the curse of Eve—and a necessary companion to women's fertility. He argued in women's favor saying, "If no food is impure to him whose mind is pure, why should that which a pure-minded woman endures from natural causes be imputed to her as uncleanness?" (Wood, 1981). He went on to say that a woman must not be prohibited from entering a church during her periods. Thus menstruation was still viewed as an infirmity, but at least it was no longer sinful. Gregory considered menstruation a normal and natural phenomenon. Yet as recently as 1963, in the *Handbook of Moral Theology*, a resource for men studying for the priesthood, purity remains an issue. Apparently the menstruating woman is unclean, but menstruation does not render the body so unclean as to prevent the receiving of Holy Communion (McGrath, 1972).

Is religion an important influence on women's attitudes toward menstruation today? Rothbaum and Jackson (1990) explored this question in a study of Jewish, Protestant, and Catholic women who were members of religious congregations in the Southeastern United States. They found that the less religious women were more likely to describe menstruation as "bothersome," but overall, the three groups of women were quite similar in their menstrual attitudes, symptoms, and expectations.

Medicine and Science: A Historical Perspective

Albertus Magnus, a leading theologian and scientist in the thirteenth century, was among the first to ascribe some benefit to menstruation. Life expectancies had changed, with women living longer than men, and Albert argued that in the curse of Eve there was a hidden mercy. As a consequence of menstruation, women were able periodically to "purge the poison from their humors in a monthly effusion of blood. Therefore, the curse now allows them *per accidens* to live longer than men" (Bullough & Voght, 1973).

Yet, for the most part, medical and scientific thought about menstruation did not differ very much from that espoused by religion. Aristotle saw menstruation as a sign of female inferiority. In his view of conception, women provided the material, formless matter that accumulated and became menstrual blood, unless this matter was imposed upon by semen contributed by the male, adding form and creating a fetus. Aristotle noted that "the physical part, the body, comes from the female, and the soul comes from the male." Saint Thomas Aquinas took this one step further, saying "the seed was the man's seed and the child was the man's child" (Bullough & Voght, 1973).

Pliny, the Roman historian who wrote in the first century A.D., also had some positive things to say about menstrual blood. He saw it as a cure for goiter, gout, and some other disorders. However, Pliny's ideas about reproduction centered on Aristotle's theory that the menses were necessary to nourish the fetus. Unaware of the role of the ovum, he explained infertility among women who did not menstruate as occurring because these women did not have the substance necessary for an infant to form.

It was not until the nineteenth century that John Power of London postulated that ovulation and menstruation were connected. And even as late as the 1890s, when the first experimental work on human hormones was being done, many American physicians did not understand that the ovaries triggered menstruation. In 1861, E. F. Pfluger demonstrated that menstruation did not occur in a woman whose ovaries had been removed. But it was not until the twentieth century that estrogen was discovered and hormonal processes as well as the timing of ovulation became more fully understood (Allen & Doisy, 1923).

Medicine did not help free women from the negative attitudes imposed by religion. Nineteenth-century doctors often began their discussions of menstruation by telling about the ancient myths that attributed magical powers to menstrual blood. They referred to its "rank smell" and then, while denying that there was any truth to the myths, they would go on to argue that menstruation made women weak, sick, and dependent. These same physicians warned that menstruation could drive some women temporarily insane, causing them to destroy furniture, attack family and strangers, and even kill their infants. Some even suggested incarceration for these poor women who were subject to such "excessive menstrual influence" (Allen & Doisy, 1923).

One of the most influential spokesmen on menstrual disability was Edward H. Clarke, professor of pharmacology at Harvard Medical School and a fellow of the American Academy of Arts and Sciences. In 1873, he wrote that although women have the right to do anything of which they are physically capable, they could not be educated and still retain good health. Clarke believed that any mental activity during menstruation would interfere with ovulation and menses. To support his thesis, he described several of his patients, young women who were ill, presumably because of hard study. He concluded that brain work destroyed feminine capability. Thus women who concentrated their energies upon education tended to lose their maternal instincts—and, presumably, their capacity as well (Bullough & Voght, 1973).

Although there were many immediate and unfavorable reactions to Clarke's ideas, he did influence a great many people. His book, *Sex in Education*, went through 17 editions over the next 13 years. Some physicians who followed Clarke exaggerated his position, among them, T. S. Clouston, a physician in Scotland who wrote about the dangers of education for women. Clouston claimed that it was medically accepted that females are more delicate than men and that "overstimulation" of the female brain will cause all sorts of difficulties, among them—stunted growth, nervousness, difficult childbirth, and even insanity.

Finally, in 1885, the Massachusetts Labor Bureau released the first statistical report on the health of American college women. Of the 705 women studied, 78% were in good or excellent health, 5% were in fair health, and 17% were in poor health. The report concluded that the health of college women did not differ from the national average (Bullough & Voght, 1973).

However, despite the publicity given to this study, attitudes about women, menstruation, and education changed very slowly. Educated women were still thought to have an insufficiently feminine frame of mind. Gynecologists talked about menstrual waves that affected the entire female being. Health experts spoke of women being dominated by their ovaries. And, in 1900, George J. Engelmann, in his presidential address before the American Gynecological Society, said that female schools should recognize the instability and susceptibility of girls during menstruation and provide rest for them at this time.

More myths and misinformation were generated by Kellogg in his book *Plain Facts for Old and Young*. He described menstruation as a time in women's lives when they were susceptible to morbid influences and vulnerable to serious derangements; he noted that many young women have permanently injured their constitutions by excessively taxing their brains during menstruation; and he warned about the dangers of exposure to cold, keeping late hours, and improper diet and dress.

Bullough and Voght (1973) have noted that as the movement for female emancipation grew, so did physicians' talk of the frailties of women. "Hard study killed sexual desire in women," according to a president of the Oregon State Medical Society in 1905. Intellectual activity also brought on hysteria, neurasthenia, dysmenorrhea, and difficult childbirth. In 1907, the *New York Medical Journal* carried an authoritative article by Dr. Ralph W. Parsons saying that higher education could only lead to physical decay and ill health in women. These medical arguments of course served to justify keeping women in their traditional roles.

Contradictory evidence was available. A careful study of the health of college and noncollege women had been published by the American Statistical Association in 1900-1901. Clarke and other physicians and scientists simply chose to ignore it. Even G. Stanley Hall, one of the outstanding psychologists of the early twentieth century, dismissed the statistical studies as inaccurate because of his own bias toward female fragility. Hall strongly opposed coeducation. He advocated special schools for girls where they could observe a monthly, four-day Sabbath during their menstrual periods. (Actually, what Hall suggested—a period of rest with the active cultivation of idleness—sounds like good advice for all of us, women and men, but it has no particular relevance to menstruation.)

Feminists of the time did try to dispute these pseudo-scientific reports and recommendations. Using both logic and scientific research, they concluded that the medically accepted facts were not facts at all, but rather attitudes derived from myths and religious dogma about menstruation and verified by physicians' experiences with women who had gynecological problems.

Mosher disputed the belief that increased activity was bad for women's health. In a study of college women between 1890 and 1920, Mosher found that during the earlier time period girls had more menstrual problems. She zeroed in on the destructive nature of women's clothing at the time—tight corsets and heavy layers of skirts—and she related the restriction of motion because of these clothes to a higher incidence of dysmenorrhea. She noted that as waists grew larger, menstrual difficulties diminished (Bullough & Voght, 1973).

In 1877, Jacobi addressed the question of rest for working women during menstruation. She concluded that frequent short rest periods were indeed desirable, but they had no special relationship to the period of menstrual flow (men would also work better if given frequent short breaks; Martin, 1987).

However, as late as 1931, authoritative books continued to say that only a minority of women were free from disability during their menstrual periods and that women should rest and refrain from physical activity for at least two days. Menstrual education has come a long way since then. Nurses, health educators, and others provide information about the anatomy and physiology of normal menstruation to girls in the schools and respond to their questions, clarifying many of the more common misconceptions. Young women are better informed today than they have ever been before. Unfortunately, some authorities are not yet similarly well informed, demonstrating that medical and scientific beliefs change slowly and sometimes get mixed up with political and social beliefs.

One of the more recent physician blunders was committed by the Baltimore doctor Edgar Berman, who in 1970 said, "If you had an investment in a bank, you wouldn't want the president of your bank making a loan under these raging hormonal influences at that particular period. Suppose we had a President in the White House, a menopausal woman President, who had to make the decision of the Bay of Pigs, which was, of course, a bad one, or the Russian contretemps with Cuba at that time?"

Never mind that Thomas Jefferson had periodic headaches; Abraham Lincoln had periodic depressions; and John F. Kennedy had a serious hormonal disorder, Addison's disease. All women are subject to cyclical hormonal changes and are therefore suspect—even to some of the so-called experts.

Why then should we be surprised when, in 1982, *The New York Times* reported that a Latin American diplomat, Jorge Enrique Illueca, soon to be president of the General Assembly of the United Nations, said during a heated debate on the war in the Falkland Islands that "Prime Minister Margaret Thatcher's actions had to be understood in the context of 'the glandular system of women.'" (Goldman, 1983).

Clearly women are different from men, and women do menstruate. However, to generalize and attribute to this difference a basic physiological and psychological weakness is bad science and perilous medicine. Though rooted in primitive and religious beliefs, attitudes toward menstruation must change.

Attitudes Toward Menstruation Today

In view of the long religious, scientific, and medical tradition of taboos and negative attitudes toward menstruation, it is not surprising to find that many negative beliefs persist in contemporary American culture. Despite the notable increase in frankness with which sexuality is discussed, many people are still uncomfortable talking about menstruation.

Although we no longer believe that menstrual blood can dull swords or cause a dog to become rabid, some misconceptions about the influence of menstruation on health, personality, and intellectual function are still with us. In 1981, the Tampax Corporation commissioned a large-scale study of attitudes toward menstruation (*The TAMPAX Report*, 1981). More than a thousand Americans ranging in age from 14 to 65 and representing all ethnic, educational, and economic segments of the population were interviewed by telephone. Some of the findings were:

- Most Americans are still reticent talking about menstruation.
- Only 35% said that it was appropriate to talk about menstruation at the office.
- More than a third said that even at home women should conceal the fact that they are menstruating.
- Eight percent said that they believed women should avoid contact with others when menstruating. (While 8% is only a small proportion of those sampled, it does represent 14 million Americans.)
- Men were more likely than women to think that it is socially acceptable to discuss menstruation openly; 38% of the men thought it acceptable as opposed to 27% of the women.

The TAMPAX Survey revealed other interesting findings as well. For example, most Americans believe that women experience a significant degree of stress during menstruation and that menstruation affects women both physically and emotionally. A substantial number believe that women cannot function normally when menstruating. And a considerable minority of both women and men still believe that it is necessary for women to restrict their physical activities and that it is harmful for women to bathe or swim while menstruating.

People's educational backgrounds and attitudes about equal opportunities for women were related to their perceptions of menstruation. Those who saw menstruation as most restrictive and debilitating were more likely to be less educated, less affluent, more politically conservative, and in the youngest or oldest age groups (55 and over, or 14 to 17).

TABLE 1.2 Highlights of the Tampax Report

Belief	Women	Men
Menstruation affects a woman's ability to think	31%	39%
Women can function as well at work when menstruating	81%	66%
Menstruation is generally painful	56%	39%
Menstrual pain is psychological rather than physical	24%	20%
Women look different when menstruating	25%	28%
Women have a different scent while menstruating	47%	51%
Women should not have intercourse while menstruating	56%	51%
It is harmful for a woman to bathe or swim while menstruating	18%	27%
Women need not restrict their physical activity while menstruating	66%	62%
Women should stay away from other people when menstruating	5%	12%

Some of the sex differences that have been found in menstrual attitudes can be seen in Table 1.2. It is striking that about one-third of men see women as being less able to function at work when menstruating, while most women deny any disability. Other studies also have found men to be less knowledgeable about menstruation than women and more likely to believe that menstruation is painful and debilitating (Golub, 1981; Golub, Daly, Ingrando, & Murphy, 1981; Parlee, 1974).

About half of both men and women say that women should not have intercourse when menstruating. However, in one study that looked at the effects of menstruation on interpersonal relationships and sexual behavior among college students, this belief was not found to be related to a lack of desire. The male subjects said that they do indeed make fewer sexual advances toward a menstruating woman, but almost 80% indicated that they were not less attracted to her. (An explanation, perhaps, for the strict Talmudic laws discussed earlier, namely, that women should not make themselves too alluring at this time.) On the other hand, only about half of the college women indicated that they were aroused and receptive to romantic overtures when menstruating (Golub, 1981).

Beliefs about menstruation are acquired at an early age and some of these beliefs are negative, reflecting cultural stereotypes rather than personal experience. Preadolescent boys and girls perceive menstruation as a symptom-laden phenomenon, associated with physical discomfort, increased emotionality, and a disruption of activities (Brooks-Gunn & Ruble, 1980; Clark & Ruble, 1978). Yet, in a study of college women's attitudes concerning menstruation-related changes, subjects were found to accept menstruation rather routinely, and they did not perceive it to be particularly debilitating. Generally these young women regarded menstruation as being predictable, bothersome, and yet a positive influence on their lives, a way of keeping in touch with their bodies and affirming their womanhood (Brooks, Ruble, & Clark, 1977). In 1988, in a study of almost 600 adolescent girls in a Boston suburb, a group of researchers from Wellesley found that girls share, to a greater or lesser degree, a belief that menstruation is normal and acceptable, while they at the same time express varying degrees of worry about and dislike for menstruation (Stubbs, Rierdan, & Koff, 1988). Apparently women's attitudes toward menstruation are mixed—both positive and negative—and they may change at different times in their lives.

Brooks-Gunn and Ruble (1986) studied differences in college men and women's attitudes about menstruation. Consistent with other research, they found that females believed that women experience both menstrual and premenstrual symptoms. Males focus on menstrual symptoms and believe the symptoms to be more severe and debilitating than do females. They also believe the symptoms to have more of an effect on women's moods. This male belief that menstruation is debilitating is hard to shake. After all, men cannot look to personal experience to validate or invalidate their beliefs. Some of the women in their lives do have menstrual discomfort, and though menstrual symptoms are generally mild to moderate, rather than severe, the men may not make this differentiation. They are not generally privy to "woman talk" that would make them aware of individual differences in women's menstrual experiences. They may not even know that there are women who have no menstrual discomfort at all.

In an attempt to look at age differences in attitudes toward menstruation, one of my students and I compared the attitudes of a group of mothers and their college-student daughters (Golub & Donnolo, 1980). The average ages of the two groups were 46 and 20 years, respectively. As expected, the daughters were found to have significantly more positive attitudes than did their mothers, and there was no particular relationship between the mothers' and daughters' attitudes. In other words, the daughters did not learn their attitudes about menstruation exclusively from their mothers. By the time they get to college, young women's attitudes are influenced by factors other than their mothers' beliefs. Interestingly, women who used tampons, those who had more liberal sexual attitudes, and those who described themselves as feminists, all had significantly more positive attitudes toward menstruation.

Educational background probably explains some of the mother-daughter differences. Only 47% of the mothers had completed one or more years of college, but those with some college education had more positive attitudes. Also, changes in societal attitudes toward women and women's changing roles probably affected the younger women's attitudes about themselves as women and their attitudes about menstruation. In this study, only 35% of the mothers considered themselves to be feminists, as opposed to 53% of the daughters.

In another study, the attitudes toward menstruation of four different groups were compared: college women, college men, professional nurses, and gay women (Golub, Daly, Ingrando, & Murphy, 1981). Significant differences were found between the women and the men, with all of the female groups demonstrating significantly more positive attitudes. However, no age differences were found. Most interesting was the finding that the gay women had the most positive attitudes toward menstruation, significantly more positive than those of either the male or female college students or the nurses. The gay women were also the most pro-feminist group. Here, as in the Tampax Report and the mother-daughter study, positive attitudes about women's rights were related to positive attitudes about menstruation.

It would be very surprising if some of a woman's attitudes toward menstruation were not also influenced by her experiences with menstrual distress. And, indeed, most of the studies that have been done do indicate that there is a relationship between attitudes and symptoms. In the past there was a tendency for researchers to blame the symptoms on women's negative attitudes. Women were accused of having menstrual pain because they rejected their identities as women. Contemporary researchers are more even-handed, turning things around and suggesting that women who have severe menstrual symptoms may come to see menstruation as debilitating and something that disrupts their lives, even if only for a few days (Woods, Dery, & Most, 1983). Thus women's symptoms are now seen as influencing their attitudes as well as the other way around. Again, it is important to recognize that women often have mixed feelings about menstruation. Positive attitudes can and do coexist with the negative. Menstruation can be seen as healthy and womanly (some suggest even "joyful") as well as a nuisance (Chrisler, Johnston, & Champagne, 1991).

In reviewing the cultural, religious, and historical roots of menstrual taboos and myths, it becomes easier to understand why they die so hard. Scientists are the products of their culture. What they study and how they study it are influenced by who they are. Sometimes a set of beliefs is not challenged because the researchers cannot conceive of any alternatives. Certainly male researchers who have never experienced menstruation would have a difficult time thinking about the positive aspects of the menstrual cycle. And few scientists over the years have found menstruation in normal, healthy women an interesting topic for their research. With the advent of the women's movement, more women have entered medicine, physiology, psychology, and sociology, and we are beginning to see more researchers addressing topics of interest to women, among them menstruation and menopause. The research is becoming far more sophisticated, taking into account biological, psychological, and sociocultural factors in trying to understand the complex ways in which menstruation affects women's lives. And we are making headway.

If a positive allusion to menstrual accoutrements can be seen in a masculine film such as *Colors*, there really is hope. I am referring to the morning duty roster meeting at which one cop says, alluding to his passive role in an ongoing bloody, drug operation, "I feel like a Tampax," only to be told by the sergeant in charge, "No, Tampax gets to go some place nice." I could not help but smile. "Macho," I thought, "but friendly."

References

Allen, E., & Doisy, E. A. (1923, September 8). An ovarian hormone. *Journal of the American Medical Association, 81,* 819-821.

Asia's lost tribe of Aryans (1984, March 5). *Time,* p. 52.

Bahrami, G. R., & Izadi, C. (1973). Religious and cultural attitudes about menstruation in Iran: Preliminary study. *Annales Medico Psychologiques, 2*(5), 637-654.

Brooks, J., Ruble, D., & Clark, A. (1977). College women's attitudes and expectations concerning menstrual-related changes. *Psychosomatic Medicine, 39,* 288-298.

Brooks-Gunn, J., & Ruble, D. N. (1980). Menarche: The interaction of physiological, cultural, and social factors. In A. J. Dan, E. M. Graham, & C. Beecher (Eds.), *The menstrual cycle* (Vol. 1, pp. 141-159). New York: Springer.

Brooks-Gunn, J., & Ruble, D. N. (1986). Men's and women's attitudes and beliefs about the menstrual cycle. *Sex Roles, 14*(5/6), 287-299.

Bullough, V., & Voght, M. (1973). Women, menstruation, and nineteenth-century medicine. *Bulletin of the History of Medicine, 47,* 66-82.

Chrisler, J. C., Johnston, I. K., & Champagne, N. M. (1991, June). *The effect of questionnaire title and presentation order on symptom reports and attitudes toward menstruation.* Paper presented at the meeting of the Society for Menstrual Cycle Research, Seattle, WA.

Clark, A., & Ruble, D. (1978). Young adolescents' beliefs concerning menstruation. *Child Development, 49,* 201-234.

Culpepper, E. E. (1974). Zoroastrian menstruation taboos: A women's studies perspective. In J. Plaskow & J. A. Romero (Eds.), *Women and Religion* (pp. 199-210). Missoula, MT: American Academy of Religion and The Scholars' Press.

Datan, N. (1986). Corpses, lepers, and menstruating women: Tradition, transition and the society of knowledge. *Sex Roles, 14*(11/12), 693-703.

Delaney, J., Lupton, M. J., & Toth, E. (1988). *The curse.* Chicago: University of Illinois Press.

Ernster, V. L. (1975). American menstrual expressions. *Sex Roles, 1*(1), 3-13.

Ford, C. F., & Beach, F. A. (1951). *Patterns of sexual behavior.* New York: Harper & Row.

Frazer, J. G. (1951). *The golden bough.* New York: Macmillan.

Goldman, A. L. (1983, September 22). U.N. leader with a mission. *The New York Times,* A8.

Golub, S. (1981). Sex differences in attitudes and beliefs regarding menstruation. In P. Komnenich, M. McSweeney, J. A. Noack, & Sister N. Elder (Eds.), *The menstrual cycle* (Vol. 2, pp. 129-134). New York: Springer.

Golub, S., & Donnolo, E. (1980). *Attitudes toward menstruation: A comparison of mothers and daughters.* Unpublished manuscript.

Golub, S., Daly, R., Ingrando, D. P., & Murphy, D. (1981). *A comparative study of menstrual attitudes.* Unpublished manuscript.

The Holy Scriptures. (1955). Philadelphia: Jewish Publication Society of America.

Lawrence, D. L. (1982). Reconsidering the menstrual taboo: A Portuguese case. *Anthropological Quarterly, 55*(2), 84-98.

Martin, E. (1987). *The woman in the body.* Boston: Beacon.

McGrath, A. M. (1972). *What a modern Catholic believes about women.* Chicago, IL: Thomas More.

Parlee, M. B. (1974). Stereotypic beliefs about menstruation: A methodological note on the Moos Menstrual Distress Questionnaire and some new data. *Psychosomatic Medicine, 36*, 229-240.

Rothbaum, B., & Jackson, J. (1990). Religious influences on menstrual symptoms and attitudes. *Women & Health, 16*(1), 63-78.

Sacks, B. (1974, July). Why I choose orthodoxy. *Ms. Magazine*, 82-84.

Schnur, S. (1985, July 18). Hers. *The New York Times*, C2.

Siegel, S. J. (1985/1986, Winter). The effect of culture on how women experience menstruation: Jewish women and *mikvah. Women & Health, 10*(4), 63-74.

Stephens, W. N. (1967). A cross-cultural study of menstrual taboos. In C. S. Ford (Ed.), *Cross-cultural approaches* (pp. 67-94). New Haven, CT: Human Relations Area File.

Stubbs, M. L., Rierdan, J., & Koff, E. (1988). Developmental changes in menstrual attitudes. *Working Paper No. 187*. Wellesley (MA) College Center for Research on Women.

The TAMPAX Report. (1981). New York: Ruder, Finn, & Rotman.

Walker, A. (1982). *The color purple.* New York: Pocket Books.

Webster's Seventh New Collegiate Dictionary. (1972). Springfield, MA: Merriam.

Wood, C. T. (1981). The doctors' dilemma: Sin, salvation, and the menstrual cycle in medieval thought. *Speculum, 6*(4), 710-727.

Woods, N. F., Dery, G. K., & Most, A. (1983). Recollections of menarche, current menstrual attitudes, and perimenstrual symptoms. In S. Golub (Ed.), *Menarche* (pp. 87-97). Lexington, MA: Lexington Books.

2

Menarche: The Onset of Menstruation

Menarche is a conspicuous and meaningful event in every woman's life. In contrast to other more gradual changes that occur during puberty, the onset of menstruation is dramatic. In *The Curse of an Aching Heart*, playwright William Alfred captures its significance. One of the characters, a woman in her sixties, recalls being frightened and embarrassed when she got her first period. She awoke with stained bedclothes and sheets not knowing what was happening to her. Confused, she ran out of the house. After walking for a while she came upon a neighbor who recognized that the girl was upset and invited her in for a cup of tea. The neighbor realized what had happened, explained menstruation to the girl, and then, in honor of the occasion, the woman gave the girl a brooch. In the play, memory of this experience was thoughtfully related to another woman more than 45 years after it happened.

Is this vignette a fluke, a bit of sentimental whimsy? Probably not. Psychological research confirms the dramatist's intuition that menarche is an important developmental event. In a study of recollections of menarche, a colleague and I found that almost all of the 137 women we studied, who ranged in age from 18 to 45, remembered their first

AUTHOR'S NOTE: Portions of this chapter appeared in S. Golub (1983). *Lifting the Curse of Menstruation.* New York: Haworth. Copyright © 1983 by Haworth Press. Reprinted by permission.

menstruation (Golub & Catalano, 1983). A majority of the women could describe in detail where they were when it happened, what they were doing, and whom they told. How many events in our lives are so vividly recalled?

Yet menarche has received little research attention until quite recently. This may be a reflection of our culture's hush-hush attitude toward menstruation in general. Anthropologists have not found this attitude to be universal. In fact, in some cultures menarche is celebrated with great joy and ritual feasting. In his book *The Forest People*, Colin Turnbull reports that among the Pygmies of the Congo the menarcheal girl is considered "blessed with the blood." Menstrual blood means life to the Pygmies, and when blood comes to a Pygmy girl for the first time, it is received with gratitude and rejoicing (Turnbull, 1962).

Even among people who are puritanical and secretive about menstruation, such as the Manus, first menstruation is associated with great ceremony. Margaret Mead (1949, p. 184) described it:

> The other girls of the village come to sleep in her house, there are large exchanges of food and ceremonial and splashing-parties in the lagoon; men are excluded and the women have a few jolly parties together—then absolute secrecy descends upon the girl's later menstruation.

There is a corresponding pubertal celebration for boys, in which their ears are pierced, but Mead notes a difference: Something is *done* to the boy, putting him in a different social status, but something has *happened* in the girl, a real physical change has occurred.

Other scientists have begun to look at both the physical and psychological aspects of menarche and at the ways in which they are inextricably linked. The body changes associated with puberty affect a girl's psychological and social development, and the girl's life experiences influence the physical changes that are occurring as well. For example, there is a relationship between exercise and the onset of menarche; and there seems to be a relationship between menarche and sexual activity. Menarche is a stressful time for some girls, less so for others. The point is that to understand the impact and meaning of menarche to adolescent girls biology, psychology, and the culture in which the girl is growing up must all be considered.

Pubertal Development

BODY CHANGES

Menarche is preceded by characteristic body changes that occur some time between the ages of 9 and 16. Breast development usually, but not always, occurs first. There is an increase in body hair, a growth spurt, and a weight gain prior to menarche, along with a change in body proportions, with the hips becoming fuller. Sweat glands become more active and a body odor develops that is thought to be related to an increase in the secretion of sex hormones from the adrenal gland (adrenal androgens). The skin becomes oilier, sometimes giving rise to skin problems. And while these external changes are going on there are concomitant changes occurring within the body: The uterus and vagina are growing (Grumbach, Grave, & Mayer, 1974).

Breast buds usually begin to form around the age of 11. Breast development is influenced by the secretion of hormones from the ovaries (estradiol), and the brain (prolactin from the anterior pituitary gland) (Wallach & Bongiovanni, 1983; Warren, 1983).

First there is a slight enlargement of the areola (the area around the nipple) and elevation of the breast as a small mound. Soon after, at about age 11, pubic hair begins to develop. Underarm hair generally appears about two years after the beginning of pubic hair development. And, on the average, menarche occurs between 12.8 and 13.2 years of age (see Table 2.1).

Pubertal development may be fast or slow. Some girls pass rapidly through the stages of breast and pubic hair development, while others move slowly. On the average, the total time for the overall process of physical transformation from child to adult is about four years (Tanner, 1978). However, some girls may take only a year and a half to pass through all the stages, while the slower developers may take as long as five years to do so. For those working or living with girls in this age group it is important to keep in mind that there can be great variation in the normal time of onset and completion of pubertal development. It is perfectly normal for a girl to begin to menstruate any time between the ages of 9 and 16, and age-mates may be at very different stages of sexual maturation. One 12-year-old can look like a woman, another very much like a child (Tanner, 1973).

TABLE 2.1 Stages of Pubertal Development in Girls[a]

Stage		Chronologic Age (years)
I	No signs of sexual development	Under 11
II	Early budding of breasts confined to periareolar region with a few tubercles; few pubic and/or axillary hairs; early prominance of labia minora and majora; initiation of increased growth velocity	10.5+/−2
III	Increased fullness of breasts with projection of areolae and nipples, many tubercles; small amount of pubic and axillary hair; moderate enlargement of labia minora and majora; dulling vaginal mucosa; maximal height growth velocity; growth of clitoris; vagina enlarges, pH becomes acid (4-5); menarche in 30%	11.5+/−2
IV	Breasts and external genitalia well developed; moderate to abundant pubic hair; onset of menarche	12.5+/−3
V	Adult sexual development; ovulation; deceleration of growth	14+/−3

Note: a. Approximations based on several sources for American girls.

There is a close relationship between menarche and the pubertal growth spurt in height. Girls start to menstruate after the growth spurt has peaked, when the rate of increase in height (height velocity) is falling. The growth spurt is nearly over at the time of menarche: Girls on the average grow only about two more inches after the onset of menstruation, though some girls do grow as much as four inches more (Tanner, 1978).

Menarche marks a mature stage in the development of the uterus but does not represent reproductive maturity. Early menstrual cycles are often irregular and between 55% and 82% of menstrual cycles during the first two years after menarche are anovulatory (in other words, menstruation occurs without ovulation having taken place). Regular menstruation may not occur for several years. However, it is important to remember that despite the apparent absence of regular monthly ovulation, any individual cycle may be ovulatory and hence potentially fertile, as indicated by the fact that there are more than

30,000 pregnancies among girls under the age of 15 in the United States each year (Brennock, 1982). These teenagers are at high risk for pregnancy complications such as low birth weight, high infant mortality, and pregnancy-induced hypertension (Leppert, 1983). In addition to the medical risks, there are tremendous social and psychological consequences associated with having a baby at 13 or 14 years of age.

WHAT TRIGGERS MENARCHE?

There is some controversy about just what it is that causes menarche to occur. Currently there are two major hypotheses, both relating menarcheal age to physical growth. However, one focuses on skeletal growth and the other on the accumulation of fat. The skeletal-growth hypothesis is based on the idea that the premenarcheal girl must reach an appropriate stage of skeletal development in order to reproduce; her body, and especially her pelvis, must be of an adequate size to carry and bear a child (Tanner, 1978). There are some data to support the idea that pelvic dimensions are significantly correlated with menstrual age (Ellison, 1982). Thus bone development can be used as an appropriate measure of developmental age in predicting when menarche will occur.

An alternative hypothesis, proposed by Frisch, suggests that the onset of menstruation is contingent upon the accumulation of fat and that a critical minimum weight for height is necessary to trigger and maintain ovulation and menstruation. Frisch notes that the greatest change during the adolescent growth spurt up to the time of menarche is a 120% increase in body fat. At menarche, girls' bodies average about 24% fat, not much different from the 28% fat found in the average 18-year-old woman. In contrast, boys at about 18 years of age are much leaner, with 14% fat. Frisch theorizes that reproduction requires energy, and the function of the stored fat is to provide readily accessible energy should it be needed for pregnancy and lactation (Frisch, 1980).

The age of menarche in the United States and much of Western Europe has declined greatly in the last 100 years, from about age 17 to just under 13. Tanner attributes the decline, sometimes referred to as the secular trend, to the acceleration of skeletal growth during this time, presumably related to better nutrition and health. In contrast, slow skeletal growth, resulting from poor nutrition or high altitude, leads to delay in the onset of menstruation. Frisch's explanation of the secular trend in menarcheal age is that girls reach 101 to 103 pounds, the average weight at menarche, sooner now, and therefore menstruation begins earlier. She points out that late menarche is associated with slower increases in body weight, such as that seen in cases of malnutrition, or among twins because they grow more slowly.

Ellison (1982) compared the two hypotheses. He used growth data drawn from the Berkeley Guidance Study in which 67 middle-class girls who were born in 1928 and 1929 were measured and weighed twice a year for 8 to 18 years. Ellison found that height velocity—the rapid spurt of growth that occurs during puberty—was the strongest correlate of menarcheal age, accounting for more than 50% of the variance. The weight factor was the second most important, accounting for 18% of the variance in menarcheal age. Thus, while there is a strong relationship between adolescent weight and menarcheal age, the effect of weight is somewhat less than that of skeletal development. Ellison makes the point that since skeletal growth tends to cease soon after menarche, natural selection would delay menarche until the pelvis could handle reproduction without the attendant complications of a pelvis that is too small, namely, difficult labor, stillbirths, or the need for Caesarean section (Ellison, 1982).

HORMONES

Although they are incompletely understood, significant hormonal changes do occur at puberty (see Figure 2.1). The female sex hormones, adrenal hormones, and hypothalamic-hypophyseal hormones are all of major importance. It is the interrelationship of these hormones that later controls the female reproductive cycle. However, endocrinologists now believe that the hormonal changes associated with sexual maturation are genetically programmed at the time of conception. The basic embryonic template is feminine. Male development is due to an intervention in this basic plan. An egg that is fertilized by a sperm carrying a Y chromosome will produce H-Y antigen, and about six weeks after conception the embryo will develop testes instead of ovaries; the testes synthesize and secrete testosterone, which leads to the development of male sexual organs. In the absence of H-Y antigen, the female embryo develops ovaries and female sexual organs (Ohno, 1978) (see Figure 2.2). By the third

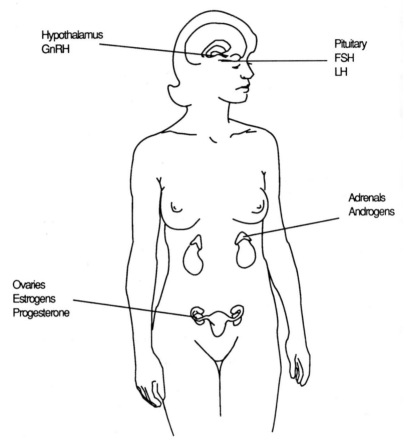

Figure 2.1. Significant Endocrine Glands and Their Hormones

trimester of pregnancy, the negative feedback system that will regulate hormonal secretions is established (see Chapter 3, Figure 3.1). During infancy the hypothalamic gonadotropin-regulating mechanism is "set" at a low level where it remains until the time of puberty when there is an increase in the secretion of follicle-stimulating hormone (FSH) and luteinizing hormone (LH) and a decrease in hypothalamic sensitivity (Petersen & Tayloy, 1980).

The adolescent growth spurt is a result of the joint action of androgens (male sex hormones) and growth hormones. A progressive

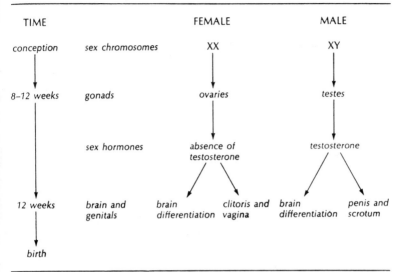

TIME		FEMALE	MALE

conception → sex chromosomes → XX / XY

8–12 weeks → gonads → ovaries / testes

sex hormones → absence of testosterone / testosterone

12 weeks → brain and genitals → brain differentiation, clitoris and vagina / brain differentiation, penis and scrotum

birth

Figure 2.2. Sequences of Prenatal Differentiation of Females and Males
Source: Hyde, J. (1991). Half the human experience.

increase in plasma dehydroepiandosterone and dehydroepiandosterone sulfate, which are weak androgens, begins about age 8 and continues through ages 13 to 15. These hormones, thought to originate from the adrenal gland, are the earliest new hormonal secretions to take place at puberty. They and the more potent androgens—testosterone and dihydrotestosterone—increase significantly as pubertal development progresses (Dupon & Bingel, 1980). Increased secretion of gonadotropins from the pituitary (FSH and LH) and sex steroids from the gonads follows.

The main female sex hormone secreted by the ovaries is estradiol, which is present in relatively small amounts in the blood until about age eight or nine when it begins to rise. This increase in blood levels of estradiol causes growth of the breasts, uterus, vagina, and parts of the pelvis. When menstruation begins, estradiol levels fluctuate with the various phases of the cycle and are controlled by pituitary FSH.

The two pituitary gonadotropins—follicle-stimulating hormone (FSH) and luteinizing hormone (LH)—are both secreted in small amounts during childhood and increase at puberty. The pubertal rise is first seen as pulses of LH that are released during sleep. This

TABLE 2.2 Pituitary and Gonadal Hormones During Puberty and
Adulthood

Pubertal Stage	Approxi- mate Age (years)	FSH (mIU/ml)	LH (mIU/ml)	Estradiol (pg/ml)	Estrone (pg/ml)	Proges- terone (ng/ml)
I	6-9	2-4	1-6	8.2	13	0.28
II	10-12	3-10	1-9	16.4	21	0.76
III	11-14	3-15	3-15	25	30	0.85
IV	12-15	4-20	4-20	47	36	1.13
V	13-17	4-20	5-25	111	61	1.51
Adult						
Follicular		5-20	5-25	24-68		0.1-1.0
Luteal		8-25	20-90	20-40		3.0-15.0

Source: Data from Bongiovanni, A. M. (1983). *Adolescent gynecology*. New York: Plenum.

sleep-associated rise in LH is not seen in either the prepubertal child
or the adult. Gradually LH is released during the daytime too (see
Table 2.2).

Menstruation, as well as earlier pubertal development, is thought
to begin with a signal to the hypothalamus from the central nervous
system. As noted above, a hypothalamic feedback system does exist
before puberty, but the hypothalamus is responsive to low levels of
LH in the prepubertal girl. Then, around the time of menarche, a
gradual change occurs, making the hypothalamic-pituitary unit less
sensitive. Higher levels of estrogen are needed. At this time there is
an increased secretion of gonadotropin-releasing hormone (GnRH),
as well as FSH and LH, and an increase in the responsiveness of the
gonads, too (Reiiter & Grumbach, 1982). The hypothalamus secretes
more FSH-releasing hormone. This neuro-hormone stimulates the
pituitary gland to release FSH, which, in turn, triggers the growth of
the ovarian follicles. As the follicles grow, they secrete estrogen,
which causes growth of the cells lining the uterus (the endometrium).
Increasing levels of estrogen in the blood also signal the pituitary to
reduce FSH and secrete LH. LH triggers the release of the ovum from
the follicle, which then evolves into the corpus luteum and secretes
progesterone and a little estrogen. If the ovum is not fertilized, the
pituitary reduces its production of LH, the levels of both estrogen and
progesterone drop, menstruation begins, and the cycle starts again.

GENETICS

Genetic factors play an important role in determining rate of growth, pubertal development, and age at menarche. Studies of identical twin sisters growing up together indicate that they reach menarche about two months apart, with the first-born twin—for some unknown reason—more likely to menstruate first (Shields, 1962). Fraternal twins differ by about 12 months. Mother-daughter and sister-sister correlations have also been reported to be significant (Chern, Gatewood, & Anderson, 1980). Swedish researchers who studied a large sample of mothers and daughters found other menstrual similarities: Significant correlations were found between mothers' and daughters' length of cycle, duration of menstrual flow, and symptoms of dysmenorrhea and premenstrual tension (Kantero & Widholm, 1971). However, lest it be thought that only mothers influence their daughters menstrual cycles, researchers believe that mother and father exert an equal influence on rate of growth and maturation. Thus a late-maturing girl is as likely to have a late-maturing father as a late-maturing mother (Tanner, 1978).

NUTRITION

There is a well-documented link between nutrition and fertility. Famine amenorrhea was reported in both world wars. Young women who are undernourished because of excessive dieting or those with anorexia nervosa often do not menstruate. And it is well known that malnutrition retards growth and will delay menarche. The fall in age at menarche that has occurred between 1830 and 1960 coincides with the increased availability of protein in the diet of developed countries during this period. In some countries, where nutrition has remained inadequate, age of menarche is comparatively high. For example, in contrast to the average age of menarche in the United States, which is now 12.8 years, in Bangladesh it is just under 16, and among certain New Guinea tribes, it is about 18 (Menkin, Watkins, & Trussel, 1980).

A study of different ethnic groups in Hawaii also suggests that nutrition and environmental factors are responsible for population differences. Goodman and colleagues compared Caucasian, Japanese, and Chinese women living in Hawaii and found no differences in age at menarche (Goodman, Grove, & Gilbert, 1983). Tanner has noted that children in urban areas are likely to have more rapid growth and earlier menarche than are children in rural areas, which is probably attributable to better nutrition, health, and sanitation (Tanner,1978). Also, girls who are heavier during preadolescence tend to reach menarche earlier (Ellison, 1982).

STRESS

Genetics, health, and nutrition are the major factors influencing the onset of menarche. However, other things may play a role as well. Recently, a theory was proposed linking early puberty with childhood stress. Drawing on sociobiology, this controversial theory suggests that girls growing up in a stressful environment will improve the chances of having their genes survive by reproducing early. Several studies report a correlation between family conflict (a home in which the father was absent or where there was parental fighting or divorce) and early sexual maturation (Goleman, 1991).

EXERCISE

Women who experience high-energy outputs, such as ballet dancers and athletes who train intensively, reach menarche at a later age and have a high incidence of amenorrhea. This is particularly true when intensive training begins at an early premenarcheal age (Frisch, 1983; Frisch, Gotz-Welbergen, McArthur et al., 1981). It is not known whether the delay in menarche seen among young athletes is due to an altered lean-fat ratio, as proposed by Frisch, or to the direct effects of exercise on hormonal secretion and metabolism (Rebar & Cumming, 1981). In a Dutch study that aimed at teasing out the effects of thinness versus activity, 649 girls between the ages of 10 and 14 were studied. The researchers found that either thinness or intensive sports activity was associated with a twofold decrease in the proportion of girls reaching menarche. And when both factors were present, there was a fourfold decrease. Thus, intensive sports activity and thinness have a synergistic effect in delaying the onset of menstruation (Vandenbroucke, van Laar, & Valkenburg, 1982).

Dancers experience differences in their breast and pubic hair development. The beginning of the growth of pubic hair follows a normal pattern but there is a delay in the beginning of the development of the breasts at puberty. Warren (1983) suggests that the mechanism for pubic hair development is not affected by the energy drain, while the mechanism affecting both breast development and menarche is suppressed. On the other hand, it may be that the other characteristics associated with successful athletic performance are also associated with later maturation.

Some investigators have expressed concern about the short-term and long-term effects of exercise on reproductive function (Rebar & Cumming, 1981). At this time it is not known whether it is an advantage or a disadvantage to have a late menarche. There is at least one report indicating that women who have their first menstrual bleeding before age 12 are twice as likely to develop breast cancer as those who have menarche at 13 or later ("Early menarche," 1983). That would make a late menarche advantageous. The consensus seems to be that exercise-related alterations in reproductive function are not serious and are readily reversible.

CLIMATIC AND SEASONAL EFFECTS

Climate has no more than a very minor effect on age at menarche. In fact, contrary to earlier beliefs, people who live in tropical countries are somewhat more likely to have a late menarche. This is thought to be related to nutrition rather than climate, for children in the higher socioeconomic groups in these countries experience menarche at about the same time as children living in temperate zones.

Season of the year does have an effect on pubertal development. Height increases twice as fast in the spring: Peak growth is seen between March and July. The greatest weight gains occur in the autumn, and girls are most likely to have their first menstruation in the late fall or early winter; conversely, they are least likely to experience menarche in the spring ("To everything there . . . ," 1980).

ACUTE AND CHRONIC ILLNESS

Under some conditions menstruation will not occur at all. For example, a girl with Turner's Syndrome, a chromosomal anomaly in which the second X chromosome is absent, will not menstruate, for she lacks ovaries. Sex hormone administration is crucial in order for these girls to attain psychosocial and psychosexual maturity. Administration of estrogen will cause the breasts to grow, and an artificial menstrual cycle may be produced by giving estrogen for three weeks followed by a week without treatment. This is important because these girls want to look, develop, and be treated like normal female adolescents (Ehrhardt & Meyer-Bahlberg, 1975).

Some illnesses can delay menarche, probably because of their effects on nutrition. This is most likely to be true in cases of ulcerative colitis, regional enteritis, cystic fibrosis, congenital heart disease, uremia, and diabetes mellitus. The timing of the onset of the illness as well as the illness per se seem to be important. For example, if diabetes develops during the initial pubertal period, menarche is delayed, whereas if it develops later, menarche may be unaffected (Warren, 1983).

Conversely, some conditions will advance the age of menarche. These include hypothyroidism, central nervous system tumors, encephalitis, head trauma, and some virilizing disorders. Inactive, retarded, or bedridden girls also reach menarche at an earlier age than their more active counterparts. Inactivity may also be the reason blind girls reach menarche at an earlier age.

Thus menarche occurs after a series of changes in hormone secretion and somatic growth. These processes are influenced by genetic and environmental factors, such as nutrition, exercise, and illness, that may accelerate or retard the onset of menstruation.

Now we turn to the psychosocial aspects of menarche and its meaning to the adolescent girl and to those around her.

Psychological Effects of Menarche on the Early Adolescent Girl

Much of the early writing about the psychology of menarche presented it as a traumatic experience. In one of the earliest psychoanalytic works about menstruation, *The Psychological Effects of Menstruation,* Mary Chadwick (1932) describes the early adolescent as ashamed of her growing breasts and pubic hair and horrified at menarche. There is no mention of the excitement and anticipation experienced by preadolescent girls who are waiting expectantly to "get it."

Early psychoanalytic theory postulated a marked increase in sex drive at puberty and an inevitable period of anxiety, worry about impulse control, and increased lability as a "relatively strong id confronts a relatively weak ego" (Freud, 1946). Benedek (1959) believed that menarche might evoke fears associated with the anticipation of pain during intercourse and childbirth.

Current psychoanalytic views are much more positive. Notman (1983) and others suggest that meeting the developmental tasks of adolescence need not be as tumultuous as was previously believed. True, the early adolescent needs to modify her attachment to her parents and develop the capacity to form relationships with peers; and, eventually, she must establish her identity as a woman and develop the capacity for intimacy with another person. However, this need not happen overnight, and the process should not cause turmoil or disintegration.

Menarche can have an organizing effect for the adolescent girl, helping her to clarify her perception of her own genitals, particularly confirming the existence of the vagina and correcting the confusion she may have had about the female genitalia. Indeed, menarche may serve as a reference point around which girls can organize their pubertal experiences, a landmark for feminine identification. Certainly the awareness of sexual differentiation between males and females does increase at menarche (Koff, Rierdan, & Silverstone, 1978).

KNOWLEDGE, ATTITUDES, AND EXPECTATIONS

What do the girls themselves say? In one study, researchers interviewed 35 White middle-class pre- and postmenarcheal girls at a summer camp. The girls had learned about menstruation from friends, commercial booklets, school, and their parents—especially their mothers. They perceived themselves as being knowledgeable about menstruation and used the appropriate terms. However, the interviewer found that the girls really did not have a good conception of what the internal organs were like or how they functioned, and they were even more inept at describing the external genitalia. Thus, despite their access to information about menstruation, the girls had not assimilated it well. They were most concerned about what to do when they got their periods, and many had mentally rehearsed what they would do in a variety of situations (Whisnant & Zegans, 1975).

Brooks-Gunn and Ruble (1980) found that both boys and girls in the seventh and eighth grades had similar and mostly negative beliefs about menstruation. For example, most believed that menstruation is accompanied by physical discomfort, increased emotionality, and a disruption of activities. Only a third thought that the onset of menstruation was something to be happy about.

Lenore Williams, a nurse educator, found more positive attitudes toward menstruation in a group of 9- to 12-year-old girls, most of whom were premenarcheal. These girls generally equated menstruation with growing up and being normal. However, about a third of them also believed menstruation to be embarrassing, 28% thought it a nuisance, 27% found it disgusting, and 23% disliked the idea that it is not controllable. The girls in this sample also believed some of the popular menstrual taboos. About half thought a girl should not swim when menstruating, and 22% believed she should not be active in sports. Many were influenced by concealment taboos, with a majority expressing concern about concealing sanitary pads and menstrual odor. A striking 85% thought that a girl should not talk about menstruation to boys, and 40% did not even think that it was all right to discuss menstruation with their fathers. And, as in the study noted above, most believed that girls are more emotional when they menstruate (Williams, 1983).

REACTIONS TO MENARCHE

What do girls actually experience at the time of menarche? In several studies menarche has been found to be an anxiety-producing or negative event. Mixed feelings, such as being "excited but scared" or "happy and embarrassed" are common (Koff, Rierdan, & Jacobson, 1981; Petersen, 1983; Woods, Dery, & Most, 1983). Most of these data were collected using interviews and questionnaires, and sometimes they were based on the recollections of older subjects, but the findings are remarkably consistent.

Petersen (1983) in looking at menarche as one part of her study of 400 middle-class suburban boys and girls in the sixth, seventh, and eighth grades found that the adolescents were remarkably inarticulate in describing their feelings about their changing bodies. Therefore, she decided that more subtle measures might be more useful than direct questions in exploring girls' feelings about menstruation. The girls were presented with an incomplete story about menarche adapted from Judy Blume's book, *Are You There God? It's Me, Margaret*. For example, the girls were given the following passage to read:

"Mom—hey, Mom—come quick!" When Nancy's mother got to the bathroom she said: "What is it? What's the matter?" "I got it," Nancy told her. "Got what?" said her mother.

The girls were then asked, "What happened next?"

Some of the girls responded that, "She told her Mom that she had gotten her period"; others said that Mom explained or helped. They were then asked, "How did Nancy feel?" About a third gave negative or fearful responses, about half were positive or pleased, and another 5% were ambivalent.

There do seem to be differences between pre- and postmenarcheal girls. Stubbs and her colleagues found that premenarcheal girls were more likely to express excitement about the growing-up aspects of menstruation. In contrast, newly postmenarcheal girls talk about negative feelings and reactions, being "grossed out," and feeling sick. It is interesting that although premenarcheal girls expect to tell their friends and talk about it with others, the newly postmenarcheal girls reported that they didn't talk much to others about it at all (Stubbs, Rierdan, & Koff, 1988).

Kumin, in a short story titled *Facts of Life*, differentiates between the expectations about menarche and its actual occurrence. She describes a group of 12-year-old girls as longing to begin to menstruate. "An eager band of little girls, itchy with the work of sprouting, sits expectant. The old reticences, embarrassments, and complaints have given way to progress. Now we have sex education, cartoon films of the reproductive tract, a beltless sanitary napkin, a slender, virginal tampon." Yet, when the first blood does indeed come, the girl is described as terribly happy and terribly sad as mother and daughter celebrate together (Kumin, 1982, pp. 9-19).

CHANGES IN BODY IMAGE

Changes in body image—the way girls see themselves—are among the most dramatic reactions to menarche. During puberty body changes occur gradually. Yet girls expect to act differently after menarche, and they perceive themselves quite differently. In a study of seventh-grade girls, Koff (1983) on two occasions approximately six months apart asked the subjects to draw male and female human figures. Of the 87 girls sampled, 34 were premenarcheal on both test

Figure 2.3a, b. Drawing of Premenarcheal Girl, Time 1 and Time 2

occasions, 23 were postmenarcheal, and 30 changed menarcheal status between the two test sessions. The findings were striking. Postmenarcheal girls produced drawings that were significantly more sexually differentiated than those of their premenarcheal peers, and a greater percentage of the postmenarcheal girls drew their own sex first. Most notable was the difference in the drawings done by the girls whose menarcheal status changed during the course of the study. Their drawings at the second testing were of womanly females with breasts and curves. These were very different from the premenarcheal, childlike drawings done at the first testing session (Koff, 1983) (see Figures 2.3, 2.4, and 2.5).

In order further to explore girls' beliefs about the change menarche would make in them, Koff and her colleagues gave a sentence-completion task to seventh- and eighth-grade girls. In response to the cue sentence, "Ann just got her period for the first time . . . ," the girls said such things as, "She saw herself in a different way," and "She felt very grown up." In response to another item, "Ann regarded her body

Figure 2.4a, b. Drawing of Postmenarcheal Girl, Time 1 and Time 2

as . . . ," postmenarcheal girls were more likely than premenarcheal girls to describe a change in body image. For example, Ann's body was "a woman's body" and "more mature than it was."

These studies clearly demonstrate that girls experience menarche as a turning point in their development, and they apparently reorganize their body images in the direction of greater sexual maturity. Postmenarcheal girls are more aware of the differences in secondary sex characteristics of males and females in general, and of themselves as women, than are premenarcheal girls of the same age. They are more mature. However, they are also more self-conscious, embarrassed, and secretive about their bodies.

The Importance of Timing

The age at which a girl experiences menarche does seem to affect her reaction to it, with the early maturing girl having a harder time.

Premenarcheal   Postmenarcheal

Figure 2.5a, b. Drawing of Girl Whose Menarcheal Status Changed

However, there is some support for the idea that the time around menarche is turbulent for most girls, regardless of when it occurs. Ulman (1984) focused on the relationship between menarche and girls' self-esteem, feelings of depression, and sense of their ability to control their lives. Her subjects were 205 girls in grades 6 through 10. Ulman hypothesized that girls initially experience menarche as traumatic, but they then adapt after a period of crisis and subsequently have greater feelings of self-esteem. She divided the girls into three groups: premenarcheal; less than two years postmenarcheal; and more than two years postmenarcheal. The girls who were postmenarcheal for less than two years had the lowest self-esteem scores and the highest scores on the measure of depressive mood. By contrast, the girls who were more than two years postmenarcheal had the highest self-esteem scores and the lowest depressive affect scores.

Recent mental-health surveys among young people in the United States, New Zealand, Canada, and Puerto Rico have highlighted certain risks: For girls, the likelihood of severe depression doubles in the year after the onset of menstruation. In a study of 1,552 young people ranging in age from 10 to 20 who live in the Albany, New York, area, Patricia Cohen, a psychiatric epidemiologist, found that severe depression reaches a peak rate of 7% in girls around 13 and 14. She concluded that there is a tremendous risk for depression in girls in the years following puberty or the onset of menstruation (Goleman, 1989).

Girls in whom menarche occurs much earlier or much later than in their contemporaries, especially girls who experience menarche early—in the sixth grade or earlier—seem to have more difficulty with it. Some of the girls in Petersen's (1983) study denied that they had begun to menstruate when they really had. When Petersen questioned the mothers of her early-maturing subjects, more than 70% of the mothers reported that menarche was very difficult for their daughters. The mothers of five of the six girls who denied having gotten their periods reported the negative aspects of the experience for them. Notman (1983) has suggested that the denial of menstruation may be related to conflicts about accepting the female role or to an attempt to delay adulthood. Certainly one of the girls in Petersen's sample who denied menstruating lends support to that view. In response to a Thematic Apperception Test card showing a middle-aged woman with a girl holding a doll, this subject described the girl in the picture as scared about growing up and asking her mother when she was going to get her period (Petersen, 1983).

When Rierdan and Koff (1985) looked at college women's recollections of the timing of their first menstrual periods and their reactions to it, they found that girls who experienced themselves as early remembered a more negative menarche than girls who experienced themselves as "on time" or late.

Unlike boys who are eager for their growth spurt and physical signs of maturity, girls would prefer to mature at the same time as everyone else. This may be because of the age difference between the sexes in the onset of puberty—boys normally start later than girls. Or perhaps it is another example of the pressure early adolescents feel to conform. Girls' attitudes about early development may also be related to the changes in their lives that occur when they develop the breasts and curves characteristic of a woman.

Peer-group support may bolster the adolescent girl's ability to adjust. One early-maturing subject in the Petersen (1983) study responded to the question of how she felt about having gotten her period by saying, "Well, I suppose I felt more grown up. I also felt a little embarrassed." Why? "Well, I knew that barely any of my friends had it and it was just kinda embarrassing, even though you know you can't tell if someone has their period. You feel different inside around your friends, like a little self-conscious" (Tobin-Richards, Boxer, & Petersen, 1983).

There is some evidence that sixth- and seventh-grade girls who are already pubertal are more likely to be dating and, somewhat paradoxically, these girls also have lower self-esteem, lower school achievement, and more behavioral problems than comparable boys and nonpubertal girls (Simmons, Blyth, Van Cleave, & Bush, 1979). Simmons and her colleagues found that pubertal development per se had little effect on the girls' self-esteem. However, the early-maturing girls who had also begun dating were more likely to indicate low self-esteem (50%, as opposed to 36%-40% of the other girls). While early dating behavior seems to be disadvantageous for girls, it has no statistically significant impact on boys.

Thus girls' self-esteem was negatively affected by early sexual maturation and ensuing social relationships while boys' self-esteem was not. Simmons suggests some reasons why this may be so. First, the sexes develop different value systems at this age. For girls, appearance and sociability assume priority, while for boys these values remain secondary. When asked to rank the importance of popularity, competence, and independence, seventh-grade girls were more likely to rank popularity first. This places a great deal of importance on other people's opinions of oneself. These girls also placed a high value on looks. Moreover, the changes in body image may be qualitatively different for girls than for boys. Pubertal boys are generally happy with their new height and muscle development. Pubertal girls are not sure whether their new figures make them better or worse looking than their peers. Further, pubertal girls' negative reactions to dating may be a result of their male partners' sexual pressures, for which the girls are not prepared. In interviews with some of these girls the researchers found them likely to express dislike for "guys trying to touch me." One subject said, "I don't really like to be kissed." It looks as if some of these girls were vulnerable, with their social and emotional maturity lagging well behind their physical development, causing confusion and contributing to their feelings of low self-esteem. This is in keeping with data from the California Adolescent Study, which show that it is the girl with accelerated growth and maturation who is at a disadvantage (Jones, 1958; Jones & Mussen, 1958). Social class may also play a role. For middle-class girls, early maturation was positively related to self-confidence, whereas working-class girls experienced a negative effect. In contrast to early maturation, late maturation, which is quite disturbing for boys, does not seem to have the same degree of negative consequences for girls. Perhaps this is because a childlike appearance is seen as feminine and attractive for women in our culture.

Impact on Relationships:
Parents, Peers, and Sex

RELATIONSHIPS WITH PARENTS

In addition to adjusting to their own changing bodies and developing closer relationships to their peers, adolescents also have the important task of establishing greater independence from parents. In view of the changes that go on in girls' perceptions of themselves at menarche, it is reasonable to expect that menarche also affects girls' relationships with family members. In Simmons' (Simmons et al., 1979) research, sixth- and seventh-grade girls who had begun to menstruate were significantly more likely to be left alone when parents were not home, to babysit, and to care more about independence from their parents. Similarly, Danza (1983) compared 48 pre- and postmenarcheal girls in the sixth and seventh grades and found that, although they were no different in age than their premenarcheal peers, postmenarcheal girls were more likely to wear make-up or a bra, to shave their legs, and to date. They also slept less on school nights, moving from nine or more hours a night toward the more usual adult eight-hour sleep cycle. Thus it seems that girls who look older (that is, have attained menarche) are also treated differently by their parents—they are allowed to act older. The postmenarcheal girls were also more uncomfortable discussing emotionally charged topics such as love, sex, drugs, and alcohol with their parents, and they reported having more conflict with parents than the premenarcheal girls did. Menarche does seem to mark the end of one phase of a girl's life and the beginning of another. No wonder it is so often fraught with anxiety.

EFFECTS ON SEXUAL BEHAVIOR

Because it marks the onset of the ability to become pregnant, menarche is important to a girl's family and community as well as to herself. In other cultures there are different tribal rituals celebrating menarche, and some societies have customs such as purdah, veiling, and virginity tests, which guard girls' reproductive potential. Economics comes into play too. Paige (1983) has suggested that there is a relationship between various methods of controlling girls' chastity and the economic resources of a particular culture. In societies where marriage bargains are important, chastity is crucial to the girl's marriageability and is rigorously controlled.

This kind of control is not seen in the United States today. Rather, the physical transformation from girl to woman and the onset of menstruation are accompanied by changes in social and sexual behavior. And, as noted above, the timing of menarche is important. Several researchers have reported that girls with an early menarche were more likely to date and pet at an earlier age than their later-maturing peers. There are also data indicating that women with early menarche begin premarital coitus earlier (Gagnon, 1983; Presser, 1978; Simmons et al., 1979; Udry & Cliquet, 1982). In an extensive study of Black and White low-income women in 16 American cities, Udry found that, compared with girls with late menarche, those with early menarche were more than twice as likely to have had intercourse by age 16. Udry also examined the relationship between ages at menarche, marriage, and first birth among women in four widely diverse countries (United States, Malaysia, Belgium, and Pakistan) and concluded that there was a clear behavioral sequence relating age at menarche to ages at first intercourse and first birth. Menarche seems to initiate a chain of events. In the United States the pattern is one of dating and other sexual behavior that increase the probability of early intercourse and childbearing.

Whether this sequence is more readily attributable to hormonal or sociocultural factors is difficult to answer. Gagnon (1983) found no significant relationship between the onset of menarche and masturbatory experience. Similarly, in their studies of children with the problem of precocious puberty (puberty beginning at six to eight years of age), Ehrhardt and Meyer-Bahlburg (1975) have found that early puberty does not automatically trigger an early sex life. Masturbation and sex play in childhood did not appear to be enhanced, and premarital intercourse did not occur earlier than normally expected. Thus at this time it seems reasonable to conclude that the timing of puberty influences when the girl, her parents, and her peers perceive her as being someone for whom dating and heterosexual relationships are appropriate, and this in turn affects her sociosexual behavior.

Overall, a girl's psychological reactions to menarche are the result of a complex interplay of biological, psychological, and social influences. Genes, hormones, environmental factors, and nutrition influence when menstruation begins. However, peer relationships, self-esteem, and the way she feels about being a woman determine how the adolescent adapts to the changes menarche imposes.

What Girls Really Need to Know

In view of the ambivalent feelings about menarche expressed by so many adolescent girls and the difficulties experienced by the early-maturing girl, it seems reasonable to ask if adequate preparation makes any difference? It probably does. Several researchers have found that subjects who report being adequately prepared have a more positive initial experience with menstruation (Rierdan, 1983). Other studies indicate a need for more and better menstrual education (Logan, 1980). In a study of 95 women from 23 foreign countries, Logan and her colleagues found that 28% complained of not having enough information. Similarly, in a large study of women in the United States, 39% reported that their preparation was inadequate. Perhaps most interesting, even adolescent girls who say that they had sufficient prior knowledge about menstruation often felt unprepared for menarche.

What do girls want to know? In a study of 97 college women's recollections of menarche, Rierdan found that the young women wanted to know about menstrual physiology and menstrual hygiene—the facts that are usually included in menstrual education materials. But, they also wanted information about menstruation as a personal event. The college students said that girls need to know about the normality of menstruation; it must be distinguished from disease, injury, and uncleanliness. They suggested that the feelings of fright and embarrassment girls experience at menarche be acknowledged as normal and that the negative aspects of the menstrual experience need to be discussed in order to provide a balanced view of menstruation. The women emphasized that girls need support and reassurance at the time of menarche, and Rierdan says, "Many referred specifically to the importance of an informed, understanding, accepting mother." Unfortunately, however, interviews with mothers of adolescent girls indicate that the mothers are not prepared to fill this role, suggesting a real need to prepare mothers to help their daughters through menarche.

Several researchers have expressed concern about the observation that postmenarcheal girls, even when they are intellectually well prepared for menstruation, report more feelings of shame, apprehension, and disgust and less pride than their premenarcheal peers (Rierdan, Koff, & Flaherty, 1985). Menstrual education today tends to be rather intellectual, emphasizing anatomy and physiology, reproductive capacity, and menstrual hygiene. The more experiential aspects are less adequately addressed. For example, girls want to know what it feels like to be menstruating. They need to be aware that women's experiences with menstruation vary a lot: Their own experiences may be different from those of their friends or other women, and periods may even differ from month to month in themselves. Certainly experiences with menstruation are different for women at different times in their lives.

Misconceptions about menstruation need to be addressed. In Rierdan's study of college women, 40% had incorrectly assumed that menstrual bleeding per se would be painful, apparently thinking that menstrual bleeding was like the bleeding associated with injuries. They did not know how much bleeding to expect. What is normal? And they were not aware of variations in the color of menstrual blood, ranging from bright red to dark brown. Similarly, there was a lack of awareness that sanitary napkins could be uncomfortable and messy. Many of the women remembered being surprised to discover that they were "annoying" and "smelly." Some did not anticipate the inconveniences that might be associated with menstruation: One has to plan for it, bring napkins to school, and have access to a bathroom.

I am reminded of the girl who got her first period at school and was upset about it. A kindly teacher started to explain what was happening to her, but the girl impatiently interrupted, "I know all about it. I just forgot to find out how to stop it when you have to go to school."

Menstrual education in the United States has come a long way in the last 50 years. However, in trying to convey menstruation as normal and natural, and in directing girls to carry on as usual, we have ignored some of the nuisance aspects of menstruation. Girls are left to find these things out for themselves, perhaps contributing to postmenarcheal feelings of shame, apprehension, and disgust. We need to acknowledge both positive and negative feelings about menstruation. In addition to the facts about physiology and hygiene, girls need an opportunity to talk about their reactions to body changes, looking older, growing up, and parental and peer expectations. Because girls' attitudes and ways of thinking change during early adolescence, menstrual education needs to be an ongoing process rather than a one-time thing. It should begin before menstruation occurs and continue throughout adolescence. Washbourn put it particularly well when she said that to emerge "from the life-crisis of menstruation implies finally trusting and liking one's body. Trusting it means being peaceful with it, knowing its potential, relaxing with the new experience of menstruation, understanding the possible good offered by the female body structure" (Washbourn, 1977, pp. 17-18).

IN SUPPORT OF A NEW TRADITION

Some psychologists have suggested that we need a "Contemporary Tradition for Menarche" in order to overcome some of the negative connotations associated with it. They believe that currently we address the physical needs of the menarcheal girl, teaching her how to take care of herself, but leaving her without the social and emotional support that she needs at this time. In order to explore what the appropriate ritual might be, Logan and her colleagues designed five short stories describing possible responses to a girl's first period and gave them to girls between the ages of 8 and 17, to mothers of girls in this age group, and to women psychologists. The most popular response of the mothers and daughters to being told about the onset of menstruation was "Congratulations, our little girl is growing up." However, the psychologists preferred, "Something special has happened," apparently acknowledging the ambivalent and even negative emotions that a girl may have about the beginning of menstruation. As for symbolic gestures, the most popular among the mothers was a toast to the girl from her mother and father, or a meal in her honor. But the daughters had reservations about this, fearing an invasion of privacy and reinforcing feelings that "everyone is watching her." The daughters preferred a hug or a kiss and a material token such as a gift or flowers. It seems dramatists often capture in a few lines what scientists seek in reams of data: William Alfred was right on target with the gift of a brooch.

References

Benedek, T. (1959). Sexual functions in women and their disturbance. In S. Arieti (Ed.), *American handbook of psychiatry* (pp. 727-748). New York: Basic Books.

Brennock, W. E. (1982). Fertility at menarche. *Medical Aspects of Human Sexuality, 16*(12), 21-30.

Brooks-Gunn, J., & Ruble, D. (1980). Menarche. In A. J. Dan, E. A. Graham, & C. P. Beecher (Eds.), *The menstrual cycle* (Vol. 1., pp. 141-159). New York: Springer.

Chadwick, M. (1932). *The psychological effects of menstruation.* New York: Nervous and Mental Diseases.

Chern, M. M., Gatewood, L. C., & Anderson, V. E. (1980). The inheritance of menstrual traits. In A. J. Dan, E. A. Graham, & C. P. Beecher (Eds.), *The menstrual cycle* (Vol. 1, pp. 123-130). New York: Springer.

Danza, R. (1983). Menarche: Its effects on mother-daughter and father-daughter interactions. In S. Golub (Ed.), *Menarche* (pp. 99-106). Lexington, MA: Lexington Books.

Dupon, C., & Bingel, A. S. (1980). Endocrinologic changes associated with puberty in girls. In A. J. Dan, E. A. Graham, and & C. P. Beecher (Eds.), *The menstrual cycle* (Vol. 1, pp. 131-140). New York: Springer.

Early menarche, more sex hormone. (1983). *Science News, 124*(5), 74.

Ehrhardt, A. E., & Meyer-Bahlberg, H. F. L. (1975). Psychological correlates of abnormal pubertal development. *Clinics in Endocrinology and Metabolism, 4*(1), 207-222.

Ellison, P. T. (1982). Skeletal growth, fatness, and menarcheal age: A comparison of two hypothesis. *Human Biology, 54*(2), 269-281.

Freud, A. (1946). *The ego and the mechanisms of defense.* New York: International Universities Press.

Frisch, R. E. (1980). Fatness, puberty and fertility. *Natural History, 89*(10), 16-27.

Frisch, R. E. (1983). Fatness, menarche, and fertility. In S. Golub (Ed.), *Menarche* (pp. 5-20). Lexington, MA: Lexington Books.

Frisch, R. E., Gotz-Welbergen, A., McArthur, J. W., Albright, T., Witschi, J., Bullen, B., Birnholz, J., Reed, R. B., & Hermann, H. (1981). Delayed menarche and amenorrhea of college athletes in relation to age of onset of training. *Journal of the American Medical Association, 246*(14), 1559-1563.

Gagnon, J. H. (1983). Age at menarche and sexual conduct in adolescence and young adulthood. In S. Golub (Ed.), *Menarche* (pp. 175-186). Lexington, MA: Lexington Books.

Goleman, D. (1989, January 10). Pioneering studies find surprising high rate of mental ills in young. *The New York Times,* C1.

Goleman, D. (1991, July 30). Theory links early puberty to childhood stress. *The New York Times,* C1, 6.

Golub, S., & Catalano, J. (1983). Recollections of menarche and women's subsequent experiences with menstruation. *Women & Health, 8*(1), 49-61.

Goodman, M. J., Grove, J. S., & Gilbert, F. (1983). Age at menarche and year of birth in relation to adult height and weight among Caucasian, Japanese and Chinese women living in Hawaii. In S. Golub (Ed.), *Menarche* (pp. 47-58). Lexington, MA: Lexington Books.

Grumbach, M. M., Grave, G. D., & Mayer, F. E. (Eds.). (1974). *Control of the onset of puberty*. New York: John Wiley.

Jones, M. C. (1958). A study of socialization patterns at the high school level. *Journal of Genetic Psychology, 93*, 87-111.

Jones, M. C., & Mussen, P. H. (1958). Self conceptions, motivations, and interpersonal attitudes of early and late maturing girls. *Child Development, 29*, 491-501.

Kantero, R.-L., & Widholm, O. (1971). Correlation of menstrual traits between adolescent girls and their mothers. *Acta Obstetrica et Gynecologica Scandinavica, Suppl. 14*, 30-36.

Koff, E. (1983). Through the looking glass of menarche: What the adolescent girl sees. In S. Golub (Ed.), *Menarche* (pp. 77-86). Lexington, MA: Lexington Books.

Koff, E., Rierdan, J., & Silverstone, E. (1978). Changes in representation of body image as a function of menarcheal status. *Developmental Psychology, 14*, 635-642.

Koff, E., Rierdan, J., & Jacobson, S. (1981). The personal and interpersonal significance of menarche. *Journal of the American Academy of Child Psychiatry, 20*, 148-158.

Kumin, M. (1982). *Why can't we live together like civilized human beings?* New York: Viking.

Leppert, P. (1983). Menarche and adolescent pregnancy. In S. Golub (Ed.), *Menarche* (p. 195-200). Lexington, MA: Lexington Books.

Logan, D. D. (1980). The menarche experience in twenty-three foreign countries. *Adolescence, 15*, 247-256.

Mead, M. (1949). *Male and female*. New York: Dell.

Menkin, J., Watkins, S. C., & Trussel, J. (1980, December). *Nutrition, health, and fertility*. Report prepared for the Ford Foundation.

Notman, M. (1983). Menarche: A psychoanalytic perspective. In S. Golub (Ed.), *Menarche* (pp. 271-278). Lexington, MA: Lexington Books.

Ohno, S. (1978). The role of H-Y antigen in primary sex determination. *Journal of the American Medical Association, 239*(3), 217-220.

Paige, K. E. (1983). Virginity rituals and chastity control during puberty: Cross-cultural patterns. In S. Golub (Ed.), *Menarche* (pp. 155-174). Lexington, MA: Lexington Books.

Petersen, A. C. (1983). Menarche: Meaning of measures and measuring meaning. In S. Golub (Ed.), *Menarche* (pp. 63-76). Lexington, MA: Lexington Books.

Petersen, A. C., & Tayloy, B. (1980). The biological approach to adolescence. In J. Adelson (Ed.), *Handbook of adolescent psychology* (pp. 117-155). New York: John Wiley.

Presser, H. B. (1978). Age at menarche, socio-sexual behavior, and fertility. *Social Biology, 25*, 94-101.

Rebar, R., & Cumming, D. C. (1981). Reproductive function in women athletes. *Journal of the American Medical Association, 246*(14), 1590.

Reiiter, E. O., & Grumbach, M. M. (1982). Neuroendocrine control mechanisms and the onset of puberty. *Annual Review of Physiology, 44,* 595-613.

Rierdan, J. (1983). Variations in the experience of menarche as a function of preparedness. In S. Golub (Ed.), *Menarche* (pp. 119-126). Lexington, MA: Lexington Books.

Rierdan, J., & Koff, E. (1985). Timing of menarche and initial menstrual experience. *Journal of Youth and Adolescence, 14*(3), 237-243.

Rierdan, J., Koff, E., & Flaherty, J. (1985). Conceptions and misconceptions of menstruation. *Women & Health, 10*(4), 33-45.

Shields, J. (1962). *Monozygotic twins.* London: Oxford University Press.

Simmons, R. G., Blyth, D. A., Van Cleave, E. F., & Bush, D. M. (1979). Entry into early adolescence: The impact of school structure, puberty, and early dating on self esteem. *American Sociological Review, 44,* 948-967.

Stubbs, M. L., Rierdan, J., & Koff, E. (1988). Becoming a woman: Considerations in educating adolescents about menstruation. *Working Paper No. 169.* Wellesley (MA) College Center for Research on Women.

Tanner, J. M. (1973). Growing up. *Scientific American, 229*(3), 34-43.

Tanner, J. M. (1978). *Foetus into man.* Cambridge, MA: Harvard University Press.

Tobin-Richards, M. H., Boxer, A. M., & Petersen, A. C. (1983). The psychological significance of pubertal change: Sex differences in perception of self during adolescence. In J. Brooks-Gunn & A. C. Petersen (Eds.), *Girls at puberty* (pp. 127-154). New York: Plenum.

To everything there is a season. (1980). *Science News, 118,* 150.

Turnbull, C. M. (1962). *The forest people.* New York: Simon & Schuster.

Udry, J. R., & Cliquet, R. L. (1982). A cross-cultural examination of the relationship between ages at menarche, marriage, and first birth. *Demography, 19,* 53-63.

Ulman, K. H. (1984, August). *Impact of menarche on self-image and mood in adolescent girls.* Paper presented at the meeting of the American Psychological Association, Toronto.

Vandenbroucke, J. P., van Laar, A., & Valkenburg, H. A. (1982). Synergy between thinness and intensive sports activity in delaying menarche. *British Medical Journal, 284,* 1907-1908.

Wallach, E. E., & Bongiovanni, A. M. (1983). Pubertal development. In A. M. Bongiovanni (Ed.), *Adolescent gynecology* (pp. 7-25). New York: Plenum.

Warren, M. P. (1983). Clinical aspects of menarche: Normal variations and common disorders. In S. Golub (Ed.), *Menarche* (pp. 229-242). Lexington, MA: Lexington Books.

Washbourn, P. (1977). *Becoming woman.* New York: Harper & Row.

Whisnant, L., & Zegans, L. (1975). A study of attitudes toward menarche in white middle class American adolescent girls. *American Journal of Psychiatry, 132*(8), 809-814.

Williams, L. R. (1983). Beliefs and attitudes of young girls regarding menstruation. In S. Golub (Ed.), *Menarche* (pp. 139-148). Lexington, MA: Lexington Books.

Woods, N. F., Dery, G. K., & Most, A. (1983). Recollections of menarche, current menstrual attitudes, and perimenstrual symptoms. In S. Golub (Ed.), *Menarche* (pp. 87-98). Lexington, MA: Lexington Books.

3

*Physiological Aspects
of the Menstrual Cycle*

Differences Between
Animals and People

Most female mammals do not menstruate. They experience a period of estrus, sometimes called "heat," a time when ovulation either has occurred or is imminent. It is only at this time that the female is actively interested in sex; when she is not in estrus, the male's sexual advances are generally rebuffed. In most animals estrus is a relatively brief period of sexual receptivity, which usually coincides with fertility.

Physiologically the menstrual cycle starts prior to estrus when the uterine lining grows under the influence of estrogen secreted by the developing ovarian follicle. Around the time when the ovarian follicle ruptures (that is, at ovulation), estrus occurs. Then, after the egg is released, the follicle becomes a progesterone-secreting corpus luteum. If fertilization occurs, estrus and ovulation are suppressed until after the birth of the fetus. If fertilization does not occur, the corpus luteum degenerates, and the uterus returns to its resting state (Symons, 1979).

In some mammals, such as laboratory rats, the estrous cycle lasts for only four or five days, and on only one of those days will the female be sexually receptive and willing to mate, namely the day on which ovulation occurs. Thus ovulation occurs spontaneously, but it is still part of an estrous cycle. If conception does not occur, the old uterine lining (endometrium) is reabsorbed and not expelled as it is in humans (menstruation). Animals that have estrous cycles do not menstruate. (The slight spotting seen in dogs is not menstrual bleeding.)

The cycle works a little differently in cats and rabbits. They prepare to ovulate several times a year, during which time they are sexually receptive (in estrus). Ovulation, which is triggered by penetration, occurs a few hours after copulation (Lein, 1979). Apparently, during copulation the penis stimulates nerve endings in the cervix and vagina. Impulses are transmitted to the hypothalamus, which secretes GnRH into the hypothalamo-hypophyseal portal system (the complex brain-hormone pathway that regulates endocrine function). Luteinizing hormone is then released, reaches the ovarian follicles, and ovulation occurs.

Thus there are two kinds of cycles found among mammals: those in which ovulation occurs after external stimulation, such as in cats and rabbits, and those in which ovulation occurs spontaneously, as in rats.

Menstrual cycles occur only in primates: some monkeys, apes, and humans. The cycle is approximately one month long, and ovulation generally occurs at midcycle. There is no period of estrus. The menstrual period is one part of the cycle, and it is characterized by a loss of blood and tissue as the endometrium sloughs off and is discharged through the vagina. The menstrual periods of nonhuman primates do not involve as much loss of blood and tissue as do those of humans. Other primates also have fewer menstrual periods, for they spend more of their reproductive lives either pregnant or nursing their young. Lactation inhibits ovulation, so nursing mothers often do not menstruate (Symons, 1979).

It is interesting to theorize about why at some point during the course of evolution estrus disappeared in mammals and the menstrual cycle evolved. With this change, sexual activity became separate from breeding; it was no longer limited to the time of ovulation.

Beach (1977) has pointed out that the sexual habits of many animals are related to other behavior patterns that are needed for the species to survive. For example, pair bonding is found in species in which the male is needed to participate in the care and rearing of the young. Thus nonreproductive sexual activity is seen among many populations of nonhuman primates as well as among humans, and all of these groups have relatively long periods of infant dependency.

Symons (1979, p. 129) speculates about marriage and the loss of estrus:

> Five or six million years ago chimpanzee-like ancestral hominids began to invade the savannah, and cooperative hunting by males became frequent and intense enough to produce substantial surpluses of meat, which set up the following selection pressures: to facilitate cooperation in the hunt, males had to reduce their sexual rivalries and to develop strong tendencies to bond with one another; at the same time, individual male-female pairs had to develop bonding tendencies in order to become effective economic and child-rearing partners—the female gathering, the male hunting, the proceeds shared with each other and with their children.

There are even further differences between the nonhuman primates and people. With greater development of the cerebral cortex, there seems to be less dependency upon the hormonal fluctuations during the menstrual cycle to affect sexual interaction. Humans share a reproductive system that is very similar to that of the apes. There is a monthly cycle of ovogenesis, ovulation, estrogen and progesterone secretion, uterine stimulation, and menstrual bleeding. However, among humans the preovulatory rise in estrogen is not clearly accompanied by increased desire and responsiveness to sexual stimulation nor to increased attractiveness to males. Hormones are a less potent control of human female sexuality and the occurrence of coitus. Vaginal lubrication occurs in response to sexual stimulation and is not dependent upon high levels of estrogen. Human female sexuality is the end result of a complex interaction of biological, psychological, and sociocultural factors. (The relationship between female sexual behavior and the menstrual cycle will be discussed more fully in Chapter 5.)

Hormonal, Systemic, and Metabolic Changes

The menstrual cycle consists of the maturation of an ovarian follicle, its release from the ovary and movement down the fallopian tube,
and the development of the corpus luteum. This process is accompanied by the growth of the endometrium. If pregnancy does not occur,
the corpus luteum regresses and the endometrium degenerates, to be
discharged from the body as the menstrual flow. These changes are
controlled by hormone messages between the central nervous system,
the hypothalamus, the pituitary, and the ovary, all operating under a
complex feedback system (see Figure 3.1).

As shown in Figure 3.2, the menstrual cycle is comprised of four
phases, each describing the state of the follicles and ova within that
phase (Hyde, 1985, p. 248). The first phase is the follicular phase
during which the ovarian follicles ripen under the influence of follicle
stimulating hormone (FSH). This period prior to ovulation extends
from approximately Day 1 to Day 14 of the cycle (Day 1 being the day
menstruation begins). The ripening follicle produces estrogen, which
inhibits the release of FSH, stimulates the release of luteinizing hormone (LH), and stimulates growth of the endometrium. The follicular
phase ends with the rupture of the follicle and release of the ovum
(the ovulatory phase). During the next phase, the luteal phase, the
corpus luteum develops in the ovary, where it secretes progesterone,
which further prepares the endometrium for implantation of the
fertilized ovum. If pregnancy does not occur, the corpus luteum
begins to regress, estrogen and progesterone levels decline, and the
endometrium begins to degenerate. Menstruation begins. During the
menstrual phase (which is a subphase of the follicular phase and
describes the days of menstrual bleeding), the endometrium is shed
along with some menstrual blood. Low levels of estrogen and progesterone cause the pituitary once again to secrete FSH, and a new wave
of follicular development begins.

HORMONE LEVELS

Figure 3.2 also shows the changes in plasma concentrations of LH,
FSH, estradiol, and progesterone during a normal ovulatory cycle. In
the follicular phase of the cycle, as the follicles mature, estrogen levels
rise slowly. FSH levels decline because of the negative feedback effect

Hormone Feedback System

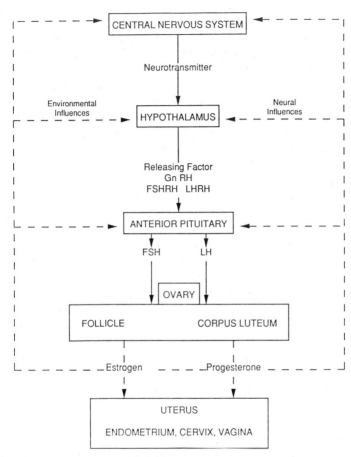

Figure 3.1. Hormone Feedback System

The menstrual cycle is based upon an intricate hormone-feedback system involving the central nervous system and hormones of the hypothalamus, the anterior lobe of the pituitary gland, and the ovaries. The hypothalamus monitors the level of ovarian hormones in the blood. Gonadotropin-hormone-releasing factor (GnRH) is secreted by the hypothalamus and causes the secretion of the gonadotropic hormones LH and FSH from the anterior pituitary. FSH stimulates the full development of a single Graafian follicle in the ovary, causing it to grow and secrete estrogen. Estrogen causes a growth of the cells lining the uterus, as well as the glands of the cervix and vaginal cells. Increasing levels of estrogen in the blood cause a reduction of FSH and dramatically magnifies the secretion of luteinizing hormone (LH). LH triggers the release of the ovum from the Graafian follicle, which then evolves into the corpus luteum and secretes progesterone and estrogen to a lesser degree. Progesterone helps to prepare the uterus to receive a fertilized egg and also signals the pituitary to slow the production of LH. If fertilization does not occur, the levels of both estrogen and progesterone gradually decline, the uterine lining begins to slough away, and menstruation begins. With low levels of estrogen in the blood, FSH production increases and the cycle begins once again.

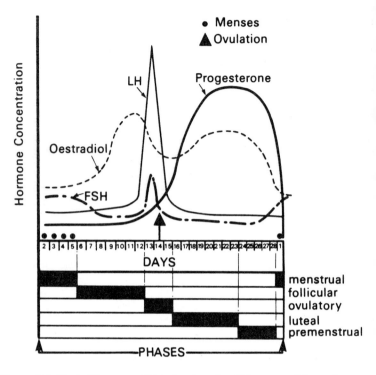

Figure 3.2. Cycle Phases and Relative Levels of Hormones Throughout
the Menstrual Cycle.

Source: Shaw, R. (1978). Neuroendocrinology of the menstrual cycle in humans. *Clinics in Endocrinology and Metabolism, 7*, 531-559. Reprinted with permission of W. B. Saunders Co.

on the brain of rising levels of estrogen. Immediately prior to ovulation, estrogen levels rise more steeply and then fall dramatically as the follicle uses up its hormone-producing cells. This signals to the hypothalamic-pituitary system that is should increase the secretion of LH, with a smaller rise in FSH. This increase in LH secretion causes the mature follicle to rupture and release the ovum.

Progesterone production increases dramatically now as the corpus luteum forms from the ruptured follicle. The luteal phase of the cycle is also characterized by a rise in plasma estrogen levels from the active corpus luteum. If fertilization of the ovum and implantation have not occurred, the corpus luteum function begins to decline about 14 days after ovulation. Lower plasma levels of estrogen and progesterone follow, as does menstruation. With the lack of inhibitory effects of the ovarian hormones, the pituitary begins to secrete more LH and FSH, and a new set of follicles begin to mature (Taymore, Berger, Thompson, & Karam, 1972).

BODY TEMPERATURE

Physiological processes in women have been found to vary in conjunction with the hormonal changes of the cycle. Most widely known is the change in body temperature that occurs at the time of ovulation (see Figure 3.3) (Hyde, 1979). Basal body temperature (the temperature just after one wakes up) is generally lower during the follicular phase; it may dip somewhat at the time of ovulation, and then it rises noticeably on the day after ovulation, generally by 0.4 degrees F or more. It continues at the higher level for the rest of the cycle. Progesterone is generally thought to be responsible for the increase in body temperature. Other indicators of an ovulatory cycle include changes in vaginal cells, cervical mucus, and urinary excretion of various hormones (Southam & Gonzaga, 1965). In fact, changes in the excretion of luteinizing hormone are the basis for the over-the-counter kits that are used to detect ovulation.

CERVICAL MUCUS

Changes in cervical mucus, either alone or in conjunction with basal body temperature, are sometimes relied upon for birth control or, conversely, to enhance the possibility of conception. Women can learn to identify the body changes linked to fertility by observing changes in cervical mucus and monitoring basal body temperature. However, it is best to learn fertility observation methods from an expert rather than from a book. A good resource is the Ovulation Method Teacher's Associations[1] (Boston Women's Health Book Collective, 1984).

Cervical glands secrete mucus throughout the menstrual cycle, and these glands respond to changing levels of estrogen. At the beginning of a new cycle, just after menstruation, when estrogen is at its lowest levels, there is a period of dryness. Then, the mucus is alkaline, thick, and viscous. As ovulation approaches and estrogen levels rise

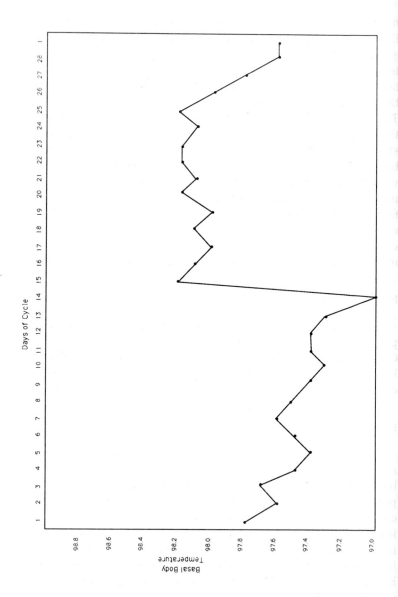

Figure 3.3. Basal Body Temperature Graph

markedly, the cervical mucus becomes more alkaline, more fluid—thin, clear, and watery—and feels very slippery. The mucus is fluid enough to flow out of the vagina and can be seen on underwear or toilet paper. If allowed to dry on a glass slide, the mucus of this period takes on a fernlike pattern. The last day of slippery mucus is called the peak day, and ovulation generally occurs on the following day. The fertile period extends from the time the mucus first appears until the fourth day after it peaks. If a woman wants to prevent conception, she must avoid all vagina-to-penis contact on fertile days. The number of fertile days varies from cycle to cycle and from woman to woman. After ovulation, under the influence of progesterone, the mucus changes noticeably, becoming thicker and less slippery. The fernlike pattern will not occur during this luteal phase, and change in mucus signals a change in fertility. The infertile phase extends from the fourth day after the slippery mucus peak day until menstruation begins (Boston Women's Health Book Collective, 1984).

BLOOD AND VITAL SIGNS

Inconsistent changes in pulse rate, respiratory rate, and blood pressure during the menstrual cycle have been reported (Southam & Gonzaga, 1965). However, two recent studies do indicate increases in heart rate and blood pressure during the premenstrual phase of the cycle (Asso & Braier, 1982; Doty, Snyder, Huggins, & Lowry, 1981).

ELECTROLYTES AND URINARY EXCRETION

There is an increase in the volume of urine excreted at the onset of menses and midcycle. Salivary composition and flow rates also have been found to be related to hormonal fluctuations. Sodium and potassium levels in saliva and the ratio of sodium to potassium change during the course of the cycle. The sodium/potassium ratio is highest during menstruation, when potassium is low and sodium is high. At ovulation the positions reverse, with potassium exhibiting its highest value and sodium its lowest (DeMarchi, 1976). Janowsky, Berens, and Davis (1973) also noted that the sodium/potassium ratio was elevated during the premenstrual phase of the cycle, along with weight and reports of negative moods.

FOOD INTAKE AND CARBOHYDRATE METABOLISM

Food intake in both women and several animal species varies significantly with the cycle; overall intake is greater during the 10 days after ovulation (Asso & Braier, 1982; Dalvit, 1981). However, the mechanisms governing these changes in appetite are not yet fully understood. In an intensive study of eight women over a 60-day period, where subjects did not know the purpose of the experiment and the experimenter did not know the timing of the cycles until after the data were collected, Dalvit-McPhillips (1983) found significant fluctuations during the course of the menstrual cycle. Subjects showed an increase in food consumption during the 10 days following ovulation. Comparison of the 10 preovulatory and 10 postovulatory days for the two cycles showed caloric intake to be significantly higher during the latter part of the cycle (Dalvit, 1981). Further analysis demonstrated that the change was primarily in carbohydrate consumption, but not in protein and fat consumption.

Many women report a premenstrual craving for sweets (Asso & Braier, 1982; Smith & Sauder, 1969), and it is possible that carbohydrate tolerance may be increased premenstrually. This is not the case among diabetic women, whose tolerance is lower at the time of menstruation and who may experience a greater need for insulin then (Magos & Studd, 1985). A dietician and a nutritionist at Kansas State University recently studied the food cravings of 83 college women for six weeks. They found that during menstruation women craved chocolate more than any other food and they craved it more than at any other time of the month (*Psychology Today*, 1985). In an earlier study of 300 nurses Smith and Sauder (1969) found a relationship between craving for food and/or sweets and premenstrual tension and fluid retention.

In fact, it does look as if a relationship exists between mood and food, particularly among those who experience mood changes. Among the nurses in the study just mentioned, those who reported a "desire to eat compulsively" or "cravings for sweets" had significantly more feelings of premenstrual tension or depression than the noncravers. And, most recently, in a prospective study, researchers at the Biological Psychiatry Branch of NIMH found a significant increase in appetite in both control subjects and in 21 patients with premenstrual syndrome. Notably, the premenstrual increase in appetite was highly correlated with self-ratings of mood—especially depression—among the patients (Both-Orthman, Rubinow, Hoban, Malley, & Grover, 1988). These researchers suggest that premenstrual syndrome may be similar to atypical depression, a disorder that also is characterized by depressive symptoms and increased appetite. They speculate that the carbohydrate craving reflects a compensatory attempt to provide the brain with tryptophan, which is necessary to correct a serotonin deficiency. Some disturbance in serotonin has been linked with depression.

WEIGHT

A weight gain of one to five pounds during the ovulatory and premenstrual phases of the cycle has been reported in about one-third of women. This increase in weight has been attributed to water, sodium, and chloride retention. When estrogens are given to humans or experimental animals, an increase in sodium and weight gain is generally seen (Southam & Gonzaga, 1965). In fact, the fluid retention that occurs during the premenstrual phase of the cycle is one of the most commonly reported symptoms. However, it is possible that a change in eating habits is also responsible (Voda, 1980).

ALCOHOL METABOLISM

Women tolerate alcohol differently at different times of the month. Jones and Jones (1976) found that drinking hits women hardest premenstrually and that they tolerate liquor best during menstruation. In an interesting and carefully controlled study, male and female college students each received 66 ml of alcohol. In addition to checking absorption and elimination rates, the subjects were given a memory task to do. The highest blood-alcohol level was found in women during the premenstrual phase, with men showing no cyclical variation (see Figure 3.4; Asso, 1983).

Alcohol impaired memory for both male and female subjects, with females suffering more impairment on a delayed recall task. These authors speculate that the sex and cycle difference may be related to the water content of the body. Men have a higher proportion of water to body weight than do women. Because alcohol is distributed throughout the body tissues in proportion to the water content, women's alcohol is less diluted, giving them higher blood-alcohol levels. Thus women were found to become more intoxicated than men

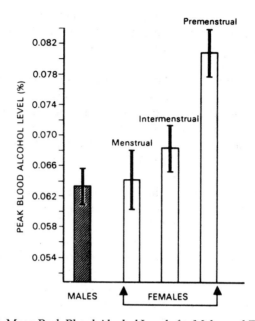

Figure 3.4. Mean Peak Blood Alcohol Levels for Males and Females
Tested at Different Times in the Menstrual Cycle

SOURCE: Jones, B. M., & Jones, M. K. (1976). Alcohol effects in women during the menstrual cycle. *Annals of the New York Academy of Sciences, 273*, 576-587. Reprinted with permission.

when given equivalent doses of alcohol at any time of the month. Interesting, too, was the finding that alcohol may increase rather than reduce anxiety during the luteal phase of the cycle (Asso, 1983).

THE SENSES

All of the senses appear to be more acute during the follicular phase of the cycle than during the luteal phase (Henkin, 1974). Around the time of ovulation women experience increased visual, tactile, and especially olfactory sensitivity (Diamond, Diamond, & Mast, 1972; Doty, Snyder, Huggins, & Lowry, 1981). Some researchers speculate that this heightened sensitivity is biologically useful, presumably increasing the likelihood of coitus and conception (Asso, 1983; Henkin, 1974). Results of studies of tactile sensitivity are contradictory, with some showing increased and others decreased sensitivity to pain midcycle. Parlee (1983) suggests that if there is a trend, it is toward less sensitivity in the premenstrual phase of the cycle, as compared with the menstrual and postmenstrual phases.

Although there is no sex difference in tactile breast sensitivity prior to puberty, after puberty women's breasts are significantly more sensitive than men's. Moreover, tactile sensitivity of the breast (the nipple, areola, and surrounding cutaneous breast tissue) varies during the menstrual cycle. It is greatest at midcycle, just prior to menstruation and at menstruation. The nipple is the most sensitive area to both touch and pain, followed by the areola, and then the cutaneous breast tissue (Robinson & Short, 1977).

Many women complain of soreness of the breasts, especially during the premenstrual phase of the cycle. Several remedies have been suggested; among the more benign are such dietary changes as reduction of sodium (salt) and xanthines (typically found in coffee, tea, and chocolate). This treatment involves no risk and seems to help some women. Some of the other suggested treatments are more controversial. Oil of evening primrose, which contains gamma-linolenic acid, has been found effective for breast tenderness. However, although it is available in pharmacies and health food stores without prescription, exact dosage has not yet been established, and this drug has not been approved by the Food and Drug Administration (Harrison, 1982). Tamoxifen, a drug used for cancer chemotherapy, which acts by inhibiting breast tissue from responding to estrogen, has been tried, too. Although side effects are not severe, premenopausal women may experience hot flashes and an increase in vaginal discharge when taking it, and the safety of this drug for long-term use has not been established (Breast Pain, 1986). Women with painful breasts need to weigh the risk of taking drugs about which little is known against relief of symptoms. For some women breast discomfort may be alleviated with dietary change or by taking an analgesic such as Tylenol.

SPEECH

The frequency of stutterers' speech disfluencies is thought to be positively related to anxiety. The more anxious a stutterer becomes, the more disfluent she will be. Hypothesizing that women would be more anxious at premenstruation than at ovulation and therefore more disfluent, a group of researchers studied 16 women (4 stutterers, 12 nonstutterers). They recorded four 3-minute speech samples and

analyzed them for repetition, revision, disrhythmic phonation, inter-
jection, and tense pauses. Consistent with their expectation, more
disfluencies were found at premenstruation among both the stutterers and nonstutterers (Silverman, Zimmer, & Silverman, 1974; Silverman & Zimmer, 1975). Unfortunately, the researchers did not use any
measure of anxiety. It would have been interesting to see if there was
a relationship between the degree of anxiety experienced and the
amount of disfluency.

Clinical Problems

In much of the literature on the menstrual cycle, the premenstrual
and menstrual phases of the cycle have consistently been cited as a
time of increased vulnerability to illness. Scarlet fever, pancreatitis,
hepatitis, influenza, pneumonia, and typhoid fever have all been
reported as occurring more frequently in the premenstrual period
(Southam & Gonzaga, 1965). Cyclical exacerbations of epilepsy have
been confirmed by most researchers (Magos & Studd, 1985). A recent
example is a study by Rosciszewska (1980), who followed 69 women
over a four-year period and found that 58% had increased seizures
premenstrually and 9% had more seizures during menstruation.

The control of diabetes is more difficult around the time of menstruation. In contrast to nondiabetic women, diabetic women have
decreased carbohydrate tolerance, their insulin requirements are
greater, and diabetic coma occurs more frequently around menstruation. Oral glucose studies in diabetics generally show a reduced
glucose tolerance at the time of menstruation, especially in women
younger than 35. This is in direct contrast to nondiabetics, in whom
oral glucose tolerance is at its highest during menstruation and lowest
in the luteal phase. Diabetic women should be aware of the possible
need to adjust their insulin dosage around the time of menstruation
(Magos & Studd, 1985).

There are cyclic changes in sensitivity to allergens. Asthma attacks
are more likely to occur during menstruation. Smolensky cites a study
of asthmatic women done by Wulfsohn in which 75% of the subjects
became worse premenstrually or menstrually (Smolensky, Reinberg,
Lee, & McGovern, 1974). Herpes commonly appears premenstrually

or at the time of menses. Skin eruptions and exacerbations of eczema often occur premenstrually. In a carefully controlled study of reactions to histamine, Smolensky and his colleagues found highest cutaneous sensitivity on the first day of the menstrual cycle and lowest sensitivity around midcycle. The difference in sensitivity is a striking 30%. Women receiving oral contraceptives did not experience the same monthly rhythm in sensitivity to histamine (Smolensky et al., 1974).

Migraine headaches are more common in females than males and may affect as many as one fifth of women, with the peak incidence between the ages of 20 and 45. In more than 60% of the cases, attacks are related to the perimenstrual phase of the cycle, hence the term menstrual migraine. There is some evidence that menstrual migraine occurs as a result of premenstrual estrogen withdrawal. The effect of pregnancy on migraine is relevant. Seventy percent of women report improvement of their migraine during the second and third trimesters when estradiol levels are consistently elevated. Somewhat paradoxically, migraine tends to improve or remit with menopause. Thus the shifting hormone levels and perhaps fluctuations in prostaglandins appear to precipitate menstrual migraine (Edelson, 1985). Several drugs have been used, with varying degrees of success, as prophylaxis or treatment, among them: propranolol, amitriptyline, ergotamine-phenobarbital-belladonna, and prostaglandin inhibitors (Raskin, 1982). Magos reports success in treating menstrual migraine with subcutaneous estradiol implants combined with cyclic oral progestogens; the combination contraceptive pill should work as well (Magos & Studd, 1985). In another study, Sargent and his colleagues found that 30 women treated with naproxen sodium experienced significantly fewer and less severe headaches during the week prior to menses than a group of placebo-treated patients (Sargent, Solbach, Damasio, Baumel, et al., 1984). However, patients in this study who also took propranolol judged their response and their overall tolerance of the propranolol to be better. The majority of patients reported a high incidence of gastrointestinal complaints associated with the naproxen.

A new drug, sumatriptan, currently being tested, offers new hope for migraine sufferers. Although the link to estrogen is uncertain, estrogen seems to affect central nervous system neurotransmitters, and some believe that a scarcity of serotonin is what causes the abnormal dilation of blood vessels associated with migraines. Sumatriptan, given by shallow skin injection, appears to cause the vessels to return to normal, thereby relieving the migraine attack and the nausea that often accompanies it (Cady, Wendt, Kirchner, Sargent, Rothrock, & Skaggs, 1991). Solbach recently reported research showing that adverse reactions are minimal, and sumatriptan is highly effective in relieving menstrual migraine headaches with dramatic, rapid improvement in pain relief and accompanying symptoms (Solbach & Sargent, 1991).

In contrast to the disorders that get worse during the premenstrual phase of the cycle, rheumatoid arthritis symptoms are least troublesome at this time. Two recent studies have shown that morning stiffness and pain and finger joint size are maximal in the early part of the cycle, when ovarian hormones are low. These data support the anti-inflammatory properties of estrogen (and to a lesser extent progesterone), which also enhances the anti-inflammatory activity of hydrocortisone (Magos & Studd, 1985).

SLEEP AND DREAMING

No clear relationship has been demonstrated between sleep and the menstrual cycle. Although women sometimes report an increase in their need for sleep and claim to take more naps during the premenstrual or menstrual phases of the cycle, the few studies that have been done are contradictory. Golub and Walsh (1985) collected sleep records for a period of five weeks from 50 college women and found no significant difference in number of hours slept across the cycle. However, Asso (1983) reports two studies in which duration of sleep was shortest at ovulation and longest premenstrually, at which time it was also more disturbed. A Belgian study suggests that there may be a relationship between cycle-related mood and changes in sleep. Cluydts and Visser (1980) studied four women in a sleep laboratory. No cycle effects were seen in three of the subjects. However, one subject showed marked changes in mood and sleep, with a lower percentage of slow-wave sleep at the time of menses. The percentage of Rapid Eye Movement (REM) sleep, which is associated with dreaming, has been reported to be higher in the follicular phase and may be related to estrogen and progesterone levels (Hoffman & Petre-Quadens, 1979). Studies of dreams and the menstrual cycle are rare, and most have only a small number of subjects, raising questions about their reliability. Yet there is a certain consistency to most of the studies. Dreams tend to be more unpleasant during the premenstrual and menstrual phases of the cycle (Swanson & Foulkes, 1967). The classic study in this area was done by Benedek who, working with an endocrinologist, could determine cycle phase based on the dream content of her psychoanalytic patients. Benedek found fears about mutilation and death, sexual fantasies, and anxiety and depression more common in the premenstrual phase (Benedek & Rubenstein, 1939). Other researchers have also reported greater sexual content and hostility around the time of menstruation (Asso, 1983).

Menstrual Synchrony

Anecdotal reports of menstrual synchrony in mothers, daughters, and sisters living together are fairly common. College roommates and close friends tell of how within a few months their periods come at about the same time. Groups of nuns living together report a similar experience. And McClintock (1971) cites a case of seven female lifeguards whose cycles fell within a four-day period of each other after they spent three months together.

McClintock hypothesized that social groupings could affect women's menstrual cycles as it does in other animals (Hopson, 1979). She studied 135 college women residing in a dormitory. The women's menstrual cycles were monitored. Three times during the academic year each woman was asked when her last and second to last menstrual periods had begun. Thus the date of onset was obtained for all cycles between late September and early April. Subjects were also asked which women they spent the most time with. The results were striking. McClintock found that roommates and closest friends did indeed experience a significant increase in menstrual synchrony. McClintock also demonstrated that the move toward synchrony was not caused by food, common stressors, light, or awareness of menstrual timing. The significant factor was time spent together. McClintock speculated about some "interpersonal physiological process" that affects the menstrual cycle but she was not able to identify just what it was that was going on during this time spent together that caused the menstrual synchrony.

Several years later, Russell (Russell, Switz, & Thompson, 1980) conducted a study in which he collected perspiration from a colleague named Genevieve Switz. She had a history of "driving" or dominating other women's cycles—that is, they became synchronous with hers when she lived with them. For the experiment, Switz wore cotton pads under her arms for 24-hour periods in order to collect perspiration. Russell then applied a liquid substance to the upper lips of 16 women volunteers three times a week for four months. Half the subjects received applications of alcohol; the others, alcohol plus Switz's underarm secretions.

The control group's cycles did not change. However, those who received Switz's perspiration had changed from an average of 9.3 days from the donor's starting day to only 3.4 days. The control group had started an average of 8.0 days away in January and by May were 9.2 days away from her, a nonsignificant change. Thus Russell showed that women need not even spend time together in order to be influenced toward menstrual synchrony. Olfactory stimulation from one woman's underarm secretions was sufficient influence to change the cycle (Russell, Switz, & Thompson, 1980).

It is now thought that menstrual synchrony is caused by pheromones, chemical substances given off by the body in small amounts and transmitted through the air. Pheromones are perceived by olfactory receptors without conscious awareness. However, the exact mechanism by which this takes place is not known. We do know that menstrual synchrony is influenced by the use of deodorants and perfumes, by whether women regularly share bathrooms, by the use of flushable tampons rather than sanitary pads, by how much time people spend together, and even by emotional factors, as will be discussed in a moment.

Stress and Menstruation

THE EFFECTS OF STRESS ON MENSTRUATION

At one time or another most women have experienced a disruption in the normal rhythm of their menstrual cycles. Often the stress of going off to summer camp or college, or experiencing a serious loss such as a divorce or the death of a loved one, will trigger early onset of menstruation or a missed period. War amenorrhea has been studied extensively. For example, during World War II the incidence of amenorrhea among nurses taken prisoner in the Philippines was 23%. And the incidence in the concentration camp Theresienstadt was 54% for a group of women facing the threat of extermination and 25% in another group who had better living conditions and did not face the threat of imminent death (Khuri & Gehi, 1981). The physiological explanations for this have become increasingly clear.

Stress results in increased levels of cortisol, a glucocorticoid released by the adrenal cortex. The path of action begins with the central nervous system: There is a psychological stressor. The hypothalamus then releases corticotropin-releasing hormone (CRH), which travels via a vascular network to the anterior pituitary. In response to CRH, the pituitary secretes adrenocorticotropic hormone, which, in turn, triggers the secretion of cortisol by the adrenal cortex. Increased amounts of norepinephrine, a brain neurotransmitter, are found in the blood around the time of ovulation. Studies suggest that the release of norepinephrine triggers the release of gonadotropin-releasing hormone (GnRH). Researchers have also found that stress promotes increased utilization of norepinephrine, with chronic stress depleting norepinephrine stores. If norepinephrine levels are low as a result of stress around the time of ovulation, the LH surge and subsequent ovulation may not occur. Chronic stress has been associated with anovulation and amenorrhea in such real-life situations as war, famine, or incarceration.

To demonstrate the effect of psychological stress on the secretion of cortisol by the adrenal gland, Marinari and her colleagues compared the cortisol responses to stress of 60 college women during the middle and premenstrual phases of their cycles. They were stressed by being asked to talk into a tape recorder and evaluate "How do you measure up to your self-expectations?" and "How do you measure up to the expectations of the people who matter most to you?" Women tested premenstrually showed greater adrenocortical reactivity to psychological stress than those at midcycle. Women on the pill did not manifest this premenstrual increase in physiological reactivity. Interestingly, there were no cycle-related changes in affective response to the task as measured by an adjective check list. The women were not aware of experiencing more stress premenstrually though their bodies responded differently at that time. Perhaps the check list was too insensitive to pick up subtle cycle-related mood changes (Marinari, Leshner, & Doyle, 1976).

Stress can inhibit ovulation. In a study of luteinizing hormone two experimental subjects were hospitalized for about a week. Blood samples were taken through an indwelling cannula every four hours. Although the subjects were admitted to the hospital shortly before they were expected to ovulate, no LH surge occurred. Blood cortisol levels remained elevated during their hospital stay. Then, within 48 hours after discharge, both women exhibited a typical LH surge, exactly what had been expected the week before (Peyser, Ayalon, Harell, Toaff, & Cordova, 1973). Lander (1988) cites a study that compared a group of 35 women who for three months during the previous year had not menstruated with an age-matched group of women under 35 with regular cycles. The women with skipped periods had experienced significantly more stressful life events, such as bereavements, than the control group.

Stress also can affect menstrual cycle length, regularity, and synchrony. Matteo (1987) studied the effect of job stress and worker interdependency on these variables in 41 women, representing five kinds of work (university department, graduate students, typing pool, emergency room nurses, recovery room nurses). The women in occupations characterized by greater levels of interdependency than stress displayed menstrual synchrony. In contrast, women who experienced high levels of anxiety and job stress were less synchronized than women with low levels of these variables. In keeping with previous work, women with high levels of anxiety and high scores on the Holmes-Rahe Schedule of Recent Life Events (a measure of life stress) had longer menstrual cycles. Regular cycles were associated with lower levels of anxiety and less life stress. Interestingly, women who lived with their sexual partners were less likely to be synchronized with their coworkers than those who did not. This suggests that regular, intimate contact with a sexual partner interferes with the mechanisms by which menstrual synchrony is established in female groups. Matteo also found that women were more likely to report daily stress in the late luteal and early menstrual phases of their cycles, raising questions as to variations in response to stress as a function of cycle phase.

STRESS AND MENSTRUAL SYMPTOMS

Many studies have demonstrated a relationship between life stress and physical illness. It is therefore not surprising that stress has also been shown to influence women's perceptions of menstrual symptoms. Wilcoxon, Schrader, and Sherif (1976) had 33 undergraduate subjects (one-third male, one-third females taking oral contraceptives, and one-third females not taking oral contraceptives) record stressful events in their daily lives, as well as symptoms and moods, over a 35-day period. Increases in impairment of concentration and stressful events were seen for both groups of women during the premenstrual phase, with a decrease in symptoms during the menstrual phase for women taking oral contraceptives. However, the data also revealed that negative affect and impaired concentration were associated to a greater extent with stressful events than with the phase of the menstrual cycle.

In a series of studies, Woods and her colleagues looked at a more representative sample of women. She selected nonpregnant women between the ages of 18 and 35 from a census listing for five neighborhoods in a large southeastern city. The women varied in racial composition and socioeconomic status. A total of 193 women were given a modified Moos Menstrual Distress Questionnaire (MDQ), and a revised version of the Holmes and Rahe Schedule of Recent Events (a measure of stress). A randomly selected subgroup of 100 women was asked to complete a daily health diary in which the women recorded daily stressors, mood, health problems, and any treatment they were getting. Total stress scores were significantly related to MDQ reports of premenstrual and menstrual pain and negative affect, as well as menstrual water retention and performance impairment. In contrast, none of the correlations between the stress scores and symptoms reported in the diary was significantly related to menstrual cycle phase. The authors conclude that this study provides modest support for a relationship between major stressful life events, daily stressors, and perimenstrual symptoms.

Further support for the link between stress and menstrual symptoms comes from a study by Siegel and her colleagues (Siegel, Johnson, & Sarason, 1979). Two hundred and forty-four female students in an Introductory Psychology class completed a battery of questionnaires, including a Life Experiences Survey, designed to assess desirable and undesirable changes in their lives during the past year, and a menstruation questionnaire. Both positive and negative life changes were significantly correlated with the number of symptoms reported. However, subjects above the median on negative life changes also reported significantly more symptoms of discomfort than subjects below the median, but this was not true for subjects experiencing positive life change. Menstrual irregularity was unrelated to life changes. Once again, women taking oral contraceptives differed from the nonusers. When the data were analyzed separately for the two groups, the researchers found that life stress and the number of menstrual symptoms experienced were significantly related only among nonpill takers. However, negative life changes were a significant predictor of menstrual pain, water retention, behavior change and bleeding in both oral contraceptive users and nonusers. Thus a relationship between negative life stress and symptoms of menstrual discomfort was supported in this study. The authors speculate about causality: Do negative life changes lead to problems with menstruation as a result of physical changes or to a greater likelihood of perceiving the symptoms as particularly bothersome? As yet there is no answer; both explanations may be true. Siegel (Siegel et al., 1979) also suggests the possibility that women under stress may intentionally or unintentionally exaggerate the discomfort associated with menstruation in order to seek succor. Perhaps they do. If successful, it sounds as if it might be an adaptive coping mechanism.

Thus the effects of stressful life events on menstrual symptoms have been seen in three studies of three different populations: university students and a community population of women ranging in age from 18 to 35 with variability in parity, occupation, income, and race. Clearly, stress is not the only factor accounting for cycle-related changes and menstrual distress, but it does appear to have a significant impact.

THE MENSTRUAL CYCLE AS A STRESSOR

Discussion of the relationship between stress and menstruation would be incomplete without a look at the flip side: How stressful is menstruation, and what factors augment that stress? A majority of women all over the world, rural and urban, of high and low social status, report physical discomfort associated with the premenstrual and menstrual phases of the cycle. For the most part these symptoms are mild and manageable. Most women do little about it; they carry on their activities both inside and outside the home. Cross-cultural reports of mood changes are also common, but more variable, ranging from about 30% in Indonesia to more than 70% in the United Kingdom and Yugoslavia. And then there is the possible stress associated with the bleeding episode itself. Women with heavier bleeding experience more pain and more anxiety (Snowden & Christian, 1983).

The way a woman responds to menstruation is influenced by cultural expectations and personal experience. Because menstrual taboos and negative cultural attitudes abound in twentieth-century America as well as in the rest of the world, the menstruating woman is subject to being devalued by the law, medicine, and religion. As previously noted, the concept of menstruation as illness still exists. Often the relatively small number of women who suffer debilitating pain at menstruation is considered the prototype, and women in general are believed to be physically and psychologically impaired by their menstrual periods.

Several studies have been designed to see whether people use the menstrual cycle as an explanation for discomfort, bad moods, or changes in behavior. Certainly both men and women believe that women do not function as well when menstruating (Golub, 1981). Further support for this hypothesis can be seen in an innovative experiment by Ruble (1977). She told subjects that their brain waves indicated that they were in either the premenstrual or intermenstrual phase of the cycle. They were then asked to fill out the MDQ describing symptoms they had experienced in the last day or two. Subjects who believed they were premenstrual had higher scores on the water retention and pain scales. The women did not actually differ in cycle phase. This study indicates that women overstate the changes in their bodies that occur during the course of the menstrual cycle, and when they think that they are premenstrual, they report more problems than when they think they are midcycle.

Menstruation also reminds a woman of her body, and most women are not particularly happy with their bodies. Twice as many high-school girls as boys want to change their looks. In one study, women consistently rated their own bodies as heavier than they would like them to be or what they thought was attractive to men. Feeling good about oneself includes feeling good about one's body. Women athletes are a lot more comfortable with their bodies than nonathletes. Studies of high-school and college women athletes have found that they have a more positive image of their bodies than nonathletes; athletic women also suffer less menstrual discomfort than sedentary women (Brooks-Gunn, Gargiulo, & Warren, 1986).

Many studies indicate a dramatic relationship between premenstrual and menstrual phases of the cycle and accident rates, acute psychiatric hospital admissions, crimes of violence, and suicide attempts. At first glance one might point to these data as demonstrating the stress of menstruation. However, Parlee (1975) has suggested a contrary interpretation: perhaps the stress of the illness or accident caused menstruation. Strong emotion may lead to hormonal shifts, changes in the endometrium, and the onset of menstruation. In order to clarify the direction of causality, we need to know whether or not menstruation occurred at the predicted time, and that hypothesis awaits further testing.

There is much more to learn about the relationship between stress and menstruation. On every level, from the hormonal to the cultural, there is a need for further research. Teasing out which is the stressor and which the response to stress and how they interact is a complex problem that is as yet unresolved.

Effects of Exercise

Many women have some change in cycle length or amount of blood loss when beginning an exercise program. The usual experience is a reduction in bleeding and shorter periods. This is no cause for concern and may even be welcomed by some. Only when taken to extremes does exercise appear to have negative consequences. For example, exercise-related amenorrhea (loss of menstrual periods) affects 7%-10% of women who engage in vigorous physical activity (Brody, 1982). However, this increases to an incidence of irregular or absent periods of up to 50% among competitive athletes.

In an article about the female athlete, Bates (1983) describes a summer program at Sargent College in which 28 women between the ages of 20 and 23 participated in an eight-week exercise experiment. The women had to run two hours a day, stay on the diet provided, and also engage in three and a half hours of moderate activity such as volleyball, softball, hiking, or cycling. Subjects were divided into weight loss and weight maintenance groups, but it was almost impossible to keep the women at weight maintenance. Menstruation ceased in 85%, and those who did menstruate had shorter cycles. However, within a few months after the end of the program, they were all back to normal, continuing to exercise, but not as hard, and gaining weight. The benefits of exercising were clear: Menstrual symptoms improved. The women had less menstrual pain and premenstrual tension, and self-esteem was much higher after the eight-week program.

Women who are under 30, have not been pregnant, had a later age of menarche, experience a weight loss of 10 pounds or more, and have a previous history of irregularity are more likely to experience exercise-related disruptions in menstruation (Baker, Mathur, Kirk, & Williamson, 1981; Lutter & Cushman, 1982). At greatest risk are long-distance runners. Amenorrhea is more prevalent among runners than among swimmers or cyclists, and runners are more affected by the number of miles run per week as well. Shangold (1985) found that the level of athletic amenorrhea increased as the body weights of the runners decreased. Affective disorders may play a role as well. In a study of 13 amenorrheic runners, Gadpaille and his associates found that 11 reported major affective disorders in themselves or in first- and second-degree relatives. In addition, eight reported eating disorders in themselves. There were no eating disorders or major affective disorders among the regularly menstruating runners, and only one had first-degree relatives with major affective disorders (Gadpaille, Sanborn, & Wagner, 1987).

The onset of menstruation may be delayed by intense physical activity. In a study of Harvard University runners and swimmers, premenarcheal-trained athletes began menstruation at an average age of 15; in contrast, postmenarcheal-trained athletes began menstruation at an average age of 13. Each year of training before menarche appears to delay menstruation by about five months. Intense physical activity before menarche was also found to contribute to irregular menstrual cycles. About 83% of premenarcheal-trained athletes had this problem, compared to only 40% of postmenarcheal-trained athletes (Exercise and Late Menstruation, 1981).

There are several reasons why amenorrhea presents a problem. Bone loss is one of them. In a study comparing nonmenstruating long-distance runners with menstruating women of the same age, height, weight, and training regimen, researchers found the bone content of the amenorrheic women to be "comparable to that of a woman 52 years old" (Menstrual Hiatus . . . , 1984). Other research confirms that amenorrheic athletes have lower vertebral bone mineral density than matched groups of normally menstruating athletes. Significant increases in bone density are seen in women who resume menstruating (Drinkwater, Nilson, Ott, & Chestnut, 1986; Riggs & Eastell, 1986).

Treatment of amenorrhea is necessary because of the risk of developing endometrial hyperplasia and adenocarcinoma from unopposed estrogen. Shangold (1985) notes that restoration of a normal hormonal milieu is desirable. There are several possible approaches: decreasing training, increasing weight and/or body fat, or, for those who do not want to change their exercise or eating habits and are not interested in fertility, taking oral contraceptives, which will provide both birth control and endometrial protection.

In a review article, Gannon (1988) explores the role of exercise in the alleviation of menstrual and menopausal symptoms. She notes that several studies have found an exacerbation of symptoms with stress. Woods and her colleagues found that the degree of daily stress women experienced was associated with the frequency and severity of PMS symptoms. And Gannon (1988) herself reported significant correlations between frequency of hot flashes and daily stressors among half of the menopausal women she and her associates studied. Both dysmenorrhea and hot flashes have been successfully treated with relaxation and other stress-reduction techniques, but what effect does exercise have on menstrual symptoms? Vigorous exercise results in increased levels of beta-endorphins. One action of these endogenous opiates is to provide analgesia. Thus exercise may decrease menstrual cramps by increasing the release of endorphins. When I was a teenager, exercise was touted as a way of reducing menstrual pain. It never worked for me. I remember thinking I hurt too much to exercise when I was having cramps. No one at that time suggested a regular exercise program, but that is precisely what seems to work. A recent study evaluated the effects of a 12-week aerobic training program on menstrual cramps. Experimental and control groups reported similar levels of symptoms before training. After training the experimental group reported significantly less severe symptoms during menstruation than the control group. There were no group differences before or after training during the premenstrual or intermenstrual phases of the cycle (Israel, Sutton, & O'Brien, 1985).

There has been relatively little research examining the effects of exercise on PMS symptoms. However, Gannon (1988) cites two studies in which women who regularly participated in sports activity experienced less PMS anxiety than nonexercising women. There are at least two possible explanations. Some researchers believe that PMS symptoms are related to a high estrogen-progesterone ratio. Exercise may reduce estrogen levels, either directly or as a result of reducing body fat (adipose tissue is one source of estrogen). Alternatively, endorphin levels are low during menstrual and postmenstrual phases of the cycle and highest during the late follicular and luteal phases. Reid and Yen suggest that PMS symptoms may be caused by abnormally elevated levels of endorphins during the midluteal phase and/or to their withdrawal prior to menstruation. If menstruation serves as a stressor, increasing these high levels of endorphins, there may be an increase in appetite. And, because these endogenous opiates tend to inhibit the production of neurotransmitters in the central nervous system, women may experience fatigue and depression. There would also be an increase in prolactin, which would lead to fluid retention, weight gain, and perhaps breast tenderness—also related to the inhibition of neurotransmitters. Finally, the body may become accustomed to higher levels of endorphins, so that when they fall just prior to menstruation, symptoms of withdrawal such as irritability, anxiety, and tension may occur. Exercise could work by stabilizing endorphin levels.

During menopause exercise can alleviate such symptoms as fatigue, depression, tension, insomnia, irritability, and weight gain because of its stress-reducing and mood-elevating effects. And it works for hot flashes, too. Hot flashes occur in conjunction with pulsations of luteinizing hormone, and both probably follow stimulation of the pituitary gland by hypothalamic gonadotropin-releasing hormone (GnRH). In premenopausal women, endorphin levels are maintained by normal cycling of ovarian hormones. However, with menopause there are decreasing levels of estrogen and progesterone and concomitant reduction in endogenous opiods, thus interfering with regulation of GnRH and thermal homeostasis. Because exercise increases endorphin levels, which decrease LH release from the pituitary, there may be a reduction in the incidence and severity of hot flashes. Two studies do demonstrate a significant reduction in the severity of hot flashes among runners and women tested before and after an aerobic conditioning program (Gannon, 1988).

This is a relatively new field, and there is a need for comparisons of different types of exercise regimens, as well as the short-term and long-term effects of exercise, and the role of diet. However, overall, the research suggests that moderate exercise has a variety of beneficial effects on menstrual and menopausal symptoms.

Note

1. Ovulation Method Teachers Association, Box 14511, Portland, OR 97214.

References

Asso, D. (1983). *The real menstrual cycle.* New York: John Wiley.

Asso, D., & Braier, J. R. (1982). Changes with the menstrual cycle in psychophysiological and self-report measures of activation. *Biological Psychology, 15,* 95-107.

Baker, E. R., Mathur, R. S., Kirk, R. F., & Williamson, H. O. (1981). Female runners and secondary amenorrhea: Correlation with age, parity, mileage, and plasma hormonal and sex hormone-binding globulin concentrations. *Fertility and Sterility, 36*(2), 183-187.

Bates, P. (1983). The female athlete: How vigorous exercise affects menstruation. *Bostonia Magazine, 57*(3), 47-49.

Beach, F. A. (1977). Cross-species comparisons and the human heritage. In F. A. Beach (Ed.), *Human sexuality in four perspectives* (pp. 296-317). Baltimore: Johns Hopkins University Press.

Benedek, T., & Rubenstein, B. (1939). The correlation between ovarian activity and psychodynamic processes. *Psychosomatic Medicine, 1,* 245-270, 461-485.

Boston Women's Health Book Collective. (1984). *The new our bodies, ourselves.* New York: Simon & Schuster.

Both-Orthman, B., Rubinow, D. R., Hoban, M. C., Malley, J., & Grover, G. N. (1988). Menstrual cycle phase-related changes in appetite in patients with premenstrual syndrome and in control subjects. *American Journal of Psychiatry, 145*(5), 628-631.

Breast pain: A new treatment. (1986, June). *Harvard Medical School Health Letter, 11*(8), 5.

Brody, J. E. (1982, September 1). Effects of exercise on menstruation. *The New York Times,* C1, 6.

Brooks-Gunn, J., Gargiulo, J., & Warren, M. P. (1986). The menstrual cycle and athletic performance. In J. L. Puhl & C. H. Brown (Eds.), *The menstrual cycle and physical activity.* Champaign, IL: Human Kinetics.

Cady, R. K., Wendt, J. K., Kirchner, J. R., Sargent, J. D., Rothrock, J. F., & Skaggs, Jr., H. (1991, June 5). Treatment of acute migraine with subcutaneous sumatriptan. *Journal of the American Medical Association, 265*(21), 2831-2835.

Cluydts, R., & Visser, P. (1980). Mood and sleep, I: Effects of the menstrual cycle. *Waking and Sleeping, 4,* 193-197.

Dalvit, S. P. (1981). The effect of the menstrual cycle on patterns of food intake. *The American Journal of Clinical Nutrition, 34,* 1811-1815.

Dalvit-McPhillips, S. P. (1983). The effect of the human menstrual cycle on nutrient intake. *Physiology & Behavior, 31,* 209-212.

DeMarchi, W. G. (1976). Psychophysiological aspects of the menstrual cycle. *Journal of Psychosomatic Research, 20*, 279-287.

Diamond, M., Diamond, A. L., & Mast, M. (1972). Visual sensitivity and sexual arousal levels during the menstrual cycle. *Journal of Nervous and Mental Diseases, 55*, 170-176.

Doty, R. L., Snyder, P. J., Huggins, G. R., & Lowry, L. D. (1981). Endocrine, cardiovascular, and psychological correlates of olfactory sensitivity changes during the human menstrual cycle. *Journal of Comparative and Physiological Psychology, 95*(1), 45-60.

Drinkwater, B. L., Nilson, K., Ott, S., & Chestnut III, C. H. (1986, July 18). Bone mineral density after resumption of menses in amenorrheic athletes. *Journal of the American Medical Association, 256*(3), 380-382.

Edelson, R. N. (1985). Menstrual migraine and other hormonal aspects of migraine. *Headache, 25*, 376-379.

Exercise and late menstruation. (1981, October 17). *Science News, 120*(16), 249.

Gadpaille, W. J., Sanborn, C. F., & Wagner, Jr., W. W. (1987). Athletic amenorrhea, major affective disorders, and eating disorders. *American Journal of Psychiatry, 144*(7), 939-942.

Gannon, L. (1988). The potential role of exercise in the alleviation of menstrual disorders and menopausal symptoms: A theoretical synthesis of recent research. *Women & Health, 14*(2), 105-127.

Golub, S. (1981). Sex differences in attitudes and beliefs regarding menstruation. In P. Komnenich, M. McSweeney, J. A. Noack, & Sister N. Elder (Eds.), *The menstrual cycle*. New York: Springer.

Golub, S., & Walsh, F. (1985). *Sleep patterns and the menstrual cycle*. Unpublished manuscript.

Harrison, M. (1982). *Self-help for premenstrual syndrome*. New York: Random House.

Henkin, R. I. (1974). Sensory changes during the menstrual cycle. In M. Ferin, F. Halberg, R. M. Richart, & R. Vande Wiele (Eds.), *Biorhythms and human reproduction*. New York: John Wiley.

Hoffman, G., & Petre-Quadens, O. (1979). Maturation of REM-patterns from childhood to maturity. *Waking and Sleeping, 3*, 255-262.

Hopson, J. L. (1979, April 28). Scent and human behavior: Olfaction or fiction? *Science News, 115*, 282-283.

Hyde, J. S. (1979). *Understanding human sexuality*. New York: McGraw-Hill.

Hyde, J. S. (1985). *Half the human experience*. Lexington, MA: D. C. Heath.

Israel, R. G., Sutton, M., & O'Brien, K. F. (1985). Effects of aerobic training on primary dysmenorrhea symptomatology in college females. *Journal of American College Health, 33*, 241-244.

Janowsky, D. S., Berens, S. C., & Davis, J. M. (1973). Correlations between mood, weight and electrolytes during the menstrual cycle: A renin-angiotensin-aldosterone hypothesis of premenstrual tension. *Psychosomatic Medicine, 35*, 143-154.

Jones, B. M., & Jones, M. M. (1976). Alcohol effects in women during the menstrual cycle. *Annals of the New York Academy of Sciences, 273*, 576-587.

Khuri, R., & Gehi, M. (1981). Psychogenic amenorrhea: An integrative review. *Psychosomatics, 22*(10), 883-893.

Landèr, L. (1988). *Images of bleeding*. New York: Orlando.

Lein, A. (1979). *The cycling female*. San Francisco: W. H. Freeman.

Lutter, J. M., & Cushman, S. (1982). Menstrual patterns in female runners. *The Physician and Sportsmedicine, 10*(9), 60-72.

Magos, A., & Studd, J. (1985). Effects of the menstrual cycle on medical disorders. *British Journal of Hospital Medicine, 33*(2), 68-77.

Marinari, K. T., Leshner, A. I., & Doyle, M. P. (1976). Menstrual cycle status and adrenocortical reactivity to psychological stress. *Psychoneuroendocrinology, 1*, 213-218.

Matteo, S. (1987). The effect of job stress and job interdependency on menstrual cycle length, regularity and synchrony. *Psychoneuroendocrinology, 12*(6), 467-476.

McClintock, M. (1971). Menstrual synchrony and suppression. *Nature, 229*, 244-245.

Menstrual hiatus can prompt bone loss in female athletes. (1984, August 4). *Science News, 26*(5), 69.

Parlee, M. B. (1975). *Menstruation and crime, accidents and acute psychiatric illness: A reinterpretation of Dalton's data*. Paper presented at the meeting of the American Psychological Association, Chicago.

Parlee, M. B. (1983). Menstrual rhythms in sensory processes: A review of fluctuations in vision, olfaction, audition, taste, and touch. *Psychological Bulletin, 93*(3), 539-548.

Peyser, M. R., Ayalon, D., Harell, A., Toaff, R., & Cordova, T. (1973). Stress induced delay of ovulation. *Obstetrics and Gynecology, 42*, 667-671.

Psychology Today. (1988, March). p. 10.

Raskin, N. H. (1982). Migraine. *Psychosomatics, 23*(9), 897-907.

Riggs, B. L., & Eastell, R. (1986, July 18). Exercise, hypogonadism, and osteopenia. *Journal of the American Medical Association, 256*(3), 392.

Robinson, J. E., & Short, R. V. (1977). Changes in breast sensitivity at puberty, during the menstrual cycle, and at parturition. *British Medical Journal, 1*, 1188-1191.

Rosciszewska, D. (1980). Analysis of seizure dispersion during menstrual cycle in women with epilepsy. *Monographs in Neural Sciences, 5*, 280-284.

Ruble, D. N. (1977). Premenstrual symptoms: A reinterpretation. *Science, 197*, 291-292.

Russell, M. J., Switz, G. M., & Thompson, K. (1980). Olfactory influences on the human menstrual cycle. *Pharmacology, Biochemistry & Behavior, 13*, 737-738.

Sargent, J., Solbach, P., Damasio, H., Baumel, B., Corbett, J., Eisner, L., et al. (1984, June 23-24). *A comparison of naproxen sodium to propranolol hydrochloride and a placebo control for the prophylaxis of migraine headache*. Paper presented at the meeting of the American Association for the Study of Headache, San Francisco.

Shangold, M. M. (1985). Causes, evaluation, and management of athletic oligo-/amenorrhea. *Medical Clinics of North America, 69*(1), 83-95.

Siegel, J. M., Johnson, J. H., & Sarason, I. G. (1979). Life changes and menstrual discomfort. *Journal of Human Stress, 5*, 41-46.

Silverman, E. M., & Zimmer, C. H. (1975). Speech fluency fluctuations during the menstrual cycle. *Journal of Speech and Hearing, 18*, 202-206.

Silverman, E. M., Zimmer, C. H., & Silverman, F. H. (1974). Variability of stutterers' speech disfluency: The menstrual cycle. *Perceptual and Motor Skills, 38*, 1037-1038.

Smith, S. L., & Sauder, C. (1969). Food cravings, depression and premenstrual problems. *Psychosomatic Medicine, 31,* 281-287.

Smolensky, M. H., Reinberg, A., Lee, R. E., & McGovern, J. P. (1974). Secondary rhythms related to hormonal changes in the menstrual cycle: Special reference to allergology. In M. Ferin, F. Halberg, R. M. Richart, and R. L. Vande Wiele (Eds.), *Biorhythms and human reproduction* (pp. 287-306). New York: John Wiley.

Snowden, R., & Christian, B. (1983). *Patterns and perceptions of menstruation.* New York: St. Martin's Press.

Solbach P., & Sargent, J. (1991). *New hope for menstrual migraine.* Paper presented at the meeting of the Society of Menstrual Cycle Research, Seattle, WA.

Southam, A. L., & Gonzaga, F. P. (1965). Systemic changes during the menstrual cycle. *American Journal of Obstetrics and Gynecology, 91*(1), 142-165.

Swanson, E. M., & Foulkes, S. D. (1967). Dream content and the menstrual cycle. *Journal of Nervous and Mental Disease, 145,* 358-363.

Symons, D. (1979). *The evolution of human sexuality.* New York: Oxford University Press.

Taymore, M. L., Berger, M. J., Thompson, I. E., & Karam, K. S. (1972). Hormone factors in human ovulation. *American Journal of Obstetrics and Gynecology, 114,* 445-453.

Voda, A. (1980). Pattern of progesterone and aldosterone in ovulating women during the menstrual cycle. In A. J. Dan, E. A. Graham, & C. P. Beecher (Eds.), *The menstrual cycle.* New York: Springer.

Wilcoxon, L., Schrader, S., & Sherif, C. (1976). Daily self reports on activities, events, moods, and somatic changes during the menstrual cycle. *Psychosomatic Medicine, 38,* 399-417.

4

Psychological Aspects of the Menstrual Cycle

The link between humor and menstruation is tenuous at best, but there is some funny stuff. Gloria Steinem's essay, "If Men Could Menstruate," is a classic. Steinem clearly turns a negative into a positive: Anything people with power have—even periods—becomes desirable (see Figure 4.1; Steinem, 1978).

Along the same lines, one of my students returned from a semester of study in England with a British ad for Dr. White's Towels and Tampons; the ad asks:

> Have you ever wondered how men would carry on if they had periods?
>
> If men had periods the cry would go up for the 3-week month, never mind the 5-day week.

The British ad also treats the nuisance aspects of menstruation more realistically than most American ads do. It says outright: "We aren't naive enough to imagine we could make your period a lot of laughs, exactly. But we're certain we can make it less of a (dare we say it?) bl**dy nuisance."

Humor attenuates anxiety, and the subject of menstrual periods vis-à-vis women's psyches is a touchy one for a great many people.

It is also an area where fallacy and controversy abound. Some researchers, and lay people as well, claim that there are no important differences between the sexes that are not culturally determined (except, of course, for the ability to carry and give birth to a baby and nurse it). Others strongly believe in the debilitating nature of menstruation; they see it as illness (or at least as not normal) and expect it to have an adverse impact on women's lives and activities. For example, anthropologist Lionel Tiger (1970) maintains, not only that there are sex differences, but that they have a basis in biology, and that women are the unfortunate victims of their cyclic hormonal variations. Tiger has even expressed concern that "an American girl writing her Graduate Record Examinations over a two day period or a week-long set of finals during the premenstruum begins with a disadvantage which almost certainly condemns her to no higher than a second-class grade. A whole career in the educational system can be unfairly jeopardized because of this phenomenon."

So which is it? Are women victims of the "m" word? What is the psychological impact of the menstrual cycle on women's lives? And, if there are cyclical changes, are they rooted in culture, physiology, or both? The answer probably is "both."

In previous chapters we have looked at the cultural and physiological aspects of menstruation. Contemporary negative attitudes find their roots in almost every culture and religion and are reflected, even today, in our language and customs. We also know that physiological processes in women ebb and flow in association with the changing hormonal environment. However, the menstrual cycle is not the only rhythm to which we respond. Biological rhythms exist in men as well as women and in the world around us. Over a 24-hour period humans experience a rhythmic fluctuation in body temperature, blood pressure, pulse, respiration, blood sugar, hormone levels, the excretion of urine, pain, allergies, and even response to medication. We are not the same from one hour to the next. Some people are aware of the changes they experience over the course of the day; some may identify themselves as "owls" (preferring to work at night), while others know that they are "larks" (most alert in the morning). Mood varies too. Mothers will readily tell you when during the course of the day or evening their babies' "cranky time" is. And the monthly cycle of women has its counterpart in men. In a year-long study of 25 male industrial workers, Rex Hersey of the University of Pennsylvania found variations in emotion within each day and over longer periods

Figure 4.1. If Men Could Menstruate

. . . So what would happen if suddenly, magically, men could menstruate and women could not?

Clearly, menstruation would become an enviable, boastworthy, masculine event:

Men would brag about how long and how much.

Young boys would talk about it as the envied beginning of manhood. Gifts, religious ceremonies, family dinners, and stag parties would mark the day.

To prevent monthly work loss among the powerful, Congress would fund a National Institute of Dysmenorrhea. Doctors would research little about heart attacks, from which men were hormonally protected, but everything about cramps.

Sanitary supplies would be federally funded and free. Of course, some men would still pay for the prestige of such commercial brands as Paul Newman Tampons, Muhammad Ali's Rope-a-Dope Pads, John Wayne Maxi Pads, and Joe Namath Jock Shields—"For Those Light Bachelor Days."

Statistical surveys would show that men did better in sports and won more Olympic medals during their periods.

Generals, right-wing politicians, and religious fundamentalists would cite menstruation ("*men*-struation") as proof that only men could serve God and country in combat ("You have to give blood to take blood"), occupy high political office ("Can women be properly fierce without a monthly cycle governed by the planet Mars?"), be priests, ministers, God Himself ("He gave this blood for our sins"), or rabbis ("Without a monthly purge of impurities, women are unclean").

Male liberals or radicals, however, would insist that women are equal, just different; and that any woman could join their ranks if only she were willing to recognize the primacy of menstrual rights ("Everything else is a single issue") or self-inflict a major wound every month ("You *must* give blood for the revolution").

Street guys would invent slang ("He's a three-pad man") and "give fives" on the corner with some exchange like, "Man, you lookin' *good!*"

"Yeah, man, I'm on the rag!"

TV shows would treat the subject openly. (*Happy Days:* Richie and Potsie try to convince Fonzie that he is still "The Fonz," though he has missed two periods in a row. *Hill Street Blues:* The whole precinct hits the same cycle.) So would newspapers (SUMMER SHARK SCARE THREATENS MENSTRUATING MEN. JUDGE CITES MONTHLIES IN PARDONING RAPIST.) And so would movies. (Newman and Redford in *Blood Brothers!*)

Men would convince women that sex was *more* pleasurable at "that time of the month." Lesbians would be said to fear blood and therefore life itself, though all they needed was a good menstruating man.

Medical schools would limit women's entry ("they might faint at the sight of blood").

Of course, intellectuals would offer the most moral and logical arguments. Without that biological gift for measuring the cycles of the moon and planets, how could a woman master any discipline that demanded a sense of time, space, mathematics—or the ability to measure anything at all? In philosophy and religion, how could women compensate for being disconnected from the rhythm of the universe? Or for their lack of symbolic death and resurrection every month?

Menopause would be celebrated as a positive event, the symbol that men had accumulated enough years of cyclical wisdom to need no more.

Liberal males in every field would try to be kind. The fact that "these people" have no gift for measuring life, the liberals would explain, should be punishment enough.

And how would women be trained to react? One can imagine right-wing women agreeing to all these arguments with a staunch and smiling masochism. ("The ERA would force housewives to wound themselves every month": Phyllis Schlafly. "Your husband's blood is as sacred as that of Jesus—and so sexy, too!": Marabel Morgan.) Reformers and Queen Bees would adjust their lives to the cycles of the men around them. Feminists would explain endlessly that men, too, needed to be liberated from the false idea of Martian aggressiveness, just as women needed to escape the bonds of "menses-envy." Radical feminists would add that the oppression of the nonmenstrual was the pattern for all other oppressions. ("Vampires were our first freedom fighters!") Cultural feminists would exalt a female bloodless imagery in art and literature. Socialist feminists would insist that, once capitalism and imperialism were overthrown, women would menstruate, too. ("If women aren't yet menstruating in Russia," they would explain, "it's only because true socialism can't exist within capitalist encirclement.")

In short, we would discover, as we should already guess, that logic is in the eye of the logician. (For instance, here's an idea for theorists and logicians: If women are supposed to be less rational and more emotional at the beginning of our menstrual cycle when the female hormone is at its lowest level, then why isn't it logical to say that, in those few days, women behave the most like the way men behave all month long? I leave further improvisations up to you.)*

The truth is that, if men could menstruate, the power justifications would go on and on.

If we let them.

—1978

*With thanks to Stan Pottinger for many of the improvisations already here.

Source: © Gloria Steinem. Reprinted from *Outrageous Acts and Everyday Rebellions* (1983) with permission.

as well. Mood cycles ranged from four-and-a-half to nine weeks, with some subjects unaware of their change in feelings and behavior (NIMH, 1970). Yet, despite the prevalence of daily, weekly, monthly and yearly cycles in our lives, we value constancy, and for the most part we deny the rhythm of our body clocks and plug ourselves into the time constraints of modern life. Thus we do not particularly concern ourselves with these other cycles. Why then the attention to adverse changes that may or may not be associated with the menstrual cycle? Several authors point to misogyny as the explanation, carefully noting that there have been few attempts to look at positive aspects of the menstrual cycle (Birke & Best, 1982). Certainly in the past the "raging hormone" hypothesis has been used to justify keeping women out of high-level jobs. Women are supposedly victims of their hormones, which render them unstable and unable to make responsible decisions. Isn't it interesting that when women are needed in the economy, such as during World Wars I and II—and now—research addressing the issue of female incapacitation burgeons, and myths about menstrual impairment diminish?

Changes in Sensation and Perception

Psychological aspects of the menstrual cycle can be divided into three major areas: sensation and perception, mood and personality, and intellectual and work performance. We are probably least aware of changes in our senses and perceptual abilities. Yet it has been reported that sight, hearing, smell, touch, and taste all reach a peak of sensitivity at the time of ovulation, and response to pain decreases at the same time (Asso, 1983). The data are most consistent for vision and smell.

When a friend and colleague of mine moved into a new house, she made the discovery that her sensitivity to odors varied at different times in her cycle. The previous family in the house had a cat, and though the cat was no longer there, the smell of the cat remained in the carpeting. My friend found that the smell bothered her, and more so at some times of the month than at others. However, she got little sympathy when she complained about it to her premenarcheal daughter and postmenopausal mother. Then she heard about a study in which a significant positive correlation was found between estrogen levels and olfactory sensitivity: Women are more sensitive than men or nonovulating women to certain odors, for example, exaltolide, a musky-smelling substance found in male urine (Asso, 1983). Now she understood what was happening. Because of their lower levels of estrogen, neither her daughter nor her mother smelled what she smelled. This knowledge helped, but she felt a lot better when she got new carpeting.

Basic sensory and perceptual processes are least likely to be influenced by sociocultural factors and therefore provide an opportunity for researchers to study a relatively pure psychological rhythm. As noted in Chapter 3, the senses appear to be more acute during the follicular stage of the cycle. In a review of the literature, Parlee (1983) found both visual and olfactory thresholds to be lower around the time of ovulation. Thus women are more sensitive to faint lights and certain odors in the middle of their cycles. However, the findings related to hearing are less consistent. In the four studies she reviewed, Parlee found that audition showed two peaks, one at ovulation and another at the beginning of menstruation, but two other studies found no phase differences for audition. Parlee did not find any consistent changes in taste, temperature sensitivity, or touch.

Sommer (1985) reviewed studies of reaction time, along with studies of sensory sensitivity and galvanic skin response (a measure of skin resistance). Consistent with the research mentioned above, the data on visual and olfactory sensitivity supported midcycle increases in sensitivity. No phase difference was found for audition, and variations in galvanic skin response were inconsistent.

The contradictory findings may be attributable to methodological problems. Differences in phase designation are common. Some researchers divide the cycle into quarters or thirds, while others make daily observations, so it is difficult to know if they are measuring the same cycle phase. Also, the assumption that there will be some kind of premenstrual or menstrual disability may influence research design, with some researchers looking for a decrement in performance around the time of menstruation. And, although the cycle-phase differences that have been found thus far tend to be small, very few replications of the research have been done. If we are to accept findings as valid, it is important that research be replicated. Because some studies report menstrual-cycle variations and others do not, Sommer wisely comments that, "it is very difficult to make clear generalizations about the psychophysiological data." It is important to keep in mind that no relationship has been found between sensory variations and hormone fluctuations.

Variations in Mood

In a study that has become a biobehavioral classic, psychoanalyst Therese Benedek, using dreams and psychoanalytic interview material, predicted where 15 of her patients were in their menstrual cycles. Meanwhile, her colleague Boris B. Rubenstein, an endocrinologist, used a record of temperatures and vaginal smears to determine cycle phase and date of ovulation. Thus he determined cycle phase on the basis of physiological evidence, while she used psychological data. Benedek and Rubenstein studied 152 cycles of 15 neurotic patients, and Benedek successfully matched Rubenstein's findings in 2,128 of the 2,261 cycles. They found consistent psychodynamic changes related to various hormonal phases. When her patients were premenstrual, Benedek found that they were restless, irritable, oversensitive to all kinds of stimuli, complained of fatigue, were fearful, and manifested emotional withdrawal, with more or less severe depression and a feeling of regret and inferiority. Because her work has often been misrepresented as overemphasizing the effects of hormonal cycles on female behavior, Benedek has clearly stated that she does not believe that these effects are as great in normal women as in the neurotic women she studied (Benedek & Rubenstein, 1939).

But what do we know about mood changes in normal women? Most of the studies done—which have used everything from questionnaires, interviews, and mood scales to projective techniques—indicate that women's moods vary throughout the menstrual cycle, with women showing the greatest feelings of well-being and self-esteem at midcycle, presumably when estrogen levels are high, and conversely, the most anxiety, hostility, and depression premenstrually, when estrogen and progesterone levels decline. Among populations of normal women, complaints of premenstrual mood changes, depression, tension, and irritability range from 30% to 95%, with the highest incidence among women over 30 years of age (Golub, 1985; Woods, Most, & Dery, 1982). However, not all women experience mood changes, and not every study finds such changes.

Research using retrospective questionnaires has been criticized and its validity questioned on the premise that women's recollection of their moods is not particularly accurate and may be influenced by stereotypic expectations (Parlee, 1973, 1974). For example, if you ask a woman what her mood was like during the premenstrual phase of her last menstrual cycle, she may tell you that she was somewhat depressed, for she expects to be depressed at that time. There is, in fact, little correspondence between retrospective reports and mood measures taken at a particular time in the cycle (Golub, 1976a). Recently, McFarlane and her colleagues had a group of women and men record their moods daily for 70 days. No menstrual-cycle-related mood changes were found. Later, when the subjects were asked to recall their average mood for each day of the week and each phase of the menstrual cycle, recollections of menstrual mood changes differed from actual (concurrent) changes. Women recalled more unpleasant moods in the premenstrual and menstrual phases than they had reported in the daily measures (McFarlane, Martin, & Williams, 1988).

Studies using more subtle measures avoid the problems of stereotypic expectations and memory failure. In 1962, Gottschalk and his colleagues designed a method for studying anxiety and hostility during different phases of the menstrual cycle. He followed five women for two or three menstrual cycles. His system consisted of having the women talk for five minutes about any experience they had had. The talk was recorded and the content then analyzed for several different kinds of anxiety and hostility. He found that four of the five women showed statistically significant rhythmical changes in anxiety and/or hostility. As expected, it was high premenstrually and low at ovulation (Gottschalk, Kaplan, Gleser, & Winget, 1962).

Using the same technique, Ivey and Bardwick (Bardwick, 1971) studied a sample of 26 college students between the ages of 19 and 22. Verbal samples were recorded at ovulation and two to three days prior to menstruation for two complete cycles. The students were asked to talk about any memorable life experience. Then, using Gottschalk's Verbal Anxiety Scale, the samples were analyzed. The findings showed consistent and significant variations in anxiety level between the premenstrual and ovulatory samples, with premenstrual anxiety significantly higher than the anxiety scores at ovulation. Bardwick notes that this difference reached the 0.0005 level of significance, which means that there were less than 5 chances in 10,000 that this difference could have been due to chance factors alone. A serendipitous occurrence further validated the findings. One young woman was interviewed on the fourteenth day of her menstrual cycle, presumably during the ovulation phase, yet the sample of her talk showed almost twice as much anxiety as her ovulation sample of the previous month. The next day she began to menstruate, two weeks early (Bardwick, 1971). The difference in mood is easy to see in the two examples of tape-recorded talks shown below.

Feelings of self-satisfaction were commonly seen at ovulation:

> So I was elected chairman. I had to establish with them the fact that I knew what I was doing. I remember one particularly problematic meeting, and afterwards, L. came up to me and said, "you really handled the meeting well." In the end it came out the sort of thing that really bolstered my confidence in myself.

In contrast, the same girl, premenstrually said:

> They had to teach me how to water ski. I was so clumsy it was really embarrassing 'cause it was kind of like saying to yourself you can't do it and the people were about to lose patience with me.

Premenstrual anxiety about injury and mutilation was seen.

> I remember the car coming down on my hand and slicing it right open and all the blood was all over the place.

The same girl at ovulation:

> We took our skis and packed them on top of the car and then we took off for up north. We used to go for long walks in the snow and it was really just great, really quiet and peaceful. (Bardwick, 1971, pp. 31-32)

This study was repeated with a larger sample of young married women, and the author again found that mood correlated with menstrual-cycle phase. However, it is important to note that not all of the subjects in Bardwick's research showed an increase in premenstrual anxiety. In her original study, for example, one subject showed no significant difference between the two cycle phases; and three subjects had other problems in their lives at the time of ovulation, leading to a situational increase in their anxiety scores that overshadowed any ovulatory good mood and eliminated any difference between the ovulatory and premenstrual testings. These exceptions, as well as research by others, support the view that not everyone has mood changes and that situational factors often overshadow menstrual-cycle effects (Rossi & Rossi, 1977; Swandby, 1981; Wilcoxon, Schrader, & Sherif, 1976).

Paige (1971) also used the Gottschalk interview technique to compare mood changes in women taking oral contraceptives with those having normal cycles. Her subjects were: (1) Women who were not taking oral contraceptives; (2) women who were taking oral contraceptives that mimic the natural cycle (sequential pills); and (3) women taking contraceptives that have a constant level of estrogen and progesterone (combination pills). Paige recorded interviews with 102 women at different phases of the cycle, and her findings lend support to the notion of a hormone-related mood shift. Women not taking oral contraceptives and those on the sequential pill showed significantly greater hostility and anxiety during the premenstrual and menstrual phases of the cycle; the women on the combination-type oral contraceptives showed no cyclic variation in mood.

So, where does this leave us? On questionnaires and in interviews many women say that their moods vary with the menstrual cycle. In addition, several studies using projective techniques have found a difference between ovulatory and premenstrual or menstrual mood. But there is also research in which no mood changes are reported, and we are left with unanswered questions about the significance of the mood change.

In order to establish the magnitude of the anxiety and depression associated with the premenstruum in normal women, and to assess its impact on personality and cognitive function, I (Golub, 1976a, b) twice gave a battery of mood, personality, and cognitive tests to 50 women, once when they were premenstrual (within four days of the onset of their next menstrual period) and again when they were intermenstrual (about two weeks after the onset of menstruation). Because premenstrual symptoms are reported to be at a peak when women are in their midthirties, the women who served as subjects were between the ages of 30 and 45. As expected, premenstrual anxiety and depression scores were significantly higher than intermenstrual scores, but the difference between the scores was small. Some comparisons of these premenstrual mood scale scores with

TABLE 4.1 Premenstrual Anxiety and Depression†

Group	Depression Scores	Anxiety Scores
Premenstrual Women	9.30	38.10
Intermenstrual Women	6.84	33.64
Female College Students	7.78	35.12
Normal Adult Women	7.80	
Female Senior Citizens	6.21	
Pregnant Women		
First Trimester	9.57	
Second Trimester	7.79	
Third Trimester	8.73	
Psychiatric Patients Depressed	16.03	54.43

Note: †Comparison with Normative Data

measures of anxiety and depression in other subjects at various times can be seen in Table 4.1.

The intermenstrual mean score on the depression scale was 6.84, about the same as that of female senior citizens (who were presumably not menstruating). The premenstrual mean score was 9.30, similar to women in the first trimester of pregnancy, and very different from those of depressed psychiatric patients, whose mean scores were about 16.

The combined mean of the premenstrual anxiety scores was 38.10, which is somewhat lower than the scores of freshman students during a college orientation session. Again, it is notable that the premenstrual anxiety scores are markedly different from the scores obtained by psychiatric patients. In other words, although the women's premenstrual mean scores are greater than those obtained at the intermenstrual testing, they are still closer to normal levels than to any pathology. For most women, changes in premenstrual anxiety and depression seem to be a relatively mild cyclical variation, approximately equivalent to the stress of being in an unfamiliar situation. And if this small change in mood is all that women in the most vulnerable age group experience, it is easy to understand why mood changes are consistently detected only when researchers use very sensitive projective techniques. Whatever the mood shift, it is time to modify our perspective: Women have cycle-related good moods, too, and investigators have begun to look at them.

Some researchers have compared the impact of life events and even the day of the week with that of the menstrual cycle on women's moods. Wilcoxon, Schrader, and Sherif (1976) studied 33 male and female undergraduates at the University of Pennsylvania for 35 consecutive days. The students, 11 males, 11 females taking oral contraceptives, and 11 females not taking oral contraceptives, completed daily self-reports that assessed moods, body awareness, pleasant activities, and stressful events. The women's menstrual-cycle phases were determined from their self-reports of menstrual flow, and the men were assigned a pseudo-cycle randomly so that they could be used as a comparison group. The males described a somewhat more stable, but less positive existence. They reported less positive mood and fewer pleasant activities than either sample of females. Both female samples experienced an increase in pain and water retention during the premenstrual and menstrual phases of the cycle. As for mood, although overall there were no significant differences among the three groups, the nonpill-taking women had a peak in their negative affect scores during the menstrual phase, while the pill-taking women peaked during the premenstrual phase. Why the difference? Presumably the nonpill-taking women experienced more menstrual discomfort. Women taking oral contraceptives have less menstrual pain and are more aware of the impending onset of menstruation; they can readily identify themselves as premenstrual, and presumably react accordingly—with an increase in anxiety and dysphoria. The authors concluded that both physiological variables and environmental events were implicated in the mood changes they found. Overall, stressful events accounted for more of the psychological changes than did cycle phase. However, Wilcoxon, Schrader, and Sherif (1976) suggest that their most important finding is the striking individual differences among the women studied, which accounted for more of the variability than either sex or cycle phase.

Variations in mood within the context of a person's life were also studied by Rossi and Rossi (1977; Rossi, 1980). Daily ratings of mood and sexual activity were collected from 67 college women and 15 college men over a 40-day period. These researchers found that Fridays are the high point of the week, with the low point occurring on Tuesdays. Men's moods were more strongly affected by the social week, with good moods enhanced on weekends. Women's moods also peaked over the weekend, especially if the woman was ovulating

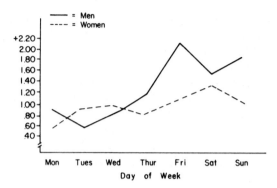

Figure 4.2. Gender Differences in Ratings of Mood by Day of the Week
Source: A. S. Rossi & P. E. Rossi. (1977). Body time and social time: Mood patterns by menstrual cycle phase and day of the week. *Social Science Research, 6,* 292. Reprinted with permission.

at the time (see Figure 4.2; Rossi & Rossi, 1977). Among the women, there was an elevation of positive moods in the ovulatory phase, while an increase in negative mood scores was seen during the luteal phase of the cycle and on the first two days of menstruation. The results suggest that the negative moods associated with menstruation are essentially somatic in character (subjects felt achy and crampy), whereas the negative moods during the luteal phase are of a psychological nature (subjects felt depressed and unhappy). However, this was not a strong pattern, largely because so many subjects showed no patterning by menstrual cycle. Rossi concludes that estrogen and progesterone levels have an effect on some of women's moods, but personal characteristics and cultural variables also contribute significantly to mood state. Many subjects showed no shift of mood by menstrual cycle, but most showed such a pattern by calendar week. The most important finding is that the variation women show across days of the week is greater than that related to cycle phase.

Changes in Personality and Behavior

Some studies show that personality as well as mood varies with menstrual-cycle phase. These personality changes have been observed in psychoanalytic interviews, on various personality tests, on the Rorschach test (a projective test using pictures that look like ink blots), and even in game-playing behavior. One researcher tested 100 women during the first 12 hours after the onset of menstruation and again intermenstrually. Using the Rorschach test, he found that at menstruation the women showed poorer overall adjustment, greater egocentricity, an increased desire for distance from others, less empathy, and decreased ability to plan, organize, and integrate (Schwarz, 1959). Unfortunately, physical symptoms were not assessed, so there is no way of knowing the relationship between these personality changes and menstrual cramps or other discomfort. It does seem likely that women would be more concerned about their own well-being if they were not feeling well.

Using a standardized personality test, the Adjective Check List, I found small but significant differences between premenstrual and intermenstrual testings on several of the personality-scale scores, specifically: Unfavorable Adjectives (the number of unfavorable adjectives used in self-description), Aggression, Succorance (the desire for comfort, care, and support), and Counseling Readiness were all higher premenstrually, while Nurturance (the desire to help or care for others) was lower (Golub, 1980, pp. 241-243). When individual adjectives were analyzed, the words most likely to appear at the premenstrual testing were: anxious, dull, impatient, intolerant, nervous, quarrelsome, and tense. In contrast, warm and peaceable were seen most frequently at the midcycle testing. Again, mean personality differences were generally small, and the differences in personality were highly correlated with changes in mood. In fact, the large number of significant correlations between mood and personality is consistent with other researchers' findings that anxiety and sadness are highly correlated with various measures of personality (Nowlis, 1965).

In a unique study of behavioral change, Oakes had women play a game of Prisoner's Dilemma to discover whether a woman plays more cooperatively or competitively at different stages of the cycle. Oakes's subjects consisted of women taking birth-control pills as well as nonpill-taking women. She found that women on the combination pill were less competitive than nonpill takers and played the game the same way at midcycle as during the premenstrual phase. Women not on the pill were found to be more competitive at midcycle. The author speculated that the competitiveness seen was a reflection of self-esteem and assertiveness, as opposed to the anger and irritability

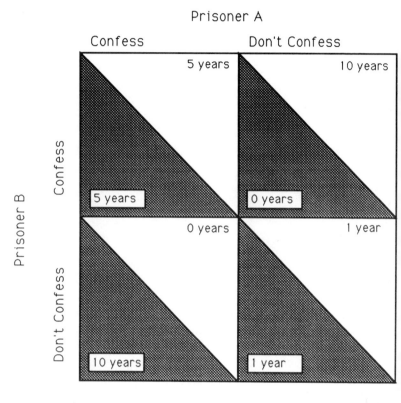

Figure 4.3. Prisoner's Dilemma

Note: The Prisoner's Dilemma game creates conflicting pressures to cooperate and compete. It is modeled after the situation in which two suspects are arrested and interrogated. If both remain silent, they cannot be convicted. But if one confesses, the confession will be used as evidence against the other, who will be given a long sentence, and the confessor will get only a light sentence. If both confess, they will both get moderate sentences. This chart summarizes the dilemma faced by two imaginary prisoners. Each prisoner can either confess or remain silent. These choices are shown along the sides of the matrix. The numbers within each cell represent the possible outcomes. Prisoner A's outcomes are shown above the diagonal line, and prisoner B's outcomes are shown below the diagonal. Thus, if Prisoner A does not confess but Prisoner B does, then A will receive 10 years and B will receive 0 years.

presumably associated with the premenstrual phase (Bardwick, 1972). (An example of a Prisoner's Dilemma game is shown in Figure 4.3; Forsyth, 1987.)

Men are generally greater risk takers than women. Research using a computer-graphic simulation of a battlefield situation in which male and female enlisted military personnel served as subjects and had to decide whether to send a tank across a mine-field with varying degrees of risk generally supported the growing body of evidence that men are more inclined to take risks than women. The researchers did not look for menstrual-cycle effects in this particular study (Hudgens & Fatkin, 1985). However, in another experiment in which subjects had to decide whether or not to send a vehicle across an intersection with varying traffic conditions and car speeds, women's risk-taking behavior did not vary with their menstrual-cycle phase (Hudgens, Dan, Chatterton, & DeLeon-Jones, 1987).

Hood (1985) videotaped social interaction among college students in a discussion group. She had 30 female subjects meet weekly for four weeks in groups of three. At each 30-minute meeting the subjects were asked to wait in the meeting room for 5 minutes (during which time they could talk about whatever they wished) before they were to begin to discuss the assigned topics. Discussion of each topic was limited to five minutes. Topics were chosen so that each subject disagreed with the other two members of the group on one of the three topics to be discussed. Menstrual-cycle stage was established in a separate procedure using a daily questionnaire. No menstrual cycle-related changes were found in task-oriented behavior, such as the frequency with which the women stated their opinions. Nor were there any phase-related differences in style of participation: initiating discussion, disagreeing, or sharing personal information. However, there was a significant cycle-related effect during the period of free, unstructured, purely social interaction. The frequency of active participation (initiating conversation) during the menstrual stage was lower than midcycle. Hood labeled this effect "menstrual quietude" and concluded that these data support the view that women are equally capable of social problem solving and task-effective social interaction at any stage of the menstrual cycle. The notion of "menstrual quietude" is supported by other studies using a different behavioral measure. It has been found that significantly fewer women volunteer to participate in a psychological experiment when they are in the premenstrual or menstrual phases of their cycle (Doty & Silverthorne, 1975).

Some recent observations by primatologists in Africa are consistent with the finding of perimenstrual quietude in women and put things in an evolutionary perspective. Biologists studying primates in Kenya have found that in the days just before the onset of menstruation female baboons seek solitude. Premenstrual baboons, whose hormonal systems are similar to those of humans, spend about 30% of their time in the trees and initiate one-third fewer contacts with other baboons than usual. The data indicate that the males do not behave differently toward the females. Rather, the females are less responsive to social overtures (Eckholm, 1985). Perhaps the idea of menstrual segregation did originate with women. What we all sometimes want to do is climb a tree and be left alone.

Cognitive Function
and Work-Related Activities

When asked on a questionnaire if they have changes in their ability to concentrate related to menstruation, about 20% of the women in one study answered yes. Then, when given a test that measures their ability to concentrate during different phases of the cycle, these same women showed no impairment (Golub, 1976b). Thus a considerable number of women believe that they are deficient when in fact they are not. This finding represents more than a methodological problem. It demonstrates the powerful influence of stereotypic ideas about menstruation on self-perception.

In 1981, when the Tampax Corporation (1981) commissioned a study of attitudes toward menstruation, more than a thousand people—a representative sample of the population—were surveyed. The results indicated that 35% believed menstruation affects a woman's ability to think and 26% believed women cannot function as well at work when menstruating. Sommer (1985) points out that these percentages, when applied to the population of the United States as a whole, indicate that more than 45 million Americans believe that women cannot function as well at work while menstruating, and more than 60 million people believe menstruation affects women's ability to think.

What evidence is there for impairment in thinking or work performance? This is not a new query; research addressing this issue dates back to 1877. In 1914, Leta Hollingworth, one of psychology's pioneers, decided scientifically to address the question of cyclical fluctuations in women's ability. Her doctoral dissertation research was an experimental study of the mental and motor abilities of women during menstruation. She compared the performance of women and men (who served as controls) on a variety of mental and motor tests over a three-month period. Not only did she find that women did as well on the various tests during their menstrual periods as at other times of the month, she also found that they performed as well as the men did (Dorr, 1915; Hollingworth, 1914; Williams, 1987; see Figure 4.4).

Many studies since then have supported Hollingworth's findings. In 1937, Orpha Lough noted:

> Few topics have been, and still are, so clothed in tradition and excess modesty as functional periodicity. . . . Traditionally women have been expected to be incapacitated, mentally and physically, during catamenial periods, commonly called "the sick time." It has been inferred, therefore that the mental efficiency of women during these periods is impaired. (Lough, 1937)

Lough challenged that assumption with a study comparing IQ test and learning performance of 96 unmarried college students at different times in the menstrual cycle. Each subject served as her own control. The Henmon-Nelson Test of Mental Ability was given between menstrual periods, and an alternate form of the test (Form B) was given during the menstrual period. The learning test involved solving simple standardized equations that were expressed in code; it took five minutes and was administered daily for 32 to 40 days. In order to keep the subjects naive as to the true nature of the research, the problem was presented as an experiment in learning. Lough found that subjects' mental efficiency during the premenstrual, menstrual, postmenstrual, and midmenstrual phases varied little. In fact there were no statistically reliable differences between average scores on the learning test for any phase of the menstrual cycle, and there were no statistically significant differences between the two forms of the Henmon-Nelson Test of Mental Ability. Lough concluded that the menstrual cycle has no statistically reliable effect upon intelligence as measured by a standardized test, and learning is not lowered during any of the phases of the menstrual cycle. In fact, Lough found a decrease in the number of errors subjects made on the second day of menstruation, which she attributed to increased effort exerted at that time.

In a review article titled "Psychological Effects of the Menstrual Cycle on Women Workers" written in 1944, Seward focused on the

"Is Woman Biologically Barred from Success?" Rheta Childe Dorr asks, as she introduces Hollingworth and her work in an article written for *The New York Times Magazine* in 1915. Leta Stetter Hollingworth's name had appeared in scientific journals in connection with some remarkable studies of the psychology of women, the first, or almost the first, made by a woman trained in science. It had been predicted that women would one day analyze their own natures, because men had never succeeded at the task, and Hollingworth had begun to do so.

Dorr then describes Hollingworth's education and what she calls "a romance remarkable for its modernity" (remember this is 1915).

The romance began in a Western university, where two students who were both interested in psychology fell in love and agreed to marry. They could not afford to marry immediately after graduation, so for two years they taught school. And this is where their paths diverge. The young man was offered a position at Columbia University, in the Department of Psychology. The salary was small but the job

promised advancement. He went to New York, and in due time the young woman followed. Soon after, they were married and set up housekeeping in a small apartment near Columbia. Of course, they could not afford a maid, so the young wife did the housework.

Now, by all the accepted laws of society and of the fiction writers, she should have been perfectly happy. She had love, a cozy little home, and a husband whose career she was helping to advance. But she was not happy. As she swept and dusted and prepared meals and put the garbage off and on the dumb waiter, the thought that her husband was congenially employed teaching psychology was not enough to make this modern young woman happy. It merely depressed her.

Until they were married, she and her husband had worked together and had done the same things. Then somehow, she stopped and he went on. Why was this? He was in line for a professorship in a department she knew as well as he, while she was doing the same work as the janitor's wife. Why? She had as good a mind and the same kind of education as her husband.

Figure 4.4. Leta Stetter Hollingworth (1886-1939)

contribution of women to the war effort. She said, "With female employment in essential war industries at an unprecedented peak, the question of possible menstrual effects becomes acute." Seward studied women ranging from college students and nurses to indus-

Marriage had not changed his status, except to improve it. Yet marriage had taken her out of intellectual work and made her into a domestic. The situation seemed entirely irrational.

Her husband agreed, and she began to look for a job as a school teacher, only to find that married women would not be hired. (At the time a married woman who had a child was dismissed instantly.) She found a position working for the city administering intelligence tests to charity cases for the Clearing House for Mental Defectives. With her earnings, Hollingworth paid for graduate study at Columbia. Under the direction of Edward Thorndike, she completed her doctoral dissertation, a study of cyclical fluctuations in ability titled, "Functional Periodicity: An Experimental Study of the Mental and Motor Abilities of Women During Menstruation." Six women and two male controls were tested daily for three months on a series of perceptual motor, and cognitive tasks. In addition, three of the women learned to type, and their progress was monitored throughout the three months of testing. Hollingworth found no evidence of impairment, no negative results during "critical periods."

Men had been writing authoritatively about menstrual impairment of mental and motor abilities of women, but they had no reliable or expert knowledge. Now that the opportunity for training and research was open to women, Hollingworth suggested that it seemed appropriate and desirable that women should investigate these matters experimentally, and she did. Her goal: a psychology of woman based on truth and accurate data, rather than opinion and magic.

Hollingworth was one of the most remarkable women in psychology in this century. She was the first to debunk the notion that women become invalids during menstruation. She was a prolific researcher, contributing to the field of education as well as psychology. And in her own life she confronted the problem of how to make an intellectual and social contribution through work while also fulfilling her other roles as a woman. Her work has been rediscovered by scholars working in women's studies, and this has led to the reissue of a once out-of-print biography, written by her husband. (Hollingworth, 1990)

Source: Dorr, R. C. (September 19, 1915). Is woman biologically barred from success? *New York Times Magazine*, 15-16. Courtesy of the New York Times Company

trial employees and pilots and found the menstrual cycle to have little effect on the woman worker. However, her focus was on dysmenorrhea and menstrual absence rates rather than any quantitative or qualitative evaluation of work performance (Seward, 1944).

Smith (1950) zeroed in on the effect of menstruation on performance in a work setting. During World War II he studied 38 women working in the electrical department of an aircraft factory, assembling equipment and constructing circuits; 46 women working in a garment factory making parachutes; and another group working in a second garment factory. The criteria of industrial efficiency were: absence rate, activity level (as judged by supervisors), and the quantity and quality of production. Smith found no differences in activity between the menstrual and nonmenstrual parts of the cycle. Absences during the menstrual period were fewer than expected, but there were more than expected during the premenstrual period. (It is notable that the differences in absences were significant only for the 39- to 50-year-old age range.) No significant differences in efficiency during the premenstrual and menstrual phases of the cycle were found, and in fact there was a trend in the direction of fewer error days during the menstrual period. Among women engaged in tasks involving a relatively high level of mental difficulty, there were significant differences in rate of production, with lowest production occurring during the premenstrual phase and highest during menstruation. In fact, during menstruation it was at such a level as to counteract the premenstrual loss. Smith concluded:

> No one phase of the menstrual cycle yields losses in efficiency more frequently than any other phase. Where significant differences occur they would appear to be the result of situational determinants rather than menstrual function.

The studies continued, becoming increasingly more sophisticated. In 1958, Wickham studied 4000 young women, exploring the possibility that the menstrual cycle might represent a source of unreliability in the testing of large groups of women. Wickham used a battery of tests, including: Ravens Progressive Matrices, Mechanical Comprehension, Arithmetic, Squares Test (a spatial task), Spelling, Instruction Test (comprehension), Mec Test (assembly of a model), and a Verbal Test. Careful analysis of all the test results revealed no statistically significant differences attributable to cycle day or phase. Wickham concluded that "no advantage would be gained by taking into account the day within the menstrual cycle on which the test was given" (Wickham, 1958).

In 1972, Sommer studied the performance on regular class examinations and the Watson Glaser Critical Thinking Appraisal of a large number of college women in an upper-division psychology class. The students ranged in age from 18 to 22. Following testing, menstrual-cycle data were obtained, and students were then categorized as to cycle phase. Data from the women taking oral contraceptives were analyzed separately. Neither the naturally cycling women nor those taking oral contraceptives showed any significant variation in test performance associated with the menstrual cycle (Sommer, 1972).

Similarly, Doreen Asso, a lecturer in the Department of Psychology at the University of London, studied the marks on final "Honours Degree Examinations" of 26 women students. Premenstrual and non-premenstrual marks were compared both within and among individuals. There was no indication of significant fluctuation with the cycle (Asso, 1985/1986).

Roger Walsh, of the University of California, Irvine, and his colleagues in Australia analyzed the scores of 244 female medical and paramedical students in all exams taken over the course of a year. They found no significant menstrual-cycle effect on examination performance and concluded that "while some persons may suffer, it does not seem that menstrual cycle effects are sufficient to handicap significantly the examination performance of the majority of female students" (Walsh, Budtz-Olsen, Leader, & Cummins, 1981).

There is a slew of other studies of the menstrual cycle and academic performance or mental work (see Sommer, 1975). Almost all show similar results: no cycle-phase effects. Obviously the stereotypic notion that women are cognitively impaired during menstruation just does not wash. However, even if we disregard the menstrual prejudices, psychologists know that emotion does affect cognition. Several studies unrelated to the menstrual cycle indicate that anxiety has a detrimental effect on problem solving, learning, and performance on standard intelligence tests; timed tests or especially difficult tasks are particularly vulnerable (Levitt, 1967; Rosenwald, 1961). Similarly, depression interferes with memory and with tasks involving flexibility, graphic expression, digit symbols, and writing speed (Hale & Strickland, 1974; Messick, 1965). So we seem to have an incongruity here: Mood changes during the menstrual cycle are substantiated by a number of studies and would lead one to expect some effect on cognition, but there do not appear to be any changes in cognitive function.

In order to directly address the issue of whether mood fluctuations are responsible for cognitive changes over the menstrual cycle, I gave a battery of cognitive tests as well as standardized mood scales to 50 women during their premenstrual phases and at midcycle. Cognitive tests were selected that have been shown to reflect the effect of depression and anxiety. The tests included measures of flexibility, speed of closure, problem solving, induction, concept formation, memory, and different components of creative thinking. Small and inconsistent differences between the premenstrual and intermenstrual testings were found for both the simple and more complex tests. As noted before in the discussion of mood, some increase in anxiety and depression was found premenstrually. However, multivariate analysis of the cognitive test difference scores showed no significant menstrual cycle effect, and no consistent relationship was found between the mood changes and cognitive performance.

The question then remains: Why doesn't the premenstrual mood shift affect cognition? One explanation has been offered by some earlier researchers and, most recently, by Judith Rodin, Professor of Psychology at Yale University. Rodin (1976) suggests that women who are aware of experiencing premenstrual anxiety or depression bolster their performance by trying harder to overcome any handicap. This may be true for some women. However, I think that the magnitude of the mood change is the more important factor in determining the effect of mood on cognition. No one disputes the fact that cognition is impaired among depressed psychiatric patients. And, in a study by Strickland, in which subjects' depression scores were considerably higher than those of the premenstrual women in this study, depression did indeed adversely affect cognitive performance (Hale & Strickland, 1974). However, for most women the magnitude of the premenstrual increase in anxiety and depression is small, and it simply is not great enough to impair women's ability to perform cognitive tasks. Thus researchers find, over and over and over again, with increasingly sophisticated research methodology, no meaningful menstrual-cycle-phase effects on women's cognitive or work performance. Yet, there is something to worry about here: We seem to be doomed by the negative stereotypes to continue to search for adverse effects.

In the fall of 1988, *The New York Times* ran a front-page story with the headline: "Female Sex Hormone Is Tied to Ability to Perform Tasks" (Blakeslee, 1988). In 1988, Doreen Kimura, a psychology professor at the University of Western Ontario, and a graduate student, Elizabeth Hampson, presented a paper at the annual meeting of the Society for Neurosciences in Toronto. They reported the results of two studies in which they found that women performed better on tasks involving verbal skill (repeating tongue twisters) or muscular coordination (finger tapping) when estrogen levels were high than when they were low. (By the way, no mention was made in the news story of any of the earlier research in this area.) In the first study, 34 spontaneously cycling women were tested twice, about 6 weeks apart: one test took place on Day 3 or 5 of menstruation, when estrogen levels are low; the other test took place during the midluteal phase when estrogen levels are presumably high. On tests of manual skill and speech the subjects showed greater speed and accuracy during the high-estrogen phase. In contrast, on the Rod-and-Frame test—a measure of spatial-perceptual skill—subjects were more accurate during menstruation (Hampson & Kimura, 1988).

The second study addressed the effect of hormone-replacement therapy on cognitive motor function in 20 postmenopausal women. When the women were taking estrogen, they performed slightly faster on a test of manual skill and articulation (Kimura, 1988).

The researchers suggest that the link between hormone levels and performance on these very specialized tasks may explain gender differences in men's and women's verbal and math skills. Not likely. The authors are generalizing from what are at most small differences in the laboratory to real-life situations. Table 4.2 shows just how small the performance differences really are. A difference in scores can be statistically significant without being of any consequence. It is also unfortunate that no male comparison group was used in either study. Testosterone levels are higher in the morning than evening, but no one has looked at how this might affect male thinking skills. The amount of attention given to this research seems once again to feed the use of the menstrual cycle to stigmatize women.

The possibility of cycle-related fluctuations should not, however, be denied. Hudgens and his colleagues at the United States Army Engineering Laboratory in Aberdeen, Maryland, recently did a study of the effects of sex and menstrual phase on hand steadiness. Men, normally cycling women, and women taking oral contraceptives

TABLE 4.2 Performance on the Rod-and-Frame and Motor Tests at
Two Phases of the Menstrual Cycle

| | Phase of Cycle | | | | |
| | Midluteal | | Menstrual | | |
Test	M	SD	M	SD	p value
Rod-and-Frame test (mean error per trial)	4.59	2.97	3.93	2.40	.02
Finger tapping (no. taps)					
Preferred hand	50.12	4.77	48.55	3.69	.01
Nonpreferred hand	46.50	5.28	44.13	4.67	.006
Purdue Pegboard (no. pegs or components)					
Preferred hand	17.63	1.63	17.53	1.33	ns
Nonpreferred hand	16.52	1.83	16.38	1.69	ns
Assembly	44.59	4.81	42.61	4.62	.0007
Manual Sequence Box					
Acquisition time (in s)					
Preferred hand	11.13	5.79	12.04	6.19	ns
Nonpreferred hand	8.88	4.08	7.88	2.73	ns
Total speeded sequencing time (in s)					
Preferred hand	13.08	5.90	16.29	8.38	.04
Nonpreferred hand	15.53	9.53	15.18	6.85	ns
Duration of criterion series (in s)					
Preferred hand	11.39	2.87	12.26	3.22	.02
Nonpreferred hand	11.17	2.51	11.98	2.98	.06

Source: Hampson, E., & Kimura, D. (1988). Reciprocal effects of hormonal fluctuations on human motor and perceptual-spatial skills. *Behavioral Neuroscience, 102*(3), 456-459. Copyright 1988 by the American Psychological Association. Reprinted by permission.
Note: Means are based on 30-34 subjects, except for duration of the criterion series on the Manual Sequence Box, in which N = 23-24, because this measure was added later.

were compared in two experiments. In the first experiment subjects were tested on a standard, laboratory hand-steadiness task. In the second experiment, subjects were tested while holding handguns of varying weights. In both experiments, the normally cycling women had by far the greatest hand steadiness. Women taking oral contraceptives were least steady, and men were intermediate. Interestingly, the normally cycling women were found to experience a significant decrement in performance during the premenstrual phase of their cycles, when their performance became similar to that of the men and the women taking oral contraceptives (Hudgens, Fatkin, Billingsley, & Mazurczak, 1987). Now, why didn't this study make the front page?

References

Asso, D. (1983). *The real menstrual cycle*. New York: John Wiley.

Asso, D. (1985/1986, Winter). Psychology degree examinations and the premenstrual phase of the menstrual cycle. *Women & Health, 10*(4), 91-104.

Bardwick, J. M. (1971). *Psychology of women*. New York: Harper & Row.

Bardwick, J. M. (1972). Her body, the battleground. *Psychology Today, 5*, 50-54.

Benedek, T., & Rubenstein, B. B. (1939). The correlations between ovarian activity and psychodynamic processes. *Psychosomatic Medicine, 1*, 245-270.

Birke, L. I. A., with Best, S. (1982). Changing minds: Women, biology, and the menstrual cycle. In R. Hubbard, M. S. Henifin, & B. Fried (Eds.), *Biological woman—the convenient myth* (pp. 161-184). Cambridge, MA: Schenkman.

Blakeslee, S. (1988, November 18). Female sex hormone is tied to ability to perform tasks. *The New York Times*, A1, D20.

Dorr, R. C. (1915, September 19). Is woman biologically barred from success? *The New York Times Magazine*, 15-16.

Doty, R. L., & Silverthorne, C. (1975). Influence of menstrual cycle on volunteering behavior. *Nature, 253*, 139-140.

Eckholm, E. (1985, June 4). Premenstrual problems seem to beset baboons. *The New York Times*, C2.

Forsyth, D. R. (1987). *Social psychology*. Monterey, CA: Brooks/Cole.

Golub, S. (1976a). The magnitude of premenstrual anxiety and depression. *Psychosomatic Medicine, 38*, 4-14.

Golub, S. (1976b). The effect of premenstrual anxiety and depression on cognitive function. *Journal of Personality and Social Psychology, 34*(1), 99-104.

Golub, S. (1980). Premenstrual changes in mood, personality and cognitive function. In A. J. Dan, E. A. Graham, & C. P. Beecher (Eds.), *The menstrual cycle* (Vol. 1, pp. 237-246). New York: Springer.

Golub, S. (1985). Menstrual cycle symptoms from a developmental perspective. In Z. DeFries, R. C. Friedman, & R. Corn (Eds.), *Sexuality: New Perspectives* (pp. 251-270). Westport, CT: Greenwood.

Gottschalk, L. A., Kaplan, S., Gleser, G. D., & Winget, C. M. (1962). Variations in magnitude of emotion: A method applied to anxiety and hostility during phases of the menstrual cycle. *Psychosomatic Medicine, 24*,(3), 300-311.

Hale, D. W., & Strickland, B. R. (1974, August). *The induction of mood states and their effect on cognitive and social behaviors*. Paper presented at the meeting of the American Psychological Association, New Orleans.

Hampson, E., & Kimura, D. (1988). Reciprocal effects of hormonal fluctuations on human motor and perceptual-spatial skills. *Behavioral Neuroscience, 102*(3), 456-459.

Hollingworth, H. L. (1990). *Leta Stetter Hollingworth: A biography.* Bolton, MA: Anker.

Hollingworth, L. S. (1914). Functional periodicity: An experimental study of the mental and motor abilities of women during menstruation. *Teachers College, Columbia University. Contributions to Education, No. 69,* pp. v-14, 86-101.

Hood, K. E. (1985, May 3-5). *Social interaction during the menstrual cycle among human females.* Paper presented at the Sixth Conference of the Society for Menstrual Cycle Research, Galveston, TX.

Hudgens, G. A., Fatkin, L. T., Billingsley, P. A., & Mazurczak, J. (1987, June 4-6). *Hand steadiness: Effects of sex, menstrual phase, oral contraceptives, practice and handgun weight.* Paper presented at the meeting of the Society for Menstrual Cycle Research, Ann Arbor, MI.

Hudgens, G. A., Dan, A. J., Chatterton, Jr., R. T., & DeLeon-Jones, F. A. (1987, June 4-6). *Performance over the menstrual cycle: Data and methodological issues.* Paper presented at the meeting of the Society for Menstrual Cycle Research, Ann Arbor, MI.

Hudgens, G. A., & Fatkin, L. T. (1985). Sex differences in risk taking: Repeated sessions on a computer-simulated task. *Journal of Psychology, 119,* 197-206.

Kimura, D. (1988, November). *Hormonal influences on cognitive/motor function in post-menopausal women: The effect of hormone replacement therapy.* Paper presented to the Society for Neuroscience, Toronto.

Levitt, E. E. (1967). *The psychology of anxiety.* Indianapolis: Bobbs-Merrill.

Lough, O. M. (1937). A psychological study of functional periodicity. *Journal of Comparative Psychology, 24,* 359-368.

McFarlane, J., Martin, C. L., & Williams, T. M. (1988). Mood fluctuations: Women versus men and menstrual versus other cycles. *Psychology of Women Quarterly, 12*(2), 201-223.

Messick, S. (1965). The impact of negative affect on cognition and personality. In S. S. Tomkins & C. E. Izard (Eds.), *Affect, cognition and personality.* New York: Springer.

NIMH. (1970). Biological rhythms in psychiatry and medicine. *U.S.D.H.E.W. Public Health Service Publication No. 2088,* pp. 110-111.

Nowlis, V. (1965). Research with the Mood Adjective Check List. In S. S. Tomkins & C. E. Izard (Eds.), *Affect, cognition and personality* (pp. 352-389). New York: Springer.

Paige, K. E. (1971). Effects of oral contraceptives on affective fluctuations associated with the menstrual cycle. *Psychosomatic Medicine, 33,* 515-537.

Parlee, M. B. (1973). The premenstrual syndrome. *Psychological Bulletin, 80,* 454-465.

Parlee, M. B. (1974). Stereotypic beliefs about menstruation: A methodological note on the Moos Menstrual Distress Questionnaire and some new data. *Psychosomatic Medicine, 36,* 229-240.

Parlee, M. B. (1983). Menstrual rhythms in sensory processes: A review of fluctuations in vision, olfaction, audition, taste, and touch. *Psychological Bulletin, 93*(3), 539-548.

Rodin, J. (1976). Menstruation, reattribution, and competence. *Journal of Personality and Social Psychology, 62,* 345-353.

Rosenwald, G. C. (1961). The assessment of anxiety in psychological experimentation: A theoretical reformulation and test. *Journal of Abnormal and Social Psychology, 62,* 666-673.

Rossi, A. S. (1980). Mood cycles by menstrual month and social week. In A. J. Dan, E. A. Graham, & C. P. Beecher (Eds.), *The menstrual cycle* (pp. 56-71). New York: Springer.

Rossi, A. S., & Rossi, P. E. (1977). Body time and social time: Mood patterns by menstrual-cycle phase and day of the week. *Social Science Research, 6,* 273-308.

Schwarz, W. (1959). The relation of functional periodicity to changes in the characteristics of emotional reactions and personality. *Dissertation Abstracts, 19,* 3372-3373.

Seward, G. H. (1944). Psychological effects of the menstrual cycle on women workers. *Psychological Bulletin, 41,* 90-102.

Smith, A. J. (1950, February). Menstruation and industrial efficiency, I: Absenteeism and activity level; II: Quality and quantity of production. *Journal of Applied Psychology, 34*(1), 1-5, 149-152.

Sommer, B. (1972). Menstrual cycle changes and intellectual performance. *Psychosomatic Medicine, 34,* 263-269.

Sommer, B. (1975). How does menstruation affect cognitive competence and psychophysiological response In S. Golub (Ed.), *Lifting the curse of menstruation* (pp. 53-90). New York: Harrington Park.

Sommer, B. (1985). How does menstruation affect cognitive competence and psychophysiological response? In S. Golub (Ed.), *Lifting the curse of menstruation* (pp. 53-90). New York: Harrington Park.

Steinem, G. (1978, October). If men could menstruate. *Ms. Magazine,* 110.

Swandby, J. R. (1981). A longitudinal study of daily mood self-reports and their relationship to the menstrual cycle. In P. Komnenich, M. McSweeny, J. A. Noack, & Sister N. Elder (Eds.), *The menstrual cycle* (Vol. 2, pp. 93-103). New York: Springer.

The TAMPAX Report. (1981). New York: Ruder, Finn, & Rotman.

Tiger, L. (1970, October 25). Male dominance? Yes, alas. A sexist plot? No. *The New York Times Magazine,* 35-37, 124-127, 132-138.

Walsh, R. N., Budtz-Olsen, I., Leader, C., Cummins, R. A. (1981, February). The menstrual cycle, personality, and academic performance. *Archives of General Psychiatry, 38,* 219-221.

Wickham, M. (1958). The effects of the menstrual cycle on test performance. *British Journal of Psychology, 49,* 34-41.

Wilcoxon, L. A., Schrader, S. L., & Sherif, C. W. (1976). Daily self reports on activities, life events, moods and somatic changes during the menstrual cycle. *Psychosomatic Medicine, 38*(6), 399-417.

Williams, J. H. (1987). *Psychology of women.* New York: W. W. Norton.

Woods, N. F., Most, A., & Dery, G. K. (1982). Prevalence of perimenstrual symptoms. *American Journal of Public Health, 72*(11), 1257-1264.

5

Sex and the Menstrual Cycle

Animal Studies

Is there a relationship between sexual behavior and the menstrual cycle? A biologist would certainly look for one. Sex ought biologically to be geared to the cycle in order to maximize the possibility of conception. Survival of the species requires reproduction, and in most species sex and reproduction are closely linked. So closely, in fact, that in some fish and amphibians ovulation is controlled by neurohormones that are released when the animals begin to engage in courting behaviors (Gray, 1970).

But what happens as we move up the evolutionary scale? Nonprimate mammals have an estrous cycle rather than a menstrual cycle, and in most female mammals, copulation is restricted to periods of estrus. Usually the estrous cycle comprises a relatively long period during which no sexual activity takes place, followed by a short period of sexual receptivity, sometimes called heat. Only during this time is copulation tolerated or encouraged by the female. Ovulation generally occurs shortly before or after the end of estrus, thus maximizing the likelihood of fertilization. In some species (rabbits and cats, for example) females prepare to ovulate several times a year, but ovulation is actually induced by mating. These animals ovulate a few hours after coitus. However, in primates—monkeys, apes, and humans—there is no estrus, presumably no peak period of sexual receptivity, and the time of ovulation is not as predictable as it is in nonprimates (Lein, 1979).

Although there are differences in cycle length among primates, the basic hormonal patterns are very similar across species: Estrogens peak in concentration near midcycle, stimulating a surge of luteinizing hormone, which in turn triggers ovulation and is followed by formation of the corpus luteum, which secretes progesterone, stimulating the uterus to prepare for implantation of the fertilized egg. If fertilization does not occur, progesterone levels drop, menstruation follows, and the cycle begins again. Testosterone levels also vary, with a peak near midcycle or just after the estradiol peak (Wallis & Englander-Golden, 1985).

Now, what are the effects of these hormonal shifts on sexuality? In several nonhuman primate species (for instance, chimpanzees and baboons) there is a cyclical swelling of the anogenital area with changes in color and skin texture. This sexual swelling increases as estrogen levels rise and then decreases as they fall. Ovulation occurs during the last one or two days of maximum swelling. The cyclical swelling of the genital area seems to serve two purposes. First, it serves as a visual indicator of sexual receptivity and attracts males. Second, as the sexual swelling increases, it includes the clitoral shaft and creates pressure, which may motivate the animal to seek sexual activity. Things are not the same in women. There is no analogous cyclical engorgement of the external genitalia. However, the entire pelvic region does undergo some fluctuation in vasocongestion, and some researchers have suggested that the premenstrual peak in sexual activity that is frequently reported in human studies may be due to pelvic vasocongestion, which contributes to heightened genital sensitivity (Wallis & Englander-Golden, 1985, p. 5).

Sex cycles are not easy to study. Research findings in this area are not consistent, and methodological problems are, at least in part, to blame. In both animal and human studies, it is often unclear what is being measured. In animals, sexual activity can be monitored by observation, but even here researchers encounter the question of who is determining the sexual interaction? Estrogen acts by increasing the female's sexual attractiveness to the male; it may also heighten the females' desire to mate. However, if one wants to determine whether there is a relationship between female sexual behavior and the menstrual cycle, the problem becomes one of teasing out whether it is the female or the male who is more interested in sex during the female's fertile period. Is the female initiating a sexual encounter or simply willing to accept male overtures?

In nature, female primates will indicate their readiness to mate by presenting their hindquarters, looking back at the male, and arching their tails out of the way (if they have one). Female chimpanzees have been seen actually grasping the male's penis and inserting it into the vagina. This certainly looks like female initiative.

When the research moves to the laboratory, there are other problems, such as those confronted by Michael and Bonsall (Primate sex, 1977) in their study of rhesus monkeys. Because males are twice as large as females, it is difficult to ascertain female sexual motivation that is not influenced by the threat of male aggression. These researchers devised a technique in which female rhesus monkeys controlled access to the males. The female's cage was divided by a movable partition. If she pressed a lever on her side, the partition rose, and she was able to go to a male partner on the other side. In a study of 17 pairs of male and female monkeys conducted during 63 menstrual cycles, females were more anxious to gain access to males right before or during ovulation than at any other time during the menstrual cycle. Male ejaculation was also greatest during this period of the cycle. And hormonal studies confirmed the relationship between sexual behavior and the females' sex-hormone status.

The hormonal changes also influence the female's attractiveness to the male. As noted above, the cyclical swelling of the genital area serves as a visual cue. In addition olfactory cues are stimulated by the presence of estrogen. Michael and his colleagues identified acids in the vaginal secretions of monkeys that serve as sex attractants. More of these acids are present at the time of ovulation (Primate sex, 1977). In fact, these olfactory cues may be more potent than the more readily observable ones. When researchers applied estrogen to the vaginas of rhesus monkeys, there was a significant increase in male interest and in the frequency of mounting. Michael also found that the acids present in the monkey's vaginal secretions were identical to those found in women. In extending this work to humans, Doty found that male subjects considered women's vaginal odors more intense and agreeable during the preovulatory and ovulatory phases of the menstrual cycle than during any other phase (Doty, Ford, Preti, & Huggens, 1975).

Thus there is a fair bit of evidence that hormones affect sexual behavior in nonhuman primates. Changes in estrogen and progesterone affect the female's attractiveness to the male. Estrogen enhances her sexual attractiveness and stimulates male mounting behavior and ejaculation. A rise in estrogen is also positively correlated with female sexual initiative. Researchers have found that giving estrogen to female monkeys who have no ovaries induces high levels of sexual interest and receptiveness: If separated from males, the females will press bars to gain access to the males. Conversely, progesterone has a disruptive effect, primarily by producing changes in vaginal secretions that reduce the female's allure. If progesterone is given, the male responds to fewer of her invitations and initiates less sexual interaction with her. There is a relationship between peak levels of estradiol, the female's seeking sexual interaction, her attractiveness to the male, and copulation in rhesus monkeys and chimpanzees and in self-reports of sexual arousal in humans as well (Wallis & Englander-Golden, 1985). Testosterone level does not appear to be related to fluctuations in sexual interest, but a normal level is needed. Monkeys that have lost both their adrenal glands and their ovaries (sources of testosterone in the female) show a dramatic decline in sexual initiative and receptivity despite treatment with estradiol. Similarly, human females who have undergone adrenalectomy also have been found to experience a diminution of sex drive, but giving them testosterone stimulates their sexual interest (Baum, Everitt, Herbert, & Keverne, 1977).

Before moving on to studies of human behavior, it is important to note that hormones alone do not determine the sexual behavior of nonhuman primates. Whether a particular female is receptive or not is sometimes determined by the approach of a more vigorous or determined male, or one who is more dominant, or one of whom the female is afraid. Similarly, a highly attractive female is likely to induce the male to be more persistent. Social factors affect sexual activity among apes and monkeys as well as humans.

Human Patterns
of Sexual Interest and Behavior

Several problems emerge in studying the relationship between the menstrual cycle and human sexual behavior. First of all, what criteria are to be used in measuring female sexuality—fantasies, arousal, masturbation, self- or partner-initiated intercourse, orgasm? Next, what are the conditions under which information is obtained? In one study, in which women were unaware of the purpose of the study, their self-reports of sexual arousal showed significant peaks near midcycle, premenstrually, and on menstrual Day 4. Women who were aware of the purpose of the study gave more conflicting reports (Wallis & Englander-Golden, 1985, p. 1). Then there is the question of which measures are best? The possibilities include: retrospective questionnaires (which are always subject to questions about validity, that is, how accurate are recollections of sexual activities?), interviews, daily reports, dreams, and different kinds of physiological measures. Also, how is cycle phase to be determined? By counting backward or forward from the last menstrual period? Or by using more physiologically based measures such as basal body temperatures, changes in cervical mucus, or blood assays of hormone levels? It is almost complicated enough to crush hopes of ever finding answers. Fortunately, some scientists persist, and over the years this research has become increasingly sophisticated.

QUESTIONNAIRE STUDIES

Most of the early research was based on data obtained using questionnaires. For example, in 1929, Davis received 2,200 responses to questionnaires mailed to women. He found that there were premenstrual and postmenstrual peaks in sexual desire, but only a small number of women reported a midcycle peak. In other questionnaire studies, as many as one-third of the women noted no particular time of increased libido. Some confirmation of this finding was seen in a more recent study (1971) in which 34% of a group of Italian women reported no peak, 26% a premenstrual peak, 24% a postmenstrual peak, and only 12% a midcycle peak (Williams & Williams, 1982). Kinsey found the highest level of sexual desire and arousal during the premenstrual and early menstrual phase, with 80% of his female subjects preferring sexual activity at these times. He also noted that orgasm occurred more frequently during this period (Kinsey, Pomeroy, Martin, & Gebhard, 1953). Evidently there is a great deal of variability in sexual desire among women, and it is difficult to assess it accurately, particularly using retrospective questionnaires.

DREAMS AND FREE ASSOCIATION

The classic study done by psychoanalyst Therese Benedek and her physiologist colleague, Boris Rubenstein, was described in Chapter 4 (Benedek & Rubenstein, 1939). Recall that Benedek could determine the menstrual-cycle phase of 15 psychoanalytic patients using their dreams and free associations taken over a period of months, while Rubenstein analyzed vaginal smears that the women had collected daily for cell and hormone activity. The results were analyzed separately so that predictions could be made about cycle phase based solely on the analytic material. The conclusions were striking: The researchers found consistent psychodynamic changes related to particular hormonal phases. In addition to looking at mood and the menstrual cycle, they looked at sexual interest. Active heterosexual drive was correlated with estrone production and passive receptivity and narcissism with progesterone production. Ovulation was associated with a period of relaxation and contentment, and heterosexual drive returned again in the premenstrual phase of the cycle. The luteal decline in sexual desire and activity was attributed to decreasing progesterone levels as the corpus luteum regressed and the premenstrual increase to increasing estrone levels.

Benedek and Rubenstein emphasized that their data were drawn from a population of neurotic women and were therefore not representative of all women. And Rubenstein further cautioned that the hormonally determined pattern of the cycle functions interactively with the "constitutional and environmental factors which determine the developmental organization of the personality" (Benedek, 1959). However, their findings are in remarkable agreement with those of other, later researchers using different methodologies.

Although Benedek and Rubenstein do not give examples of their subjects' dreams in their published work, they do note that impending menstruation was often associated in the psychoanalytic material with references to excretory functions, fears of injury, or inferiority feelings. Indeed, when Swanson and Foulkes (1968) monitored four women in a dream laboratory over a period of 11 consecutive weeks, they found that the sexiest dreams—those highest in sexual content—occurred during menstruation when waking sexual desire was lowest.

In her book *Creative Dreaming*, Patricia Garfield (1974) observed that there was a lower incidence of dream recall during menses and a high peak of dream recall during the middle of the cycle, but she made no observations as to dream content.

Over the last 10 years I have recorded nonpatient dreams, my own and those of students and other family members. In reviewing them recently, I found, like Garfield, that very few dreams occurring during menstruation were remembered, and the themes were remarkably similar to those described by Benedek. For example, this dream from a 40-year-old woman:

> I was in a public bathroom. It was a large room with booths on both sides. A weirdo man was looking into the booths. I was menstruating and I took out a bloody tampon and began chasing him with it. I was going to smear menstrual blood on his face.

Recall that Benedek's three themes were excretory function, fear of injury, and inferiority feelings. Here we see menstruation placed within the context of elimination (the public bathroom), a threat (invasion of privacy), and action aimed at overcoming feelings of vulnerability. Rather than feeling inferior, this woman was going to teach the man a lesson by frightening him; she was going to make him bloody.

A college student's dream:

> My friend Lisa was in the bathroom and I was talking to her. She was really excited because she just came back from a date and she was having another date with this guy's best friend.

Again there is a reference to excretory function: Lisa is in the bathroom. And the feelings of inadequacy here are social: Lisa has two dates and I have none.

Another college student:

> My roommate Karen and I were in a small bedroom. There was a large window with blinds. We were getting dressed to go to a football

game. We both had on bathrobes. I pulled up the blinds to see what the weather was like. It was snowing. And as we were looking out the window a small, heavy man with brown glasses was coming toward the window. I told Karen to hide. We thought he left but he came right up to the window, reached in and began to pull me out. I was screaming to Karen to do something but she just stood there. Then I lifted my foot up and pulled his glasses off with my toes.

Although there is no bathroom in this dream, it is set in a bedroom; the bathrobes and drawn blinds indicate a very personal and private setting. At first there is a threat of invasion of privacy as the man comes toward the window. Then fear of injury and feelings of vulnerability become salient as he reaches in and grabs her and she screams for help. The dream ends with the young woman regaining power by fighting back and knocking the glasses off this "small, heavy man with brown glasses." The dreamer does two things to cope with her fears: She removes the threat by eliminating his ability to see, and she diminishes the man by making him undesirable.

It has been suggested that feelings of helplessness, powerlessness, or low self-esteem are predominant themes in premenstrual and menstrual dreams and free associations. While feelings of vulnerability are present in the dreams described above, there is also a tendency that has not been noted elsewhere: to act rather than to remain a passive victim. It is unfortunate that no information about life events or free associations were collected along with the dreams, and therefore these samples were not analyzed for sexual fantasies or themes. One wonders what relationships might be found among dreams, sexuality, and mood.

DAILY REPORTS OF SEXUAL ACTIVITY

Daily reports of coitus and orgasm represent a much more concrete and, some would say, objective measure. In 1937, McCance and his colleagues did a very careful study in which they obtained daily recordings from 166 women of mood, sexual feelings, symptoms, and behavior, including intercourse (McCance, Luff, & Widdowson, 1937). Subjects were White, educated, middle-class women between the ages of 20 and 47 (110 single women, mean age 29; 56 married women, mean age 31). In all, 780 cycles were recorded. McCance found that sexual feeling and intercourse rose rapidly from a menstrual phase low and were maximal on Day 8 of an average 28-day cycle. This was true for both married and single women. Following this peak, frequency declined up to Days 15-17 and was then stable until falling off at the onset of menses. There was a slight rise in the frequency of sexual feelings premenstrually, but not in coitus.

Two of the most prolific researchers in this field, Naomi Morris and Richard Udry, began their program of research designed to explore the epidemiologic patterns of sexual behavior in the menstrual cycle somewhat serendipitously (Morris & Udry, 1982). While working on another study, they collected daily sexual data from 40 premenopausal, married, working women, most of whom were not high-school graduates. When they graphed these subjects' reports of intercourse and orgasm, they found that midcycle reports were approximately twice as high as those one week before or after menstruation. A low point was reached four days prior to the onset of the next menstrual period, followed by a recovery just prior to menstruation. They noted with surprise that this pattern was much like that seen in rhesus monkeys, and they began to wonder whether this pattern was replicable.

They first sought confirmation in a sample of 48 middle-class, college-educated women who kept daily calendars for the Institute for Sex Research at Indiana University. The data represented more than 800 menstrual cycles. They noted differences between single and married women, with the single women showing a rise in the rate of intercourse toward the middle of the cycle, followed by a decline in the latter half of the cycle and a brief recovery before the next menstrual period. Among the married women there was no midcycle peak in rate of intercourse, but there was a luteal phase decline. Because these women had provided data for a number of years, it was also possible to look at individual patterns. This showed that some women clearly had cycle-related changes, while others did not.

Morris and Udry next studied 51 women who were participants in a double-blind study designed to measure the effects of contraceptive hormones on sexual behavior. They found a midcycle rise in the probability of intercourse and orgasm, and a luteal phase depression. The luteal decline in both orgasm and intercourse was erased by birth-control pills. Overall, the three groups showed similar findings: The lowest rates of coitus and orgasm occurred during menses, there was a decline in sexual activity during the luteal phase, and there was a tendency toward a periovulatory maximum, with a small premenstrual peak two to four days before the next period.

In an attempt to address the problem of differences in menstrual-cycle length, Morris and Udry charted the data in five different ways. They noted that counting days from menstruation, either forward or backward, is no substitute for physiological measures of ovulation. They concluded that (1) the most consistent feature was a rise in sexual behavior about six days before presumed midcycle, and (2) there was a luteal decline in sexual behavior (Morris & Udry, 1982, p. 151).

This pattern has been supported by several other studies (James, 1971; Williams & Williams, 1982). James combined data from McCance's and Morris and Udry's studies with his own, and the resulting pattern showed highest rates of intercourse postmenstrually, with a sharp decline thereafter. There was also a midcycle rise, low rates during the luteal phase, and a premenstrual rise during the last two to five days of the cycle (James, 1971, p. 164).

Adams, Gold, and Burt (1978) made an important advance when they focused on female-initiated sexual activity. These authors hypothesized that menstrual-cycle effects should be apparent only in female-initiated behaviors and that including male-initiated behaviors simply complicated the issue. They asked 35 White, college-educated, married women, between the ages of 21 and 37 to complete questionnaires recording all of their sexual experiences daily. Data were collected over three cycles. Women who were not taking the pill showed definite ovulatory rises in masturbation, fantasy, and female-initiated heterosexual activity (coitus and caressing). Women using oral contraceptives showed no peak at midcycle and their female-initiated heterosexual activity was "unexpectedly low." There were also premenstrual and postmenstrual peaks in female-initiated heterosexual behavior for all of the women, and increased autosexual behavior during menstruation. Gold and Adams (1981) concluded that the postmenstrual peak was probably related to both cognitive and hormonal factors.

Finally, in a study of mood, sexuality, hormones, and the menstrual cycle, Sanders and her colleagues (Sanders, Warner, Backstrom, & Bancroft, 1983) collected daily records of mood, sexual interest, sexual activity (with a partner, masturbation, and orgasm) along with a rating of the subjective quality of the experience, from a group of 66 women in their early thirties, one-third of whom were patients at a

PMS clinic. The PMS group differed from the other subjects in having longer and more painful menstrual periods, and they were more likely to be married and working at home caring for small children. Blood samples were taken several times a week, and plasma estradiol, progesterone, androstenedione, and testosterone were measured. Significant phase differences were found in feelings of well-being, physical distress, and sexual feelings in the group as a whole (Sanders et al., 1983). Further analysis of these data showed a peak in sexual activity during the postmenstrual phase with initiation by the woman or by both partners more likely to occur at this time, and, as one might suspect, there was a relationship between mood and sexuality. Women experiencing a deterioration in feelings of well-being during the luteal phase showed a comparable pattern in their sexual feelings. There was no evidence of an increase in sexual interest or activity around the time of ovulation. Hormone levels were unrelated to the mood changes, but a high correlation between testosterone levels and the frequency of masturbation was found in those women who masturbated (Backstrom, Sanders, Leask, Davidson, Warner, & Bancroft, 1983; Bancroft, Sanders, Davidson, & Warner, 1983).

Cycle-Related Physiological Changes

EROTIC STIMULATION IN THE LABORATORY

Masters and Johnson were the first to study human sexual response in the laboratory using methods of direct observation (Masters & Johnson, 1966). They found a sexual-response cycle in both sexes that includes four phases: excitation, plateau, orgasm, and resolution. The two basic processes that occur in women are vasocongestion (engorgement of the pelvis and vaginal wall) and myotonia (a generalized increase in muscle tension). What follows is a brief summary of the physiological changes occurring in women during the sexual response cycle.

In the excitement phase of the cycle the vagina becomes moist as fluids seep through the vaginal walls. This phenomenon is sometimes referred to as vaginal "sweating." Several other physical changes occur as well. There is a thickening of the vaginal wall, ballooning of the top two-thirds of the vagina, and clitoral tumescence. During the plateau phase, vasocongestion continues, an orgasmic platform develops in the outer third of the vagina, the breasts and uterus become enlarged, the clitoris retracts, and there are also autonomic responses, such as increases in pulse and respiratory rate. During orgasm there is a series of rhythmic contractions of the orgasmic platform and the uterus. Orgasm triggers a release of muscle tension and vasocongestion, and the body returns to its unaroused state during the resolution phase (Hyde, 1979).

Masters and Johnson (1966) did not study menstrual-cycle variations in women's sexual response cycle. However, they did investigate uterine response to stimulation during menstruation. Fifty women agreed to participate during the period of their heaviest flow. A speculum was placed in the vagina to provide a full view of the cervix throughout the entire cycle; all the women achieved orgasm by automanipulative techniques. During the orgasm, menstrual fluid was observed spurting under pressure from the uterus through the opening in the cervix (the external cervical os). Masters and Johnson concluded that these observations provide further clinical evidence of strong uterine contractions in response to effective sexual stimulation; the objective clinical observation also supports many women's subjective reports that sexual activity during menstruation temporarily increases menstrual flow.

On a clinical note, Masters and Johnson recognized the cultural interdiction against sexual activity during menstrual flow and clearly state that there is no clinical evidence to support the notion that coital activity during menstruation causes physical distress. Thus, there is no medical contraindication to coition or masturbation during menstruation. In fact, 43 of the 331 women in their sample reported that they frequently used automanipulative techniques at the onset of menstrual flow to relieve dysmenorrhea. Orgasm increased the rate of menstrual flow, reduced pelvic cramping, and frequently relieved their menstrually associated backaches.

Picking up on the work of Masters and Johnson, Bardwick (1970) measured changes in uterine contractions in response to sexual and nonsexual stimuli during each of four phases of the menstrual cycle. She found no relationship between menstrual-cycle phase and uterine contractions.

Several other laboratory studies using only subjective reports of sexual arousal are of dubious value because there was no concomitant objective measure of arousal. In a study that compared subjects' self-reports of the degree of their sexual arousal with actual recordings of physiological changes Heiman (1975) found a significant lack of correlation between the two measures.

In a methodologically solid laboratory study of 30 regularly cycling women between the ages of 20 and 30, Schreiner-Engel and her colleagues measured sexual arousal by both self-report and photoplethysmographic recordings of vaginal congestion and vaginal pulse amplitude (Schreiner-Engel, Schiavi, Smith, & White, 1981). Plasma estradiol, progesterone, and testosterone were determined by radioimmunoassay, and measurements were taken during the follicular, ovulatory, and luteal phases. Sexual arousal was defined as a woman's response to a known erotic stimulus. Although there were marked and consistent individual differences in sexual arousability, a pattern of menstrual phase differences enterged. Significantly higher levels of vaginal vasocongestion were found during the follicular and luteal phase than during the ovulatory phase. The same pattern of subjectively assessed increases in arousal was observed, but the differences were not significant. Correlations between hormones and subjective and objective assessments of arousability were low and for the most part not significant. These findings are consistent with other recent reviews of the literature focusing only on studies using daily records: There is a postmenstrual and premenstrual peak in sexual arousal, rather than a peak at ovulation. However, Schreiner-Engel et al. note that each woman showed a consistency in her capacity for sexual arousal relative to other women that was not linked to the phase of the menstrual cycle, and she cautions that there is a need for studies in which women are followed for several cycles, using hormonal determinations and concurrent assessments of other sexual responses, such as orgasmic capacity or sexual satisfaction (Schreiner-Engel et al., 1981, p. 204). Two subsequent studies by other investigators failed to document a relationship between phase of the menstrual cycle and vaginal response to erotic stimuli. At this time it seems safe to say that researchers have failed to find a relationship between sexual activity and cyclic changes in estrogen and progesterone during the menstrual cycle (Segraves, 1988).

A few words about testosterone: Awareness of the link between androgens and sexuality stems from the late 1950s when women who underwent adrenalectomy following mastectomy and oophorectomy for breast cancer reported sudden and total loss of libido. When the androgens were replaced, their sex drive returned to its former level.

Thus there is evidence of a relationship between testosterone and sexual arousability. When Schreiner-Engel divided her subjects into subgroups, the high-testosterone group exhibited a higher capacity for sexual arousal, assessed subjectively and physiologically, than the low-testosterone group. There were also considerable differences in masturbation frequency and the occurrence of sexual dreams between the two groups. Similarly, Bancroft and his research team found that mean testosterone levels were correlated with masturbation frequency, though not with sexuality involving a partner (Bancroft, Sanders, Davidson, & Warner, 1983, p. 509).

In studies of surgically menopausal women who received either an estrogen-androgen drug, separate estrogen or androgen, or a placebo, Sherwin and her colleagues found that exogenous androgen enhanced the intensity of sexual desire and arousal and the frequency of sexual fantasies (Sherwin, Gelfand, & Brender, 1985). Further, a comparison of three groups of women receiving an estrogen-androgen preparation, estrogen alone, or no hormones clearly showed that women who received the estrogen-androgen preparation reported significantly higher rates of sexual desire, arousal, fantasy, coitus, and orgasm (Sherwin & Gelfand, 1987).

A look at testosterone levels in both husbands and wives showed no relationship to their sexual behavior, but the wives' self-rating of sexual gratification was significantly correlated with their own plasma testosterone levels (Persky, Charney, Lief, O'Brien, Miller, & Strauss, 1978). Evidently, despite a wide range of individual differences, there is a relationship between testosterone level and sexual behavior in women. However, no link has been demonstrated between testosterone and variability of sexual experience across the menstrual cycle.

The Effect of Social Factors on Sexual Behavior

Clearly, hormones alone do not determine sexual behavior in women. Mood, personality, opportunity, anatomy, and physiology all play a role, and women differ greatly from each other. If there is a relationship between sexual behavior and the menstrual cycle, it seems to be one in which coital frequency is at a low during menstruation, rises rapidly to a maximum during the follicular phase, and then gradually declines over the rest of the cycle, perhaps with a slight increase around ovulation. Then, just before menstruation there is another slight increase before it falls again to its menstrual low. Several explanations for the perimenstrual pattern have been offered:

- greater desire after menstrual abstinence, that is, making up for lost time
- feeling good after feeling bad, improved feelings of physical well-being after menstruation
- avoidance of pregnancy
- a rise premenstrually in anticipation of forthcoming abstinence
- greater sexual pleasure because of premenstrual pelvic vasocongestion

A recent study by Margie Ripper (1987), a social scientist at Flinders University of South Australia, demonstrates a pattern similar to most of the others described here. However, Ripper examined the influence of the day of the week on sexual interest as well as that of menstrual-cycle phase. She collected daily measures of mood and sexual interest from 55 women, mostly in their thirties, married, and with children. She compared the effects of both the menstrual cycle and the social week—that is, weekday versus weekend—and found evidence of a significant menstrual-cycle effect on both mood and sexual interest. Sexual feelings were high in the preovulatory phase and dropped rapidly after ovulation, with a low occurring during menstruation, at which time the women reported being disinterested in sex. An analysis of the social week effect showed that "on weekends the women felt significantly more relaxed, calm, submissive, trusting and sexually interested" (Ripper, 1987, p. 21).

THE INFLUENCE OF ATTITUDES

The low incidence of intercourse during menstruation is easiest to explain socioculturally: Most likely, it is directly related to the belief that sex should be avoided at this time. In an international study conducted by the World Health Organization of more than 5000 women in 14 sociocultural groups in 10 countries, 90% or more of the women in Egypt, India, Indonesia, Jamaica, Korea, Mexico, the Philippines, and Yugoslavia held this belief. A marked difference in attitude occurred only in the United Kingdom, where only about half the women thought that intercourse should be avoided during menstruation. The reasons given for this avoidance vary. Among some of the women it was religious belief (avoidance is a teaching of the Islamic faith). In other cultures hygienic, health, or aesthetic reasons were given, and some women simply found the idea "abhorrent" or "just not right." Those subjects with higher socioeconomic background and/or more education were more likely to continue sexual activity during menstruation (Snowden & Christian, 1983).

Men and women in the United States are remarkably similar to their British counterparts. In the 1981 Tampax study of attitudes toward menstruation, 51% of American men and 56% of American women agreed that women should not have intercourse while menstruating. Approval of a taboo on intercourse during menstruation varies by region: 62% of Southerners, 40% of Westerners, 51% of Midwesterners, and 54% of Easterners agree with it (*The TAMPAX Report*, 1981).

I found some thought-provoking gender differences in attitudes about sex during menstruation in a study of 100 Northeastern college students. The women said that they were significantly less affectionate, less prone to arousal, and less interested in romantic overtures or sexual intercourse when menstruating. However, comparable attitudes were not reported by the men. Of the college men, 86% said that they would have intercourse with a menstruating woman, but only 46% of the women shared their interest. These findings lend support to the idea that women control the diminution in sexual activity during menstruation (Golub, 1976). In a follow-up study of 90 college women, more than half were not comfortable with intercourse during menstruation, and most cited messiness (51%) and pain (24%) as the reasons for avoidance (Golub, Danis, & Kanelos, 1981). The concern with messiness led me to wonder whether women who used tampons were more comfortable with their bodies and would hold more positive attitudes toward menstruation or more liberal sexual attitudes. Not so. In a study of 50 college students the attitudes of tampon users were no different from those of nontampon users (Golub, Porter, & Jaycox, 1982).

Even among Masters and Johnson's subjects (obviously a nonrepresentative group), only 52% of the women expressed an interest in sexual activity during menstruation. Very few objected on the basis of religious concerns, and most had no objection to sexual activity during their menstrual periods provided they felt well, had a willing male partner, and were not at peak menstrual flow.

Emily Culpepper, who gives workshops on menstruation to groups of adult women, asks them about their experiences with sex during menstruation. She has found that some women find menstruation a time of heightened erotic arousal, while others say they cannot possibly imagine feeling sexual during their periods (Culpepper, 1985).

With researchers generally displaying a lack of conviction about the existence of a universal menstrual-cycle-related rhythm for human sexual behavior, it is appropriate to speculate about the way in which attitudes about engaging in sexual intercourse during menstruation might affect the actual incidence of coitus and autosexual activities (both fantasy and masturbation). Gold and Adams graphed the mean number of acts of intercourse in two groups of women, one that abstained during menstruation and one that did not. Both groups showed increased levels of intercourse prior to menstruation. Then there was a sharp decline in intercourse during menstruation among the abstainers, with a dramatic rise postmenstrually. However, there was somewhat less variability in the mean rate of intercourse among the women who did not abstain during menstruation (Gold & Adams, 1981, p. 675). In a study of seven lesbian couples who did not use contraceptives and had no fear of pregnancy, Matteo and Rissman (1984) found no decline in sexual encounters during menstruation and no evidence of pre- or postmenstrual peaks in sexual behavior. There was a midcycle increase in the number of reported orgasms, lending support to the idea of heightened sensitivity around the time of ovulation. These researchers suggest that gay women may be less inhibited about initiating sexual activity during menstruation than heterosexual women or men; this would certainly be in keeping with my finding that gay women have more positive attitudes toward menstruation.

The Social-Hormonal Link

Attitudes affect behavior. But what about the behavioral-hormonal link. Can social life influence hormones? Maybe so. Over the years there have been anecdotal reports from families, roommates, nuns, and nurses of menstrual synchrony: women who live together cycling together.

In 1971, McClintock showed that women who lived together or were close friends became adapted to each other's cycles so that they were menstruating at about the same time (see Chapter 3 for more details; McClintock, 1971). A few years later this finding was confirmed in another study of 79 college women: close friends, neighbors, and random peers. Over a four-month period the differences in the date of menstrual onset of close friends become markedly smaller, while neighbors and random pairs stay about the same (Graham & McGrew, 1980). Both researchers concluded that the significant factor in causing the cycles to synchronize was the amount of time the individuals spent together. It is now known that pheromones (chemical substances given off by the body and perceived through the nose) drive these cycles.

If close contact with other women affects their menstrual cycles, what about contact with men? Here the data are contradictory. McClintock found that women seeing males less than three times a week had significantly longer cycles. Two other studies did not find a significant correlation between cycle length and the amount of social interaction with males (eating, studying, dating) (Graham & McGrew, 1980, p. 245; Quadagno, Shubeita, Deck, & Francoeur, 1981). However, Veith and her colleagues found that women who spent two or more nights with men during a 40-day period had a significantly higher rate of ovulation than those spending one or no nights with men, though there was no effect on cycle length (Veith, Buck, Getzlaf, Van Dalfsen, & Slade, 1983).

In another example of a possible social-hormonal link, Sanders and her colleagues found that women who were married or living with a man had lower testosterone levels than those living alone (Sanders & Bancroft, 1982). Further, women working full time had higher testosterone levels than those working part time or in the home as housewives. These are difficult findings to explain: Are the higher testosterone levels cause or effect or neither?

Money and Ehrhardt (1972) have studied the interaction of sex hormones and behavior for many years. One group of their subjects is of particular interest here. A group of 25 girls who were exposed to androgens while still in utero because of congenital adrenal hyperplasia, a condition in which the cortex of the adrenal glands produces excessive amounts of androgenlike hormones, was followed for a period of years. These girls were more likely to be "tomboys." They had a high level of physical energy and engaged more frequently than a control group in vigorous outdoor play and boys' sports. Although the girls clearly identified themselves as girls, they had little interest in playing with dolls and were more likely to express the intention of having a nondomestic career, or of combining career with family. It is too great a leap to infer that hormones determine whether a woman will choose career over domesticity, particularly today when a majority of women work outside the home. However, the link between androgens and high energy levels or heightened sex drive is certainly worth exploring further.

Returning to the pheromonal influence of men on menstrual-cycle length and fertility: In a series of studies, Cutler and her colleagues at Philadelphia's Monell Chemical Senses Center and the University of Pennsylvania School of Medicine have found significant relationships between sexual behavior, hormone levels, and cycle length (Cutler, Garcia, Huggins, & Preti, 1986; Cutler, Garcia, & Krieger, 1979; Cutler, Garcia, & Krieger, 1980; Cutler, Preti, Huggins, Erickson, & Garcia, 1985). It seems that male scents can change a woman's menstrual cycle. Women who had regular weekly heterosexual activity had menstrual cycles of about 29 days. In contrast, women who were celibate or engaged in sporadic (less than weekly) coital behavior tended to have lower levels of estradiol and a high frequency of aberrant cycle lengths, which tend to be associated with anovulatory and infertile cycles (Cutler, Garcia, Huggins, & Preti, 1986). The highest incidence of fertile-type basal body temperature rhythms and high estrogen levels was found among women who had weekly sex. The total amount of coital behavior was not related to any of the hormones assayed—consistency of the behavior was relevant. However, women with aberrant length cycles tended to have lower levels of estradiol (Cutler, Garcia, Huggins, & Preti, 1986, pp. 496-502).

The link between weekly sex and high estradiol levels also held up in a prospective, double-blind study of perimenopausal women. Here Cutler et al. found hot flashes and sexual behavior to be inversely related to each other. Perimenopausal women who were coitally active at least once a week showed higher levels of estrogen than their age-matched pairs who were less sexually active. No difference in testosterone levels was found between the weekly and less-than-weekly groups. The more sexually active women had a milder menopause (Cutler, Garcia, Huggins, & Preti, 1986, p. 497).

The relationship between weekly sexual activity and a 26- to 33-day cycle is striking. In the college women there were no short cycles among the weekly coitally active women, and there were fewer long cycles in this group. Very short cycles reflect greater potential for infertility; longer cycles may be fertile, but there are fewer fertile days per year. Thus there may be an association between infrequent sexual activity and infertility (Cutler, Garcia, & Krieger, 1980).

These data suggest that coital activity throughout the entire cycle serves some function. Luteal-phase activity is just as necessary as follicular-phase activity to get the desired cycle regularity. This lends support to the notion that nonovulatory coital activity is important for physiological as well as social reasons. A relationship exists between heterosexual activity and menstrual-cycle normality as well as between heterosexual activity and fertility. And that goes for men as well as women. In men, higher weekly ejaculation frequencies are associated with higher sperm quantity and quality. Cutler and colleagues suggest that perhaps regular coitus serves to "prime the reproductive system" as well as impregnate it.

An observation made by this group warrants further study: A delayed age at first coitus was found in a group of infertile women. Apparently optimum fertility is obtained if first coitus occurs within seven years after the onset of menarche. The suggestion here is that patterns of sexual behavior throughout the life cycle may influence fertility.

In another demonstration of the effect of odor on the hypothalamic-gonadal axis, male and female "essence" was made from the underarm secretions of seven male and female volunteers who wore underarm pads for 18 to 27 hours a week over a three-month period. Male essence, mixed with alcohol, was applied to the upper lips of six women with abnormal menstrual cycles and no current sexual relationship. These women's cycles speeded up or slowed down toward 29.5 days. The irregular cycles of the control groups remained the same. In the second study, 10 women who received female essence likewise showed a significant trend toward synchronized menstrual periods after only a few cycles. The control group showed no such change. The Monell Center has filed applications for four pheromone patents (Leo, 1986). Apparently, underarm odors have effects similar to those of regular sexual intercourse, although perhaps the odor effects are weaker. Male scent may be used some time soon to regulate the menstrual cycle, correct certain kinds of infertility, and perhaps even relieve menopausal symptoms.

It is tempting to speculate about the weekly rhythm. Why does the week seem to provide the best interval for marking human reproduction patterns and fertility? And where does the Sabbath come in? Did those cultures that marked time in this way reproduce more successfully? Going back to the question posed at the beginning of this chapter: Is there a relationship between sexual behavior and the menstrual cycle? The answer is clearly yes. But in reviewing the literature, one is forced to acknowledge the interactive nature of the variables: Cyclical variations in hormone levels apparently affect sexual behavior (perhaps directly and certainly indirectly), but social and sexual behaviors affect reproductive hormones as well.

References

Adams, D. B., Gold, A. R., & Burt, A. D. (1978). Rise in female-initiated sexual activity at ovulation and its suppression by oral contraceptives. *New England Journal of Medicine, 299*(21), 1145-1150.

Backstrom, T., Sanders, D., Leask, R., Davidson, D., Warner, P., & Bancroft, J. (1983). Mood, sexuality, hormones, and the menstrual cycle, II: Hormone levels and their relationship to the premenstrual syndrome. *Psychosomatic Medicine, 45*(6), 503-507.

Bancroft, J., Sanders, D., Davidson, D., & Warner, P. (1983). Mood, sexuality, hormones, and the menstrual cycle, III: Sexuality and the role of androgens. *Psychosomatic Medicine, 45*(6), 509-516.

Bardwick, J. M. (1970). Psychological conflict and the reproductive system. In J. M. Bardwick, E. Douvan, M. S. Horner, & D. Gutmann (Eds.), *Feminine personality and conflict* (pp. 3-30). Belmont, CA: Brooks/Cole.

Baum, M. J., Everitt, B. J., Herbert, J., & Keverne, E. (1977). Hormonal basis of proceptivity and receptivity in female primates. *Archives of Sexual Behavior, 6*(3), 173-192.

Benedek, T. F. (1959). Sexual functions in women and their disturbance. In S. Arieti (Ed.), *American handbook of psychiatry* (pp. 727-748). New York: Basic Books.

Benedek, T. F., & Rubenstein, B. B. (1939). The correlations between ovarian activity and psychodynamic processes. *Psychosomatic Medicine, 1*, 245-270.

Culpepper, E. E. (1985). *New attitudes of women toward menstruation.* Paper presented at the meeting of the Society for Menstrual Cycle Research, Galveston, TX.

Cutler, W. B., Garcia, C.-R., Huggins, G. R., & Preti, G. R. (1986). Sexual behavior and steroid levels among gynecologically mature women. *Fertility and Sterility, 45*(4), 500.

utler, W. B., Garcia, C.-R., & Krieger, A. M. (1980). Sporadic sexual behavior and menstrual cycle length in women. *Hormones and Behavior, 14*(1), 63-172.

utler, W. B., Preti, G., Huggins, G. R., Erickson, B., & Garcia, C.-R. (1985). Sexual behavior frequency and biphasic ovulatory type menstrual cycles. *Physiology and Behavior, 34*(5), 805-810.

utler, W. B., Garcia, C.-R., & Krieger, A. M. (1979). Sexual behavior frequency and menstrual cycle length in mature premenopausal women. *Psychoneuroendocrinology, 4*, 297-309.

utler, W. B., Garcia, C.-R., Huggins, G. R., & Preti, G. (1986). Sexual behavior and steroid levels among gynecologically mature premenopausal women. *Fertility and Sterility, 45*(4), 496-502.

oty, R. L., Ford, M., Preti, G., & Huggens, G. (1975). Changes in the intensity and pleasantness of human vaginal odors during the menstrual cycle. *Science, 190*, 1316-1317.

arfield, P. L. (1974). *Creative dreaming.* New York: Simon & Schuster.

old, A. R., & Adams, D. B. (1981). Motivational factors affecting fluctuations of female sexual activity at menstruation. *Psychology of Women Quarterly, 5*(5), 670-680.

olub, S. (1976). Sex differences in attitudes and beliefs regarding menstruation. In P. Komnenich, M. McSweeney, J. A. Noack, & Sister N. Elder (Eds.), *The menstrual cycle* (Vol. 2, pp. 129-134). New York: Springer.

olub, S., Danis, R. M., & Kanelos, K. (1981). *Young college women's attitudes about sexual behavior throughout the menstrual cycle.* Unpublished manuscript.

olub, S., Porter, H. A., & Jaycox, C. (1982). *Attitudes regarding sexuality and menstruation held by tampon users vs non-tampon users and their reported comfort with their bodies.* Unpublished manuscript.

raham, C., & McGrew, W. C. (1980). Menstrual synchrony in female undergraduates living on a coeducational campus. *Psychoneuroendocrinology, 5*, 245-252.

ray, P. (1970). *Encyclopedia of the biological sciences.* New York: Van Nostrand Reinhold.

eiman, J. R. (1975). Women's sexual arousal: The physiology of erotica. *Psychology Today, 9*, 91-94.

yde, J. S. (1979). *Understanding human sexuality.* New York: McGraw-Hill.

ames, W. H. (1971). The distribution of coitus within the human intermenstruum. *Journal of Biosocial Science, 3*, 159-171.

insey, A. C., Pomeroy, W. B., Martin, C. E., & Gebhard, P. H. (1953). *Sexual behavior in the human female.* Philadelphia: W. B. Saunders.

ein, A. (1979). *The cycling female.* San Francisco: Freeman.

eo, J. (1986, December 1). The hidden power of body odors—male pheromones are good for women's health. *Time*, 67.

asters, W. H., & Johnson, V. E. (1966). *Human sexual response.* Boston: Little, Brown.

atteo, S., & Rissman, E. F. (1984). Increased sexual activity during the midcycle portion of the human menstrual cycle. *Hormones and Behavior, 18*, 249-255.

cCance, R. A., Luff, M. E., & Widdowson, E. E. (1937). Physical and emotional periodicity in women. *Journal of Hygiene, 37*, 571-611.

cClintock, M. K. (1971). Menstrual synchrony and suppression. *Nature, 229*, 244-245.

Money, J., & Ehrhardt, A. A. (1972). *Man and woman, boy and girl*. Baltimore an London: Johns Hopkins University Press.

Morris, N. M., & Udry, J. R. (1982). Epidemiological patterns of sexual behavior i the menstrual cycle. In R. C. Friedman (Ed.), *Behavior and the menstrual cyc* (pp. 129-154). New York: Marcel Dekker.

Persky, H., Charney, N., Lief, H., O'Brien, C. P., Miller, W. R., & Strauss, D. (1978 The relationship of plasma estradiol level to sexual behavior in young wome: *Psychosomatic Medicine, 40*(7), 523-535.

Primate sex preference at ovulation. (1977, February 19). *Science News, 111*, 118-11

Quadagno, D. M., Shubeita, H. E., Deck, J., & Francoeur, D. (1981). Influence of ma social contacts, exercise and all-female living conditions on the menstru. cycle. *Psychoneuroendocrinology, 6*(3), 239-244.

Ripper, M. (1987, June). *A comparison of the effect of the menstrual cycle and the soci. week on mood, sexual interest and self-assessed performance*. Paper presented at th meeting of the Society for Menstrual Cycle Research, Ann Arbor, MI.

Sanders, D., Warner, P., Backstrom, T., & Bancroft, J. (1983). Mood, sexuality, ho mones and the menstrual cycle, I: Changes in mood and physical stat Description of subjects and method. *Psychosomatic Medicine, 45*(6), 487-501.

Sanders, D., & Bancroft, J. (1982). Hormones and the sexuality of women—th menstrual cycle. *Clinics in Endocrinology and Metabolism, 11*(3), 639-659.

Schreiner-Engel, P., Schiavi, R. C., Smith, H., & White, D. (1981). Sexual arousabili and the menstrual cycle. *Psychosomatic Medicine, 43*(3), 199-214.

Segraves, R. T. (1988). Hormones and libido. In S. R. Leiblum & R. C. Rosen (Eds. *Sexual desire disorders* (pp. 271-311). New York: Guilford.

Sherwin, B. B., Gelfand, M. M., & Brender, W. (1985). Androgen enhances sexu. motivation in females: A prospective, cross-over study of sex steroid admin istration in the surgical menopause. *Psychosomatic Medicine, 47*(4), 339-351.

Sherwin, B. B., & Gelfand, M. M. (1987). The role of androgen in the maintenance (sexual functioning in oophorectomized women. *Psychosomatic Medicine, 49*(4 397-409.

Snowden, R., & Christian, B. (1983). *Patterns and perceptions of menstruation*. Ne York: St. Martin's Press.

Swanson, E., & Foulkes, D. (1968). Dream content and the menstrual cycle. *Journ. of Nervous and Mental Disorders, 145*, 358-363.

The TAMPAX Report. (1981). New York: Tampax Corp.

Veith, J. L., Buck, M., Getzlaf, S., Van Dalfsen, P., & Slade, S. (1983). Exposure to me influences the occurrence of ovulation in women. *Physiology and Behavio 31*(3), 313-315.

Wallis, J., & Englander-Golden, P. (1985). *Female primate sexuality across the menstru. cycle*. Paper presented at the meeting of the Society for Menstrual Cyc. Research, Galveston, TX.

Williams, G. D., & Williams, A. M. (1982). Sexual behavior and the menstrual cycl In R. C. Friedman (Ed.), *Behavior and the menstrual cycle* (pp. 155-176). Ne York: Marcel Dekker.

6

Experiencing Menstruation: Menstrual Bleeding and How Women Handle It

The Advantages of Menstruating

n terms of morbidity and mortality, nature's bias seems to differ from hat of society. Women live longer than men and are less vulnerable o a number of diseases. Whether this is due to an advantage con-veyed by being female or to a disadvantage inherent in being male is not yet known. However, menstruation may have something to do with the fact that women are less vulnerable than men to heart disease until after menopause. Speculating that blood viscosity might be a factor, two medical researchers proposed that it may be the bleeding itself—the monthly loss of blood—that protects women (Vaisrub, 1977). Recognition of the benefits of menstrual bleeding is not new. The second-century-A.D. Greek physician Galen made a similar observation, and he urged men to bleed themselves. Even earlier, ceremonies in which men cut themselves and bled, simulating men-struation, were seen among primitive tribes. And bloodletting as a medical treatment was popular from the time of Hippocrates (460-377 B.C.) until the middle of the nineteenth century. However, a more likely explanation of the low incidence of heart attacks in premeno-pausal women is the presence of ovarian hormones. Estrogens have a salutary effect on the blood, increasing levels of high-density lipo-protein cholesterol (the good cholesterol) and reducing levels of low-density lipoprotein cholesterol (the bad cholesterol) in a manner that is thought to protect against heart disease. Studies of hormone replacement therapy in menopausal women show a 50% reduction in the risk of a coronary attack in women using unopposed oral estrogen (Barrett-Connor & Bush, 1991). It thus seems to be estrogens rather than the bleeding per se that is protective.

Variation in Cycle Length

If asked how long a normal menstrual cycle is, most people will respond "about 28 days." And that is reasonably correct. Yet few women menstruate regularly every 28 days. By definition, the length of the menstrual cycle is the number of days from the first day of a bleeding episode through the day before the onset of the next consec-utive bleeding episode. In a one-year study of 2,316 women between the ages of 15 and 44 at the Center for Population Research in Washington, D.C., researchers found that 77% of the women had average cycle lengths between 25 and 31 days. The modal length was 27 days. The arithmetic average was 29.1 days, with a standard deviation of 7.46 days. About 5% of women have very irregular cycles. When these cycles were omitted from the calculations and only cycles between 15 and 45 days were considered, the average length dropped to 28.1 days, with a standard deviation of 3.95 days (Chiazze, Brayer, Macisco, Parker, & Duffy, 1968).

Thus, the 28-day figure is useful, but only as a broad guideline. There is variation in cycle length both among women and within the same woman. The degree of irregularity is such that only 13% of the women in the study mentioned above had cycles that varied by less than six days over the course of the year. The remaining 87% had variations of seven or more days.

AGE AND VARIABILITY

Variation in menstrual-cycle length with respect to age has been confirmed in several studies. Treloar and his colleagues gathered data from more than 2,700 women over a 30-year period, thus representing nearly 3000 person years of menstrual history. They found that variability of menstrual-cycle length was greatest in 15- to 19-year-olds and lowest among the 25- to 39-year-olds, reaching a minimum between 35 and 39 years. A slight increase in variability follows for women aged 40 to 44 years (Treloar, Boynton, Behn, & Brown, 1967).

Chiazze and his collaborators (Chiazze et al., 1968) at the Center for Population Research collected more than 30,000 menstrual cycles. They found that although 27 days was the modal length for the entire sample, this length was most likely to be seen in the three older age groups, women between 30 and 44 years of age. A modal length of 28 days was found in groups aged 15 to 29. However, in no age group did 28-day cycles occur more than 16% of the time.

As a menstrual cycle researcher, I can vouch for the variability in women's cycles. When I was trying to test women during the four days prior to the onset of menstruation and at midcycle, without letting them know what I was doing, I "caught" my subjects when I wanted them only about half the time. Typically, the women would indicate on a questionnaire that they had a 28- or 29-day cycle. I would schedule a testing session accordingly, and then they would begin to menstruate on Day 24, or not begin to menstruate until Day 32. It happened all the time.

Vollman (1977) arranged data collected from 594 women and 30,261 menstrual cycles according to gynecologic age, that is, the number of years after menarche. As shown in Figure 6.1, the mean length of the menstrual cycles formed a U-shaped curve, falling steeply from 35.0 to 29.8 days during the first four years of menstruation and then dropping slowly to about 27 days after 28 years of menstruation, after which it gradually rose to 44 days at the gynecologic age of 40 years.

Both Vollman's and Chiazze's findings are similar to those of Treloar. The greatest variation in cycle length occurred in the premenarcheal and premenopausal years, that is, the menstrual cycles are typically longest at the extremes of the reproductive years. This trend toward longer intervals is more marked in the premenopausal years. Less variation in cycle length occurred in women between 20 and 40 years old, with the least seen among subjects about the age of 36. However, even in this group the range for 98% of the cycles varied between 20 and 43 days with a standard deviation of 9.9 days.

As for the correlation between consecutive cycles, several studies indicate that the length of each cycle is not related to the length of the one that preceded it (Presser, 1974). Very short cycles (less than 24

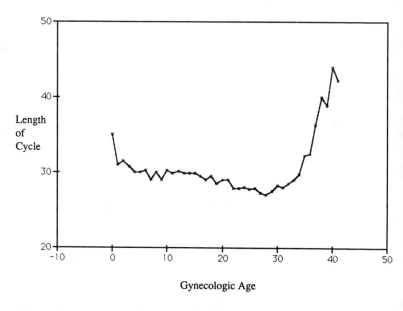

Figure 6.1. Variation in Cycle Length With Age

days) or very long cycles (more than 45 days) were generally followed by cycles within a 25- to 39-day range. Less than half of the cycles were within two days of each other, but about three-fourths occurred within five days of the previous cycle.

Whether anovulation could be producing the differences in the length of the menstrual cycle at various ages is a relevant question. Age appears to be highly correlated with the incidence of anovulation. However, in an extensive review of the literature, Presser (1974) found that studies of only ovulatory cycles had results similar to those that did not control for ovulation. Therefore, whether cycles are ovulatory or not, there seems to be a relationship between age and cycle length.

THE ROLE OF CELIBACY AND
ORAL CONTRACEPTIVES

Sexual activity, or simply contact with men, also influences menstrual timing. Women who spend more time with men tend to have a greater number of regular menstrual cycles (29 ± 3 days), whereas women who have sporadic sexual activity or are celibate have a higher frequency of aberrantly short and long cycles (<26 or >33 days). And, as noted in Chapter 5, researchers at the Monell Chemical Senses Center found that exposure to extracts derived from men's or women's perspiration can affect menstrual cycles.

While women are taking oral contraceptives, their cycles are very regular because they are artificially controlled. However, menstrual-cycle length and regularity may change and become irregular for a while when use of the pill is discontinued. In one study, irregularity was marked in the first two postpill cycles, with an average increase in cycle length, but by the third cycle there was a tendency to return to original menstrual-cycle patterns.

UNPREDICTABILITY

Perfect regularity in menstrual rhythm is rare to nonexistent. In addition to age and sexual activity, life changes, both positive and negative, may alter the cycle. For example, the number of cycles often decreases within a 90-day period after illness, surgery, or accidents (Smith, 1991). Regularity within three or four days is the best we can hope for and is most likely to occur between ages 20 and 40. For women who do worry about it, it is perhaps most important simply to know that menstrual-cycle irregularity is normal. What impact does this have on women's lives?

The more unpredictable the onset of menstruation, the more potentially troublesome it is. How does one plan one's life around this phenomenon, which influences work, play, and sex, among other things? As just one example, a major difficulty in the use of natural family planning for birth control stems from the variability of menstrual-cycle length. One cannot predict times of fertility (namely the three days preceding ovulation and the one day following it) on the basis of calendar alone. Thus women must use basal temperatures and observations of body changes and cervical mucus to enhance the reliability of establishing when ovulation actually occurs. As noted in Chapter 3, basal body temperature dips at the time of ovulation and then rises noticeably on the day after. Similarly, cervical mucus changes as ovulation approaches: It becomes more abundant and changes from being sticky and viscous to a thinner, more watery, slick consistency. A woman who examines her own cervix just before ovulation will find that the cervix is more difficult to reach—it is located somewhat higher in the pelvis because high estrogen levels enhance the contraction of the broad ligaments supporting it. The cervix also feels softer and the os is slightly open. After ovulation the cervix is easier to reach, becomes firmer, and the os is closed. Originally designed for Catholic couples, the system of natural family planning using basal body temperature and observations of the cervix and cervical mucus can be used by others who want to give up artificial contraceptives. However, to make the rhythm method work, careful attention must be given to cyclical physiological changes, and couples must abstain from intercourse or use other methods of contraception during fertile periods (Keefe, 1976).

Menstrual Fluid:
Composition and Bleeding Patterns

Despite the fact that menstrual cycles are not necessarily regular and that each woman has her own mean and variability (both of which change with age), for most women the duration and volume of menstrual bleeding has been shown to be fairly constant throughout a woman's mature life.

Menstrual fluid is a combination of blood from the endometrium, endometrial cells, and mucus from the cervix and vagina. A variety of organic compounds, minerals, and hormones have been identified in menstrual fluid. Prostaglandin F, a hormone-like substance, has been found in high concentrations in the menstrual fluid of women with severe dysmenorrhea. The pH of menstrual fluid is alkaline and is reported to range between 6.9 and 7.5. Menstrual blood is more viscous than peripheral venous blood, although it has a much lower hematocrit. In one study, the menstrual discharge was found to behave like "an oil-based paint, having small particles suspended in a thick fluid" (Reame, 1985). Menstrual fluid viscosity was also found to be highest on Day 1 of menses and gradually dropped during subsequent days of flow. In a World Health Organization study, menstrual blood—as compared with other blood—was described by women as darker in color, thicker in texture, and having a "mild but distinctive odour" (Snowden & Christian, 1983).

Although the average menstrual blood loss is said to be about 30 ml (about one fluid ounce), the normal range is anywhere from 20 to

60 ml. Because most women do not go around measuring their menstrual blood loss, as some researchers do, it is useful to know that a completely wet pad absorbs about 90 ml and a tampon 40 ml of menstrual blood. Average flow is of four days' duration, but, once again, there is a great deal of variation from one woman to another. In one study of 476 randomly selected Swedish women between the ages of 15 and 50 years, Hallberg and his associates found that the youngest and oldest groups had significantly different amounts of blood loss. The 15-year-old age group lost less blood (about 34 ml) and the 50-year-old group lost more blood (about 62 ml) than did the other groups. The authors suggest that the lower blood loss seen among the younger subjects may be a function of methodology: There were fewer tampon users in this group, and more blood is lost to measuring error when only napkins are used for collecting menstrual flow. However, the influence of sexual activity and parity cannot be ruled out. Among the older women the higher incidence of heavy bleeding was thought to be due to a higher frequency of problems such as fibroids, which are more common in the perimenopausal years and are often linked to heavy menstrual bleeding. Within the 23- to 45-year-old age group, age did not affect menstrual blood loss: It ranged from about 40 ml to 49 ml (Hallberg, Hogdahl, Nilsson, & Rybo, 1966).

Menstrual blood loss is thought to be a major factor influencing iron balance and hemoglobin concentration in women. A hemoglobin of 12 g/100 ml blood is considered normal. Hallberg and colleagues found that women with a menstrual blood loss greater than 60 ml had lower concentrations of plasma iron and hemoglobin.

The upper normal limit of menstrual blood loss is 76.4 ml. This is consistent with the finding of increased frequency of iron deficiency in subjects with menstrual blood loss of 61-90 ml or more. More than 40% of these women had abnormally low hemoglobin levels. The loss of iron in menstruating women is about 0.6 mg daily. If a woman is consuming the recommended daily intake of 15 mg (with 10% absorption), that leaves 0.9 mg after menstrual losses. Thus Hallberg's study indicates that iron balance will be maintained and blood hemoglobin levels will be normal with blood losses up to 63 ml, assuming a daily intake of 15 mg of iron. Blood loss of more than 80 ml is pathological.

Generally speaking, women are not good judges of the amount of their menstrual blood loss. In one study almost 40% of women with abnormal blood loss described their bleeding as small or moderate

(Hallberg et al., 1966, p. 342). And in another study, 37% of the women with heavy blood loss considered their bleeding to be moderate, and 4% considered it scanty. Conversely, 14% of the small-blood-loss group considered their bleeding heavy. Perhaps what women need is a frame of reference, such as the scale introduced by Snowden (1977) ranging from 1 (very heavy—need to change highest absorbency tampon or pad every 1-2 hours) to 5 (very light—hardly bleeding, one daily change needed).

Women with heavy bleeding show no change in length of menses or in distribution of total menstrual loss. It is the same as that associated with normal menstrual loss. Women with excess bleeding do lose heavily, but they do so over short periods of time.

FACTORS INFLUENCING MENSTRUAL BLOOD LOSS

Studies of monozygotic and dizygotic twins indicate that hereditary factors influence blood loss. And although American and European populations on average experience similar amounts of menstrual blood loss, there has been at last one report of a primitive tribe in which women experience a total menstrual period of only a few drops that lasts only half an hour. In a study offering further support for genetic differences, Goodman and her colleagues compared characteristics of menstruation of Caucasian, Japanese, and Chinese women living in Hawaii. They found that heavy flow and menses lasting more than five days were reported significantly more often by the Caucasian women than by the other two groups (Goodman, Grove, & Gilbert, 1984). In a Swedish study, a significant correlation was found in duration of flow between mothers and daughters (Kantero & Widholm, 1971).

Although evidence about the effects of parity or the birth weight of children on menstrual blood loss is contradictory, parity was associated with increased menstrual bleeding in both Caucasians and Japanese in Goodman's study and has been implicated in other studies as well (Rybo, 1966). Snowden and Christian (1983) found that although the majority of women in all parity groups reported a bleeding duration of three to four days, of those who reported the shorter episodes of one to two days, a disproportionate number were women with seven or more pregnancies.

Airline flight attendants have been reported to have a greater amount of flow in addition to menstrual cycle irregularity. Whether this is due to the stress of travel, high altitudes, or disruption of circadian rhythms is not known at this time. However, in one study of women vacationing at a high altitude, researchers found a shortening of the menstrual period and prolongation of the cycle (Prill & Moar, 1971).

Birth-control pills result in less blood loss and shorter, more regular periods, while IUDs cause an increase in menstrual flow and may lengthen bleeding episodes. Copper and progestogen-containing IUDs are associated with less menstrual blood loss and cramping than the inert types.

Season affects length of flow, with longer flows in winter and spring, and shorter flows during the hot summer months (Datta, 1960). Time of day is significant too. In a study of menstrual flow rate, Reame (1985) found that samples collected during the day were more than twice as high as those collected overnight while subjects were sleeping.

Several studies report that most blood (about 76%) is lost during the first three days. The most profuse bleeding is seen on Day 2. It is notable that despite large differences between individuals, differences in the same person are small. Women who bleed heavily tend to do so for most of their period, while women who bleed lightly do so throughout their period. Thus the length of the bleeding episode is much less variable and hence more predictable than the length of the cycle. In the World Health Organization study, most women report a bleeding episode of four to five days' duration, with respondents taking oral contraceptives reporting a lighter loss, one to three days, and IUD wearers a heavy loss of more than six days duration. The accuracy of these predictions is high: 88% of the women were on target or over—or underestimated by only one day. Contrast this with predictions about when they would get their next period, where 8% were unwilling to make any predictions and only 31% were able to make a prediction accurate to within one day; 22% were inaccurate in their estimates by as much as a week or more. Snowden and Christian note that "in all cultures studied the majority of women were unable to predict accurately the onset of their next bleeding episode" (Snowden & Christian, 1983, p. 83).

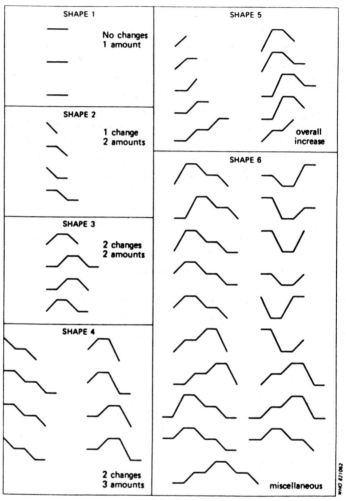

Figure 6.2. Typical Bleeding Shapes

Source: Snowden, R., & Christian, B. (1983). *Patterns and perceptions of menstruation*. New York: St. Martin's Press. Reprinted with permission by Groon Helen, publishers.

Note: The amount of bleeding is represented vertically and the number of days is plotted horizontally.

BLEEDING SHAPE

Very few studies have been concerned with patterns of bleeding during menstruation, that is, how bleeding on the first day compared with the whole menstrual period. The World Health Organization study collected these data and introduced a new concept: "bleeding shape." Bleeding shape refers to the perceived amount of blood lost on each day, and the changes in amounts of bleeding during the entire menstrual bleeding episode. In looking at Figure 6.2 it is clear that in Shape 1 there is no change in daily amount of bleeding; in Shape 2 there is one change, from a greater to a lesser amount; Shape 3 describes two changes and two amounts; Shape 4 has two changes but ends in light bleeding; in Shape 5 there is an increase; and all other bleeding patterns are lumped together as Shape 6. The most common shape is Shape 3 (32%), closely followed by Shape 2 (30%). Shape 4 and Shape 1 were seen less frequently (15% and 10%, respectively). More than 90% of the women reported at least one change in the amount of blood loss, and the greatest number reported a heavier loss at the start of the bleeding episode and a smaller loss as the period proceeds.

Women who experience no changes in amount (Shape 1) generally experience a shorter, lighter bleeding episode, whereas women who experience a decreasing amount of blood loss or irregular patterns (Shape 4 or Shape 6) tend to have longer and heavier bleeding episodes.

Most women bleed between three and four days (48%) or between five and six days (35%). Longer bleeding episodes were found among women living in urban as opposed to rural areas. Age seems to be a factor among women reporting short bleeding episodes (one to two days): The majority were over 30.

The perceived amount of bleeding does affect behavior. Women with heavier bleeding were more likely to report that they reduced the amount of physical work they undertook and increased their amount of rest during menstruation. This was not true for the duration of bleeding. However, both amount and duration of the bleeding episode affected mood and physical discomfort. The greater the amount or duration of bleeding the greater the likelihood that physical discomfort and a mood change would be reported.

Bleeding shape did not affect the type of protection used. Rather, this depended upon perceived blood loss. The heavier the blood loss and the longer the duration of bleeding the more likely the woman was to use pads. Tampon users were more likely to report light bleeding.

One of the purposes of the World Health Organization study was to acquire information about attitudes toward changes in menstrual bleeding patterns that might occur with different methods of contraception. The majority of women (71%) said that they would not accept a contraceptive that would induce amenorrhea. When asked if they wanted more or less bleeding than they currently experienced, most women said that they did not wish to experience any change. However, women with longer duration of bleeding and heavier flow expressed greater preference for less blood loss. The researchers concluded that contraceptives would be most acceptable if they did not change the amount of blood loss, ensured that bleeding episodes were of relatively short duration and occurred regularly, permitted the predictability of bleeding episodes, and did not result in blood that differed in color or consistency from menstrual blood (Snowden & Christian, 1983, pp. 142-143).

Menstrual Accidents

Most women see menstruation as a very private and personal matter. Menstrual bloodstains on clothing are considered shameful, and many women wear darker, looser-fitting clothes during menstruation. Yet menstrual accidents are really quite common—and, given the lack of predictability of the onset of menstruation, not surprising. When a random sample of 103 women in the New York metropolitan area was asked whether they had ever got their period when they were not prepared for it, 61% said that they had. Some examples:

I was at the beach and didn't realize I was supposed to be getting my period, but I did. I realized it before it went through my bathing suit, but I didn't have anything with me. I went to the First Aid Station and they didn't have anything. There was nothing in the bathroom. I was an hour away from home. So I walked around and asked "girls" if they had a tampon. I was so embarrassed. A very nice woman came to my aid. She even gave me an extra tampon for later in case I needed it. After that I put one in the glove compartment of my car for emergencies.

I was sleeping over at my cousin's house. When I woke up there was blood on the sheets. I was too embarrassed to tell anyone, so my sister and I changed the sheets and took them down to the laundry room without anyone knowing.

I was on the bus and right before my stop I got up and saw blood on the seat. I had a napkin on, so I got nervous. I sat right back down and passed my stop because I didn't want anyone to notice. I got off at the last stop which was four stops after mine and walked home from there.

I was in class and I felt it coming on. I took my friend's long coat and wore it until lunch time. Then I went home. One good thing, I missed my afternoon classes.

Four other women described incidents in which they wrapped jackets—their own or someone else's—around their waists until they got home. And sometimes there are other surprises:

One night while I was washing dishes after supper, my little brother laughed and yelled to my mother that I had sat in ketchup.

I was at a writer's workshop on a lunch break. I had my period and was wearing a tampon but suddenly, while walking back for the afternoon session, I began to gush. I dashed into a nearby shop, told the woman there I had started to bleed heavily, and begged to use the rest room. I was frantic. She was kind. What a mess! I cleaned up with toilet paper and fortunately had a fresh napkin to put on. I did make it back to the workshop.

It was my third or fourth date with the man I would later marry. We were out with some friends of his. Driving home—in the friend's car—I realized that I had soaked through my tampon, underwear, dress and probably the back seat of the car. I somehow managed to get out of the car and into my apartment without dying of embarrassment and they (the men) didn't mention it for years.

It is notable that many of the women recalled precisely what they were wearing when they had an accident: "I was wearing lavender pants," "I was wearing tennis shorts," "I was wearing a white gown," "I was wearing a pink dress," "I really liked that sexy grey and black dress."

More than 75% of the women said that they did not rely on machines in public rest rooms for sanitary protection. In order to be prepared, 16.5% carried menstrual protection with them all the time, 35.8% carried it when they expected their periods, 33% carried it while menstruating, and only 14.5% never carried tampons or napkins (Golub, "Embarrassing moments," n.d.). That may be just as well, for the machines are not universally available, and almost every woman has found herself, at one time or another, in the frustrating position of facing a broken, empty, or nonexistent sanitary napkin dispenser when she needed it. A survey by Market Opinion Research in 1985 found that 65% of all women feel that employers, stores, and businesses fail to take their needs for feminine hygiene products seriously (*Ms.*, 1985). How true!

Menstrual Hygiene Products: History and Current Status

I use an exercise in my social psychology classes—a simulation of a disaster—in which small groups of students are asked to draw up a list of the 10 things they would want to have in their "survival cells." Perhaps because I teach at a women's college and students are less embarrassed than they would be in a co-ed situation, menstrual protection appears—along with blankets, first aid kits, and books—on almost every list.

The history of menstrual products is interesting. Women have almost always used some sort of sanitary protection. Tampons and pads have been made of cloth, paper, vegetable fiber, cotton, wool, or grass, depending of course upon availability. In the days of the Roman Empire, women used cloth bandages; in ancient Japan, they used paper tampons; and in Africa, there were pads made of grass or moss.

Between 1854 and 1914 some 20 different patents for sanitary napkins or menstrual receptacles were taken out in the United States. The first commercial disposable pad, Lister's Towels, was introduced by Johnson & Johnson in 1896. However, we know very little about how women felt about this new product. We do know that it did not fare well in the marketplace and was eventually withdrawn, probably because of difficulties in advertising its availability.

It is hard to believe that only 70 years ago American women were washing and reusing pads made of old, soft sheets. Sanitary napkins as we know them are an outgrowth of a discovery made by French nurses during World War I. The nurses found that the cellulose material used for bandaging wounds absorbed menstrual blood better than cloth diapers, and they began to use the bandages. After the war, the Kimberly-Clark Corporation found itself with a surplus of bandage material, learned that the army nurses had found the material useful for menstrual pads, and began manufacturing "sanitary" pads. Sanitary napkins went commercial in 1921 when "Kotex," the first successful disposable sanitary napkin was produced and marketed, followed soon after by "Modess."

Lillian Gilbreth, an industrial psychologist (in addition to being the mother of 12 children made famous in the biography *Cheaper by the Dozen*), was asked by Johnson and Johnson in 1926 to conduct a market and consumer analysis on the use of sanitary napkins (Bullough, 1985). She distributed 3000 questionnaires to high-school students, college women, and business and professional women from Boston to Grand Forks, North Dakota, and from Detroit to Baltimore. The findings of the more than 1000 questionnaires that were returned are still of interest today. Gilbreth concluded that only a fraction of the available market had been reached by the manufacturers in spite of the number and variety of commercial napkins offered. And, to a large degree, the napkins offered on the market did not meet or satisfy consumers' demands.

There were some other interesting findings:

- On average each consumer uses 11 napkins per month
- The average duration of menstrual life is 32 years
- Thus, each woman during her menstrual life would require a total of 4,576 napkins

Since 1921, the sanitary napkin has changed and improved: Pads are smaller; they adhere to panties with a thin strip of adhesive rather than being attached to a sanitary belt with pins or clips; and they are now even biodegradable and flushable. The leading brands are: Kotex, made by Kimberly-Clark, commanding about 55% of the market; Modess, made by Johnson & Johnson, reaching about 35% of buyers; and Confidets, made by the Scott Paper Co., with about 10% of purchases.

Tampax entered the market in 1933. At first, it was an object of scorn, derision, and controversy because tampons were thought to destroy a young woman's virginity, but this myth was subsequently refuted, and tampons gradually gained acceptability, with additional brands entering the market. Currently, Tampax is the leading tampon manufacturer, with Playtex number two, and Kotex tampons in third place. In contrast to women in Europe, most women in the United States prefer tampons with applicators, finding them easier to insert. Both European and American women are generally happy with tampons, citing comfort, lack of mess and unpleasant odor, invisibility under clothes, ease of use, and ease of disposal as reasons for their satisfaction. The initial insertion of a tampon has become a new American puberty ritual. Many of us can identify with the cartoon drawings in which two girls, with much embarrassment, buy a box of tampons and then go through contortions in trying to insert one for the first time (Bretecher, 1980). However, despite the belief that the relative freedom with which women engage in recreational activities is associated with the use of tampons during menstruation, a majority of women worldwide still use only napkins or other kinds of external protection. Sommer notes that at the end of 1989 there was no factory in the entire USSR that manufactured tampons (Barbara Sommer, personal communication).

In the World Health Organization's cross-cultural study, considerable variation was found in the type of protection used during menstruation. Most women used external pads and, in general, more women used homemade pads of cloth, cotton wool, or toilet paper than store-bought pads. The cloth pads are usually washed and used again. In some cultures (India and Indonesia) extra clothing, such as panties or additional petticoats, are also worn as protection. In Pakistan, some women and schoolgirls wear black trousers during their periods, and Filipino women are reported to wear thicker dresses with black or red over-skirts. In Egypt 27% of the women reported using no protection at all: They believe that it interferes with normal blood flow and is unhealthy. Generally, there is a tendency for urban, high-status, educated women to use store-bought pads and rural, low-status, uneducated women to use homemade pads. Of course in poor and rural areas store-bought pads are both uneconomical and frequently unavailable (Snowden & Christian, 1983, p. 52).

A relationship also exists between the amount of bleeding and the kind of menstrual protection used. Women who are taking oral contraceptives experience less blood loss and tend to use internal tampons, whereas women wearing an IUD experience heavier bleeding and tend to use pads or pads and tampons together. Bleeding shape does not seem to affect the type of protection used. Rather, tampon or napkin use is dependent upon the total blood loss during the bleeding episode and the duration of bleeding.

In studying tampon absorbency, Consumers Union found that the research method used influences which tampons perform better. When the tampon is simply dunked into a container of liquid and weighed, tampons that expand lengthwise (such as Tampax) excel; however, when the tampon is tested using a device called a "Syngyna," which simulates a vagina, tampons that expand in a radial fashion (such as Playtex and Pursettes) do best (Consumer Reports Books, 1980). The difference between regular- and super-sized tampons is not size, but weight. The supers weigh about 25% more and are more absorbent. This is also true of pads, with super-sized pads achieving increased absorbency with increased weight.

Some women's groups advocate homemade tampons made from sponges. They note that one kitchen sponge can be made into four tampons, which last for as long as six hours of heavy flow. The sponges can be sterilized by boiling and then reused, making them the most economical method available (Delaney, Lupton, & Toth, 1988, p. 141).

The frequency with which sanitary protection is changed depends upon the volume of the blood loss and the degree of discomfort experienced. Weather, working conditions, and body weight are all factors.

Methods other than tampons and napkins have been tried. In the late 1960s, the Tassett Co. of California introduced the Tassaway, a bell-shaped plastic cup that fit into the vagina to catch the flow. It could periodically be emptied, washed, and reinserted, making it potentially more economical than disposable products. If inserted properly, the Tassaway would not leak, and it could hold more fluid than the average tampon. However, some women found the Tassaway uncomfortable or messy to remove—many women object to methods that require them to put their fingers into their vaginas. The Tassaway did not survive the vagaries of the marketplace and is no longer available. However, some women use their rubber diaphragms to catch the menstrual flow or to enable them to have nonmessy sex during menstruation.

Some women worry about the health effects of using tampons. They express concern that tampons could lead to vaginal or bladder infections, or to erosion of the cervix. Several studies have found no adverse physiological or clinical effects associated with the normal use of tampons. However, many physicians advise against the use of "deodorant" tampons or pads because of the possibility of irritation or allergic reaction to these products. An important cause for concern is Toxic Shock Syndrome.

Toxic Shock Syndrome and the Need for Tampon Labeling

First described in 1978, Toxic Shock Syndrome (TSS) is an acute illness whose signs and symptoms include: fever (usually more than 104 degrees); rash; hypotension (a sudden drop in blood pressure that may lead to shock); involvement of three or more organ systems (for example, vomiting or diarrhea, muscle pain, and kidney, liver, or blood dysfunction); and peeling of skin, especially on the palms and soles. TSS came into public view in the spring and summer of 1980 when it was linked with the use of tampons by previously healthy, menstruating women, some of whom died.

In 1981 the Institute of Medicine formed a medical committee in order critically to review and analyze data related to TSS, evaluate what was known, and stimulate appropriate new research (Institute of Medicine, 1982). The committee found that more than 1,600 cases of TSS were reported nationally through April 1982, 92% of which were associated with menstruation. Of the menstrual cases, 98% occurred among tampon users. The fatality rate for cases reported in 1981 was about 3%. A strong association was found between the occurrence of TSS and the presence of Staphylococcus aureus, a bacteria known to cause other human diseases. Women between the ages of 15 and 19 accounted for approximately one-third of the menstrual cases. Recommended treatment includes the use of antibiotics to combat infection, treatment of hypotension, and correction of fluid and electrolyte imbalances.

Although TSS is a relatively rare illness, it can be fatal. Thus the committee concluded that although the etiology and epidemiology were not completely understood, some preventive measures could be taken. They suggested that because most cases were associated with tampon use, a research priority would be the development of tampons that did not enhance the user's risk of getting TSS; it was also important to identify susceptible persons who would benefit from tampon avoidance. Finally, there was a need to educate both the public and health professionals in order to foster informed decision making.

The committee specifically recommended that:

1. Women who have already had TSS should be advised not to use tampons. Postpartum women should be informed that use of tampons may increase TSS risk.
2. Women, especially adolescents, should be advised to minimize their use of high-absorbency tampons.
3. Physicians and other health professionals should be informed about the variations in presentation of nontampon-associated cases that have occurred, should be alerted to the symptoms of TSS, and should be encouraged to report all definite and probable cases, as well as suspected cases. Physicians also should be advised that treatment of TSS patients with beta-lactamase-resistant antibiotics apparently decreases the chance of recurrence. (Institute of Medicine, 1982)

What has been learned since 1982? The number of reported cases has steadily declined from 319 in 1983, to 97 in 1986, and about 75 in 1987. The death rate has also dropped dramatically from 10%-12% to 2%-3%. TSS is a rare disease with an estimated incidence of two to four cases per 100,000 women per year; and only 55% of the cases in 1987 were related to menstruation. In nonmenstrual cases, TSS can begin with a skin infection, a burn, an insect bite, or a postoperative wound. This public-health success story is attributable to public education, tampon labeling (since 1982, the FDA has required labels advising that the use of the lowest absorbency needed may minimize the risk of toxic shock), and to changes in the chemical composition of tampons that have been made by the manufacturers (McDonald, 1988).

Rely tampons, the Proctor and Gamble brand implicated in many early cases, were made of polyester foam and carboxymethycellulose.

They were taken off the market in September 1980. Brands currently sold are made from cotton and rayon and are less absorbent. Studies by the Centers for Disease Control have found the risk of TSS is 33 times greater for tampon users than for nonusers, and the risk generally increases as the absorbency of the tampon increases, regardless of the chemical makeup of the tampon. For each 1 g increase in tampon absorbency, the risk of illness increased 37%. Thus the preferential use of low-absorbency tampons now on the market is likely to reduce further the risk of TSS. However, researchers have also noted that because labeled tampon absorbencies were not standardized between different manufacturers, it was difficult for consumers to make informed choices based on actual absorbency (Rome, Wolhandler, Dieckmann, & Kahn, 1987).

Esther Rome and Jill Wolhandler of the Boston Women's Health Book Collective, and representatives from other women's health advocacy groups have been working for years to develop labeling of tampon absorbencies. In 1982 they participated, with representatives from various tampon manufacturing companies, on a task force of the American Society for Testing and Materials. The task force's charge was to develop a standard test method for measuring tampon absorbency and a means for expressing absorbency on tampon labeling. They met frequently for more than three years, agreed on appropriate methods of testing tampon absorbency, but could not reach agreement on uniform absorbency labeling.

Finally, in September 1988 the Food and Drug Administration (FDA) concluded that manufacturers would not voluntarily agree to provide absorbency information that would facilitate interbrand comparisons of tampons, so the FDA moved to impose a standardized testing and labeling system. The new regulations require that the labels for tampons reflect standard absorbency levels. The terms "junior," "regular," "super," and "super-plus" now conform to specific standard levels of absorbency. An ounce of water weighs about 28 g. A "junior" tampon is one that absorbs 6 g or less of water in a standardized test; in contrast, a "super-plus" absorbency tampon would absorb 12-15 g.

The attention focused on tampons by TSS has generally served women well. People began to talk more openly about menstruation. Researchers, physicians, and women themselves began to ask questions about tampons: "What are they made of?" and "What effect do hey have on the vagina?" We learned that new superabsorbent ampons (containing polyacrylate rayon) were being used.

At a meeting of the Society for Menstrual Cycle Research in May 1985, Rome put one of these new tampons into a glass of water and passed it around. The water turned cloudy and there were particles floating in the liquid. She said, "Look carefully and think about what happens to those bits and pieces in your vagina." At that time there was no available research addressing the safety of these new fibers for use inside the vagina, but reports began to appear in the medical literature linking tampons with microulcerations and ulcers of the vagina as well as increased risk of TSS. Could these particles enter the lymph system through vaginal ulcers and cause problems in other parts of the body? Nobody knew. Consumer groups called for more biocompatibility testing: measuring the effects of tampons and tampon ingredients on living tissue. Subsequently, as research demonstrated a decrease in the incidence of TSS associated with changes in tampon composition, superabsorbent tampons were taken off the market (Petitti & Reingold, 1988). Later it was found that regardless of the chemical composition of the tampon, increasing absorbency increased the likelihood of developing TSS.

The Boston Women's Health Book Collective offers some valuable guidelines regarding tampons:

1. Choose a tampon with the lowest absorbency you can use. A used tampon should slide out easily when you pull on it. It is too absorbent if it sticks to your vagina.
2. Avoid perfumed, "deodorant," tampons because the scent may irritate your vagina.
3. Tampons made of plain cotton rather than new ingredients may be the safest.
4. Take care in using applicators to avoid scratching or pinching vaginal tissue. (Rome, Wolhandler, Dieckmann, & Kahn, 1987)

Rome and her colleagues point out that there is a number of things we simply do not know about using tampons. For example: How long should a tampon be used before it is changed? Can the particles that come off a tampon cause problems in the vagina? What germs are on tampons when we buy them (they are not sterile)? Few women want to give up the convenience, comfort, security, and easy disposability of tampons. However, tampons can be improved. Unfortunately that will only happen if the public becomes more aware of the need for further research to address the questions raised here and if women demand the development of safer tampons.

References

Barrett-Connor, E., & Bush, T. L. (1991, April 10). Estrogen and coronary heart disease in women. *Journal of the American Medical Association, 265*(14), 1861 1867.

Bretecher, C. (1980). The first tampon. In G. Kaufman and M. K. Blakely (Eds.), *Pulling our own strings* (pp. 18-21). Bloomington: Indiana University Press.

Bullough, V. L. (1985). Merchandising the sanitary napkin: Lillian Gilbreth's 1927 survey. *Signs, 10*(3), 615-627.

Chiazze, Jr., L., Brayer, F. T., Macisco, Jr., J. J., Parker, M. P., & Duffy, B. J. (1968). The length and variability of the human menstrual cycle. *Journal of the American Medical Association, 203*(6), 89-92.

Consumer Reports Books. (1980). *The Medicine Show* (pp. 214-223). Mount Vernon, NY: Consumers Union.

Datta, N. (1960). Influence of seasonal variations on the reproductive cycles in women. *Population Review, 4*, 46-55.

Delaney, J., Lupton, M. J., & Toth, E. (1988). *The curse.* Chicago: University of Illinois Press.

Golub, S. (n.d.) Embarrassing moments: Recollections of menstrual accidents. Unpublished manuscript.

Goodman, M. J., Grove, J. S., & Gilbert, Jr., F. I. (1984). Recalled characteristics of menstruation in relation to reproductive history among Caucasian, Japanese and Chinese women living in Hawaii. *Annals of Human Biology, 11*(3), 235-242.

Hallberg, L., Hogdahl, A., Nilsson, L., & Rybo, G. (1966). Menstrual blood loss—a population study. *Acta Obstetrica et Gynecologica Scandinavica, 45*, 320-351.

Institute of Medicine. (1982). *Toxic shock syndrome.* Washington, D.C.: National Academy Press.

Kantero, R., & Widholm, O. (1971). Correlations of menstrual traits between adolescent girls and their mothers. *Acta Obstetrica et Gynecologica Scandinavica, Suppl 14*(4), 30-36.

Keefe, E. F. (1976). Physicians help make rhythm work. *New York State Journal of Medicine, 76*(2), 205-208.

McDonald, W. (1988, September 4). Toxic Shock: A success story. *The New York Times.*

Ms. (1985, February), 13(8), 18.

Petitti, D. B., & Reingold, A. (1988, February 5). Tampon characteristics and menstrual toxic shock syndrome. *Journal of the American Medical Association, 259*(5), 686-687.

Presser, H. B. (1974). Temporal data relating to the human menstrual cycle. In M. Ferin, F. Halberg, R. M. Richart, & R. L. Vande Wiele (Eds.), *Biorhythms and human reproduction* (pp. 145-160). New York: John Wiley.

rill, H. J., & Moar, H. (1971). Changes in the menstrual cycle during stay at high altitude. *Medizinische Klinik, 66*(27), 986-989.

eame, N. (1985). Menstrual health products, practices, and problems. In S. Golub (Ed.), *Lifting the curse of menstruation* (pp. 37-51). New York: Harrington Park.

ome, E., Wolhandler, J., Dieckmann, J., & Kahn, R. P. (1987). *Tampons, are they safe?* Published by the Boston Women's Health Book Collective.

ybo, G. (1966). Menstrual blood loss in relation to parity and menstrual pattern. *Acta Obstetrica et Gynecologica Scandinavica, 45, Suppl. 7,* 25-45.

mith, K. R. (1991). *Life events and variations in menstrual cycle length.* Paper presented at the meeting of the Society for Menstrual Cycle Research, Seattle, WA.

nowden, R. (1977). The statistical analysis of menstrual bleeding patterns. *Journal of Biosocial Science, 9,* 107-120.

nowden, R., & Christian, B. (1983). *Patterns and perceptions of menstruation.* New York: St. Martin's Press.

reloar, A. E., Boynton, R. E., Behn, B. G., & Brown, B. W. (1967). Variation of the human menstrual cycle through reproductive life. *International Journal of Fertility, 12*(1), 77-126.

aisrub, S. (1977). Sex determinants of heart disease. *Journal of the American Medical Association, 237*(5), 477.

ollman, R. F. (1977). *The menstrual cycle.* Philadelphia: W. B. Saunders.

7

Dysmenorrhea: Painful Periods

Pain is so commonly associated with menstruation that many pe
ple—professionals as well as lay persons—dismiss it as normal.
"normal" means most women have it, then perhaps it is. In the Wor
Health Organization study of women in 10 different countries, t
majority reported physical discomfort in conjunction with menstr
ation (Snowden & Christian, 1983). In other studies of nonpatie
populations (women who were not seeking medical treatment)
Europe and the United States, the reported incidence of prima
dysmenorrhea ranges from 3% to 70%, with the wide range attribu
able to differences in the population surveyed and the definition
dysmenorrhea used for the study (Dingfelder, 1981; Morrison
Nicolls, 1981). It is frequently said that about 50% of all wom
experience some form of dysmenorrhea, while 5% to 10% experien
pain severe enough to be incapacitating for an hour to three days
each month (Lamb, 1981). There are two types of dysmenorrhe
primary dysmenorrhea, in which the pelvic organs are normal, ar
secondary dysmenorrhea, where there is some underlying pelv
pathology, such as tumors or endometriosis.

Primary Dysmenorrhea

Primary dysmenorrhea is the most common menstrual disorder nd is often cited as the single greatest cause of lost school or working ays among young women (Ylikorlkala & Dawood, 1978). Some 10%) 14% of young women in their late teens and early twenties are bsent from classes monthly because of dysmenorrhea. Friederich 1983) has expressed concern that because of its potential impact on 1e academic success of young women, this may have subtle but >ng-range implications for women who are training for their future ccupations.

The economic impact of primary dysmenorrhea is important. Vomen with severe dysmenorrhea miss more workdays than women /ith mild or no dysmenorrhea. A recent study addressing the issue f workdays lost because of pain found menstrual pain to be the sixth 1ost common complaint, with 24.5 million workdays lost because of : each year (The high cost of pain, 1985).

Feminist researchers worry that statistics such as these will be used) justify discrimination against women in the workplace. Yet women o not lose more workdays each year because of illness than do men. .nd there is evidence that despite widespread complaints of men-trual pain, most women carry on and have a very low incidence of /ork absenteeism resulting from menses (Lamb, 1981, p. 103; Garling c Roberts, 1980). One explanation may be that the incidence of ysmenorrhea declines as women get older.

.GE AND DYSMENORRHEA

There seems to be a relationship between age and dysmenorrhea. ienerally the incidence is low around the time of menarche and ecomes more severe some time in the next two years. Because of the requent occurrence of anovulatory cycles during the first year, dys-1enorrhea is usually not seen until after six months of cyclic men-truation (Widholm & Kantero, 1971). However, some women report 1e onset of pain during the first year, and in one study 30% of the /omen reported that pain started with the earliest menstrual periods 3olub & Catalano, 1983).

Several studies document the rapid increase in the incidence of ysmenorrhea during the teen years. Bickers (1960) found that the incidence of menstrual cramps in girls under the age of 15 is less than 5%, but from age 15 to 22 the incidence rises progressively, going from 5% to 30%. Similarly, Widholm and Kantero (1971, p. 22) found that the incidence of dysmenorrhea more than tripled, going from 7.2% to 25.6% in the five years after periods began. Overall, 38% of the more than 5000 girls they studied had pain occasionally, and 13% experienced it regularly. In his study of 839 wives of graduate students Moos (1968) found that the younger women, those under 21, complained significantly more of menstrual pain than did the women over 31 years of age. Thus, dysmenorrhea generally begins in the early teens and becomes most severe in the late teens and early twenties.

After the high incidence of dysmenorrhea seen during the teen years, it seems to decrease gradually with increasing age. Kessel and Coppen (1968) found a significant negative correlation between menstrual pain and age in their sample of 500 women between the age of 18 and 45. And in a recent study, Woods and her colleagues found that severe dysmenorrhea was reported by 20% to 25% of the 18- to 25-year-old women, but by only 7% of the 31- to 35-year-old age group (Woods, Most, & Dery, 1982). So there is a decline in both the incidence and severity of menstrual pain after age 25 or 30 (Golub, 1985).

The next question that comes to mind is: Is it just getting older that makes a difference, or does it have something to do with childbearing? It is difficult to separate the effects of age and parity, for a women get older, they are more likely to bear children. However anecdotally women often say that their periods got better after they had a child, and in the past physicians used to tell women who complained of dysmenorrhea that it would disappear when they had a baby. Old wives' tale? Probably not. In a study of 890 women Svennerud (1959) found the frequency of dysmenorrhea to be similar in married and unmarried women in the 20- to 24-year age group However, in married women the frequency of dysmenorrhea decreased more rapidly with age. Although these data were not examined for the effect of parity, it can be assumed that the married women were more likely to have had children. Similarly, more than 30% of a group of women between the ages of 30 and 45 reported that childbirth had altered their menstrual cramps (Golub & Catalano, 1983 p. 57). And in a study of perimenstrual symptoms in which the effect of parity was specifically addressed, researchers found that women who had been pregnant were significantly less likely to experience menstrual cramps than were the women who had never been pregnant (12.5% versus 21%; Woods, Most, & Dery, 1982, p. 1260).

It seems reasonable to conclude that both age and parity affect the incidence and severity of primary dysmenorrhea, though why pregnancy makes a difference remains a mystery. The increase in uterine vascularity and blood supply that occurs during pregnancy and persists afterwards has been offered as one explanation. Dysmenorrhea has been called uterine angina, and the increased blood supply may relieve the pain caused by uterine contractions and ischemia (a lack of blood due to constriction or blockage of a blood vessel; Dingfelder, 1981, p. 876). Other suggestions have been proffered: a change in pain-sensitive nerves in the uterus during pregnancy; the formation of less prostaglandin[1] or less sensitivity to prostaglandin after pregnancy; dilation of the cervix that allows for unobstructed menstrual flow; and, for some as yet unknown reason, age alone (Dysmenorrhea, new . . . , 1981). However, despite the fact that many women do experience relief from menstrual pain after pregnancy or with the passage of time, this is by no means a universal phenomenon. More than 30% of the 30- to 45-year-old women Golub and Catalano studied reported that nothing had altered their menstrual cramps over the years (Golub & Catalano, 1983, p. 57). Dysmenorrhea remains a problem for a large number of women throughout their menstrual lives.

PSYCHOLOGICAL ASPECTS

In the past, women who complained to their physicians about menstrual pain were often told, "It's all in your head." What could be less helpful or more provocative? A favorite cartoon of mine shows a doctor's office, with a man in a white coat sitting behind a big desk and a young woman in the patient's chair. He is saying, "It's all in your head." She, distraught, unscrews her head and flings it across the room at him.

The lay press, medical texts, and many psychologists supported the idea of a psychogenic factor in the etiology of dysmenorrhea, and for many years psychologists looked for a link between personality or femininity and menstrual disorders. Most of the studies have been correlational in nature, for example, showing a relationship between menstrual complaints and negative attitudes toward menstruation.

Unfortunately, these studies sometimes were interpreted as indicating that psychological problems caused menstrual symptoms. This kind of research is a good example of the way in which the attitudes of researchers shape their hypotheses and their interpretations of research findings. A more reasonable explanation, from a dysmenorrheic woman's perspective, is just the opposite: Menstrual discomfort leads to negative attitudes about menstruation. Recent work has failed to find a causal link between attitudes and symptoms (Lawlor & Davis, 1981; Stolzman, 1983). The World Health Organization's cross-cultural survey found wide differences in attitudes from one culture to another. The percentage of women who viewed menstruation as an illness ranged from 3% in Pakistan to 67% in Egypt, with a great deal of variability in the attitudes of the women sampled in other countries. Yet, the incidence of menstrual symptoms varied far less across cultures, with 50% to 70% of the women in the 14 groups sampled reporting discomfort prior to or during menstruation ((Snowden & Christian, 1983, pp. 58-59). Thus culture may shape attitudes toward menstruation, how a woman feels about herself when she is menstruating, and whether or not she seeks medical treatment for menstrual symptoms, but culture and negative attitudes do not cause dysmenorrhea (see Table 7.1).

It has also been proposed that menstrual symptoms have something to do with a rejection of traditional role expectations: "Women who do not like being women get dysmenorrhea." Research findings are contradictory. Some studies find significant correlations between symptoms and low-role acceptance, while others find precisely the opposite. Some researchers imply that accepting one's role and being feminine (nice, well behaved, deferent, and passively attractive) are psychologically healthy attitudes. Others disagree. Gannon (1985) asks whether it is really better (healthier) for women to accept passivity—the traditional woman's role—or to rebel against the inferior position thrust upon them in our society? Certainly no conclusions can be drawn about the relationship between menstrual pain and gender-role orientation at this time.

Psychological factors do play a role in the experience of menstrual distress. Women with pain during menstruation or heavy menstrual bleeding also experience feelings of anxiety, tension, and depression (Paige, 1973; Gannon, 1985, p. 73; Golub & Harrington, 1981). However, the reasonable explanation seems to be that the mood changes are the *result* of menstrual symptoms rather than the *cause* of them.

TABLE 7.1 Beliefs and Behavior Associated With Menstruation

Percentage of respondents believing:	Egypt	India, Hindu High Caste	India, Hindu Low Caste	Indonesia Javanese	Indonesia Sundanese	Jamaica	Korea	Mexico	Pakistan Sind	Pakistan Punjab	Philippines	United Kingdom	Yugoslavia Non-Moslem	Yugoslavia Moslem
Menstruation is necessary for femininity	96	95	96	58	85	61	79	57	33	84	95	42	52	61
Menstruation is "dirty"	88	69	48	82	93	33	34	53	58	40	41	7	41	68
Menstruation is like "sickness"	67	20	7	19	14	37	22	26	5	3	61	7	24	53
Intercourse should be avoided during menstruation	98	97	94	94	98	91	91	90	88	86	90	54	94	94
Washing hair should be avoided during menstruation	16	18	2	58	61	21	11	14	36	16	68	5	38	32
Cooking should be avoided during menstruation	1	79	75	1	2	27	2	3	3	3	6	0	5	19
Bathing should be avoided during menstruation	42	8	3	7	2	18	72	20	47	44	72	10	45	34
Visiting friends/relatives should be avoided during menstruation	55	49	56	2	2	39	7	16	12	7	24	0	27	13
Physical discomfort prior to or during menstruation	58	58	55	65	70	61	53	51	68	50	62	57	60	69
Mood changes prior to or during menstruation	42	44	40	34	23	42	52	38	58	39	48	71	65	73
Decreased work during menstruation	10	58	46	12	7	19	14	7	14	11	19	15	12	18
Increased rest during menstruation	21	72	43	18	15	29	28	11	36	22	27	22	21	41

Source: Snowden, R., & Christian, B. (Eds.). (1983). *Patterns and perceptions of menstruation*. New York: St. Martin's Press. Reprinted with permission by Groom Helm, publisher.

Despite efforts to demonstrate that dysmenorrhea is related to poor personal adjustment, no relationship has been found between neurotic tendencies and dysmenorrhea (Coppen & Kessel, 1963).

SYMPTOMS AND ETIOLOGY

Primary dysmenorrhea is defined as painful menstruation without any evidence of physical abnormality (Budoff, 1980). Women describe menstrual cramps as sharp pains in the lower mid-abdomen; the pains may radiate to the lower back or upper thigh. Some women complain of a more congestive type of pain, which is described as a steady, dull ache, sometimes radiating down the legs and to the suprapubic area. The pain may be accompanied by headache, nausea, and vomiting (Ylikorlkala & Dawood, 1978, p. 833).

Typically, dysmenorrhea starts between 2 and 12 hours before the onset of flow (or at the onset of menstrual flow) and lasts about 24 to 36 hours. It is generally agreed that dysmenorrhea occurs only in ovulatory cycles and is somehow related to ovulation. In an ovulatory cycle, estrogens and progesterone are produced cyclically and foster the development and shedding of the endometrium. Before ovulation there is a progressive increase in estrogens, which is accompanied by proliferative changes in the endometrium. After ovulation, the corpus luteum produces progesterone, which converts the proliferative endometrial tissue to secretory endometrium. Although estrogen levels are higher in the first part of the cycle and progesterone higher in the second part, both are continuously produced. Changes in uterine activity throughout the cycle are modulated by circulating levels of estrogen, progesterone, and prostaglandins (Dawood, 1981a).

A breakthrough in our understanding of dysmenorrhea came in 1957 when V. R. Pickles, a British physician and physiologist at Sheffield University, discovered a substance in menstrual fluid that stimulated uterine smooth-muscle contractions, specifically, contractions of the myometrium during menstruation. This stimulant was later found to contain prostaglandins. The two prostaglandins present in menstrual fluid with the capability of initiating uterine contractions are PGF2-alpha and PGE2. Prostaglandins are present throughout the body and regulate many physiological processes, including reproduction, inflammation, blood pressure, blood clotting, and hormone activity. During the menstrual cycle, as progesterone levels drop, uterine prostaglandin levels begin their dramatic rise, and the uterus becomes responsive to them. In anovulatory cycles, in the absence of increased progesterone, there is no increase in endometrial prostaglandins, and subsequent menstruation is not painful (Pickles, Hall, Best, & Smith, 1965; Dawood, 1981a, pp. 24-39).

Pickles was the first to demonstrate that the prostaglandin concentrations in the menstrual fluid of dysmenorrheic women were higher than that in the menstrual fluid of women who did not have dysmenorrhea. Others have confirmed this observation and have shown that some of the breakdown products of PGF2-alpha are increased on the first day of menses in women with dysmenorrhea. The laborlike pain and other symptoms of dysmenorrhea, such as diarrhea, vomiting, and nausea, are well-known side effects seen when PGE2 or PGF2-alpha is given to induce labor.

Studies in which menstrual fluid has been collected from tampons in order to monitor menstrual prostaglandins have provided information about the total amount of prostaglandin released and total menstrual fluid volume. Strong correlations have been found between the quantity of prostaglandins released and the clinical symptoms experienced (Dawood, 1981a, p. 39).

Thus, evidence now exists that women with dysmenorrhea have higher levels of menstrual and endometrial prostaglandins. It is also known that prostaglandins produce menstrual pain in three ways: by increasing uterine contractions, by causing ischemia due to reduced uterine blood flow because of the excessive contractions, and by increasing sensitization of pain fibers. However, whether these high concentrations of prostaglandins are due to increased production, abnormal release, or decreased breakdown of prostaglandins is not yet clear (Friederich, 1983, p. 97).

In women who suffer from dysmenorrhea, uterine activity is abnormal. Experiments designed to measure uterine contractions date back to before 1900. However, a great leap in the sophistication of these measurements and in knowledge of uterine physiology was made in the mid-1970s when microtransducers were introduced. These very small measuring devices translate one form of energy to another; thus changes in pressure or temperature can be recorded. Microtransducers enable researchers to monitor several different sites inside the uterus and thereby visualize uterine contractions. In doing so they have found that contractions generally begin at the fundus (the large upper end of the uterus), that they vary during the menstrual cycle according to the hormonal status of the uterus, and that each woman has her own unique pattern of uterine contractility.

The proliferative phase of the cycle is characterized by short, frequent contractions of relatively small amplitude. Around the time of ovulation, the contractions become more frequent, and the amplitude is reduced, making the uterus relatively quiescent. This is thought to enhance sperm migration. After ovulation, in the secretory phase, there are fewer contractions but their amplitude increases to "prelaborlike" contractions before menstruation. At menstruation there are frequent high-amplitude contractions. Women with dysmenorrhea have a hypercontractile pattern: Contractions that are more frequent (6-12 every 10 minutes, as compared to 3-10 in normal cycles) and of higher amplitude (stronger than those seen during labor). It is thought that this hypercontractility of the uterus results in a decrease in blood flow to the uterine muscle and hence ischemia, which causes the pain (Friederich, 1983, pp. 93-94; Lundstrom, 1981).

Although primary dysmenorrhea is related to ovulation, the roles of estrogens and progestins are not clear. Hormone levels in the blood do not necessarily reflect what goes on in the uterus. The pituitary hormones, oxytocin and vasopressin, do affect uterine activity, but there is no agreement as to specific effects. Research has shown that when oxytocin levels are low or when the ratio of vasopressin to oxytocin increases, uterine contractions are dysrhythmic and painful. Dysmenorrheic women seem to have higher vasopressin levels, but it is unclear whether the higher levels are responsible for increased uterine activity, or whether they are the result of pain and/or other changes in women with dysmenorrhea (Dawood, 1981a, p. 23).

TREATMENT

When Grandma suggested brandy in tea or a glass of sherry for menstrual pain, she was on the right track. Relatively small doses of alcohol are effective in relieving menstrual pain, and, contrary to what one might expect, it does not serve as a sedative or analgesic but rather works by reducing uterine activity, for it inhibits the secretion of oxytocin and vasopressin. However, alcohol does have its limitations, and one is forced to agree with the physician who concluded that, "the well known side effects of alcohol preclude its practical use in young women with dysmenorrhea" (Fuchs, 1982).

TABLE 7.2 Some Nonprescription Drugs for Dysmenorrhea and Premenstrual Symptoms

Drug	Ingredients	Purpose
Midol Original	Acetaminophen 325 mg Pyrilamine Maleate 12.5 mg	analgesic, pain relief antihistamine, relief of tension, irritability, cramps
Midol Maximum Strength	Acetaminophen 500 mg Pyrilamine Maleate 15 mg	see above
Midol PMS	Acetaminophen 500 mg Pyrilamine Maleate 15 mg Pamabrom 25 mg	see above mild diuretic, for relief of water retention and related symptoms
Pamprin	Acetaminophen 400 mg Pyrilamine Maleate 15 mg Pamabrom 25 mg	see above
Premsyn PMS	Acetaminophen 500 mg Pyrilamine Maleate 15 mg Pamabrom 25 mg	see above
Nuprin Advil Trendar	Ibuprofen 200 mg	antiprostaglandin, for pain

In deciding what is the appropriate treatment for a particular woman, the first step is a gynecological examination and a thorough medical history. If the examination is normal and menstrual cramps are mild, aspirin or other over-the-counter preparations may be suggested. Aspirin is a mild antiprostaglandin, and many of the nonprescription drugs contain aspirin in combination with other drugs, such as caffeine, which provides a stimulant effect, or mild diuretics for relief of the symptoms of water retention (see Table 7.2).

However, if dysmenorrhea is more severe, an oral contraceptive or one of the prostaglandin synthetase-inhibiting drugs is needed. Oral contraceptives prevent ovulation and thin the uterine lining, so prostaglandin production is reduced. If contraception is desired, this is an appropriate choice. Friederich (1983, p. 99) notes that "any of the low dose estrogen-progestin combinations taken from day 5 to day 25 of

TABLE 7.3 Prostaglandin-Inhibiting Drugs Approved by the FDA for Use in the Treatment of Dysmenorrhea

Generic Name	Brand Name	Dosage and Instructions for Use
Ibuprofen	Motrin	400 mg, every 4 hours as necessary
Mefenamic Acid	Ponstel	500 mg to start, then 250 mg every 6 hours as necessary
Naproxen	Naprosyn	500 mg to start, then 250 mg every 6 to 8 hours as needed. Total daily dose not to exceed 5 tablets
Naproxen Sodium	Anaprox	550 mg to start, then 275 mg every 6 to 8 hours as needed; total daily dose not to exceed 5 tablets

the cycle can be prescribed if the examination and history are completely negative for pathology."

For women who do not need contraception and do not want to take hormones for 21 days in order to relieve pain that occurs for one or two days a month, the antiprostaglandins (also called nonsteroidal anti-inflammatory drugs) are the medications of choice. These drugs interfere with the synthesis or action of prostaglandins and are available over the counter in mild form but require a prescription for higher dosages (see Table 7.3). Clinical trials in which the patient takes the medication under study, another analgesic, and a placebo during different cycles and records her responses on each cycle have shown about 80% success rates for the antiprostaglandins. The medication is begun at the onset of flow. It is usually absorbed within 15 to 20 minutes and generally does not have to be taken for more than 48 hours. The fact that these drugs act quickly and are excreted rapidly increases their safety and reduces the likelihood of side effects. However, some people do experience side effects. The more common ones include gastrointestinal symptoms, such as nausea, heartburn, and epigastric pain. These can sometimes be reduced or eliminated by taking the medication with milk or food. Less frequently seen side effects are dizziness, skin rashes, drowsiness, headache, bronchospasm, changes in vision and hearing, and hematologic symptoms.

Keep in mind that many of the adverse side effects were seen in patients being treated for arthritis, where higher dosages and long-term use are more common. Nonetheless, contraindications to the use of antiprostaglandins include: chronic inflammation or ulceration of the gastrointestinal tract; aspirin-induced asthma, or bronchospasm, or other allergic reaction to aspirin; sensitivity to the specific drug; kidney disease; or use of anticoagulants (Budoff, 1980, p. 67; Friederich, 1983, p. 100; *Physician's Desk Reference*, 1986).

As previously noted, studies indicate that 80% to 85% of women respond to antiprostaglandin drug therapy. And, if one medication does not work, Budoff (1981) has found that by switching to another drug—or a second, third, or even a fourth—more than 95% of women will respond. She believes the improvement with one antiprostaglandin but not another lies in "individual chemical idiosyncrasy." She also notes that if a patient develops resistance to a drug (it works for several months and then ceases to give relief), switching to another drug is often effective. Behavioral treatments also have something to offer in the treatment of primary dysmenorrhea. Pain is experienced differently by different women and perhaps even by the same woman at different times. The pain actually experienced by a woman with dysmenorrhea has both a physical and a psychological component. Each person's unique body structure and biochemical individuality contribute to the organic component of pain. Psychosocial factors, such as ethnicity, stress, previous learning, and perceived ability to control the pain, contribute to the psychological component of pain. For example, in one study Italian and Jewish patients showed more pain than did Irish and Old American (*sic*) patients (Zborowski, 1969). Learning has been found to influence menstrual symptoms. Nursing students who had been encouraged to adopt a sick role when menstruating or whose mothers had modeled menstrual distress reported significantly more menstrual symptoms as adults (Whitehead, Busch, Heller, & Costa, 1986).

Some success has been reported in the treatment of dysmenorrhea using muscle relaxation and biofeedback techniques. In one study, Heczey (1980) divided 44 college women into four treatment conditions. In the biofeedback group, subjects were trained in progressive skeletal-muscle and mental relaxation. They also received hand-warming thermofeedback during the first four sessions, and during the last four sessions a thermo-probe was inserted by the subject into her vagina to encourage her to learn to elevate vaginal temperature.

The individual autogenic training condition group received individual relaxation training without the biofeedback. A group autogenic training condition group received autogenic training in subgroups of four. The subgroups were also encouraged to spend time discussing their problems and successes. The control group comprised 10 students who were exposed to the experimenter weekly in a classroom setting. Dysmenorrhea was completely alleviated in 54% of both the biofeedback and individual autogenic training groups and in 33% of the autogenic training group. Decrease in dysmenorrhea was significantly correlated with a decrease in bleeding. Some of the other findings are of interest as well. The autogenic training with biofeedback was most effective in alleviating symptoms of dysmenorrhea. However, the group training seemed to have a therapeutic effect above and beyond that related to the relaxation process. Those subjects who shared their problems and successes in addition to taking autogenic relaxation training experienced the greatest reduction in negative affect after treatment. Clearly there is a place for psychological interventions in the treatment—and perhaps in the prevention —of dysmenorrhea. Education about menstruation and dysmenorrhea, pain-control strategies, imagery, relaxation techniques, and biofeedback all warrant further investigation.

In summary, for mild to moderate dysmenorrhea the recommended treatment includes aspirin or other over-the-counter medications, relaxation training (with or without biofeedback), warm baths, and perhaps an alcoholic beverage for medicinal purposes if the situation permits. For severe dysmenorrhea, oral contraceptives or prostaglandin-inhibiting drugs are the treatment of choice. If dysmenorrhea is still unrelieved, other gynecological problems, such as endometriosis, polyps, cervical stenosis, or pelvic inflammatory disease, should be ruled out.

Secondary Dysmenorrhea

ETIOLOGY AND SYMPTOMS

In secondary dysmenorrhea there is some kind of pelvic pathology that leads to painful menstruation. Laros (1981) further divides secondary dysmenorrhea into the following subclasses:

TABLE 7.4 Clinical Characteristics of Dysmenorrhea

Clinical Characteristics	Primary	Secondary		
		Spasmodic	*Congestive*	*Obstructive*
Age of onset	6 months to 4 years after menarche	Years after menarche	Years after menarche	With very 1st period or shortly there-after
Relationship of pain to onset of menstrual flow	Just prior to and on 1st and 2nd day of flow	Variable	Several days before flow	3rd or 4th day of flow
Duration	4 to 48 hours	1-5 days	3-4 days	3-5 days
Character	Crampy	Crampy	Constant, heavy feeling	Crampy or stretchy
Severity	Variable	Variable	Variable	Usually severe
Site	Lower abdomen	Lower abdomen	Lower abdomen, may be more severe on one side	Generally unilateral
Radiation	Back and thighs	Back and thighs	Back	Thigh and flank
Associated feelings	Associated faintness, nausea, and vomiting	Menorrhagia	Leukorrhea menorrhagia, dyspareunia, tenesmus	Depends on site of lesion

Source: Laros, Jr., R. K. (1981). Secondary dysmenorrhea (excluding endometriosis). In M. Y. Dawood (Ed.), *Dysmenorrhea* (pp. 155-164). Baltimore, MD: Williams & Wilkins. Reprinted with permission. © (1981), the Williams & Wilkins Co., Baltimore.

obstructive, spasmodic, and congestive. This categorization is helpful in establishing a diagnosis and subsequently working out a treatment plan. Differences in the symptoms associated with each subtype and comparison with primary dysmenorrhea are shown in Table 7.4.

Obstructive dysmenorrhea is due to a congenital abnormality in the development of the uterus. This results in a partially developed uterus lined with endometrium, which cycles in response to hormonal stimulation but, because there is no opening to the vagina or an inadequate opening, menstrual flow cannot escape, leading to a build-up of pressure, increased absorption of prostaglandins, and pain. Surgery to correct the abnormality is the appropriate treatment (Laros, 1981, p. 160).

Spasmodic dysmenorrhea is characterized by pain that is similar to primary dysmenorrhea. There is uterine hyperactivity, leading to an inadequate supply of blood to the uterine muscle, which produces pain. Benign tumors, such as submucous fibroids and endometrial polyps, intrauterine contraceptive devices, cervical stenosis (narrowing), heavy bleeding with the passage of large clots, and membranous dysmenorrhea are all conditions associated with spasmodic dysmenorrhea (Laros, 1981, pp. 156-157).

Treatment depends upon the diagnosis and severity of the symptoms. Many women have fibroids growing in the walls of the uterus. They are generally harmless and do not require treatment. However, if they become very large and impinge on other organs, or if bleeding is abnormally heavy and accompanied by pain, surgery—either a myomectomy to remove the fibroids, or a hysterectomy—may be indicated.

If an IUD is causing severe dysmenorrhea, one of the prostaglandin synthetase inhibitors may provide relief. The presence of an intrauterine device leads to an increase in endometrial tissue prostaglandin levels. The antiprostaglandins, such as ibuprofen and naproxen, have been shown to relieve both the dysmenorrhea and heavy bleeding associated with the use of an IUD (Dawood, 1981b). If the drugs are ineffective, removal of the IUD is indicated.

Dilatation and curettage (D & C) is the treatment of choice for some conditions. Cervical stenosis, a narrowing of the cervix, may be congenital or caused by a previous abortion or surgical procedure. In either case it can be corrected by a D & C in which the cervix is dilated and tissue removed as necessary. Endometrial polyps, which grow on the lining of the uterus, may also be removed by D & C. However, Rosemary Reiss (personal communication) cautions that D & C is a much overused procedure, and while it would be appropriate in the case of cervical stenosis or polyps, it is not appropriate for most patients with dysmenorrhea or even menorrhagia (excessive menstrual bleeding).

Menorrhagia and membranous dysmenorrhea are associated with heavy bleeding as well as pain. There are several possible courses of treatment: first, hormone therapy with an estrogen-progestin combination; second, a prostaglandin antagonist; third, a tocolytic agent (a drug that reduces uterine contractility), such as nifedipine; and last, hysterectomy (Laros, 1981, p. 163).

Congestive dysmenorrhea pain is of a more achy quality and is associated with a feeling of heaviness. It generally begins several days before the onset of menstrual flow and continues longer than does the pain of spasmodic dysmenorrhea. Some of the causes of congestive dysmenorrhea are endometriosis (an abnormal growth of endometrial cells outside the uterus), adenomyosis (a benign growth of the endometrium into the uterine muscle), chronic inflammation of a fallopian tube or other pelvic inflammatory disease, or an inflammation in some other organ, such as colonic diverticulitis.

Inflammation of the fallopian tubes, ovaries, or other organs causes pain. Treatment is aimed at curing the infection. Antibiotics are the first treatment of choice. If medical treatment is ineffective, surgery may be necessary (Laros, 1981, p. 163).

Endometriosis

Endometriosis is one of the most common causes of dysmenorrhea and is also a major cause of infertility (an estimated 25% to 40% of women with an infertility problem have endometriosis). Thus it warrants more detailed consideration here. It affects an estimated 10% to 15% of premenopausal women, and the incidence appears to be increasing. Because it is less common in countries where women are more often pregnant and therefore menstruate fewer times, endometriosis has been called "the career woman's disease," and the increased incidence in recent decades has been attributed to changes in life-style and the current practice of delaying pregnancy until the late twenties or thirties. The hypothesis is that women today have more menstrual cycles than women in the past, and therefore the opportunity for endometriosis to develop has increased. Others argue that physicians are more aware of endometriosis now and therefore more likely to make the diagnosis than they were years ago. A recent study did find that women with short menstrual cycles and heavy menstrual flow are at increased risk for endometriosis (Endometriosis risk factors . . . , 1986).

Endometriosis is caused by the spread and growth of endometrial tissue from the lining of the uterus to other organs, particularly the ovaries and fallopian tubes, although patches have been found on the intestine and in other parts of the body. These endometrial cells respond to the same hormones as do those within the uterus; thus they thicken, enlarge, and bleed. This may cause cysts, scarring, and pain.

How the disease begins is not yet known. One theory is that endometriosis is caused by the implantation of endometrial cells that are regurgitated through the fallopian tubes into the peritoneal cavity during menstruation. This would explain the presence of endometrial tissue on the ovaries and adjacent structures. However, some physicians believe that every woman pushes blood out through her tubes every month, yet every woman does not develop endometriosis. Also, this theory does not explain why endometriosis can appear at such distant sites as the lungs or the lymph nodes. Another theory postulates that an inherited factor exists that increases susceptibility to endometriosis. In a study of 123 patients who had been diagnosed by laparoscopy as having endometriosis, women who had a mother or sister with endometriosis had a seven times greater risk than women without an affected relative. And there was an even stronger genetic relationship in cases of severe endometriosis: The incidence in the familial group was 61%, compared to 24% in the nonfamilial group. Further support for the role of a genetic factor is the very low incidence of endometriosis (1.6%) found in a sample of 1,027 Israeli women. Similarly, in a study of 2,669 laparotomies performed at two predominantly Jewish hospitals in New York City, only a 2.7% incidence of endometriosis was found, higher than the Israeli figure but still far below the national average. In contrast, two studies of Japanese women revealed 8.9% and 9.2% incidences of endometriosis (Older, 1984).

Pain and/or infertility are the complaints that most commonly bring the patient with endometriosis to the gynecologist. The pain is characteristically located in the lower abdomen; it may be either unilateral or bilateral and is often associated with pelvic soreness throughout the month. Backache and painful intercourse or bowel movements are other common symptoms of endometriosis. In contrast to the cramping pain of primary dysmenorrhea, which usually begins before the flow, becomes severe in the first few hours of menstruation, and generally is gone within 24 to 48 hours, the pain associated with endometriosis often starts a few days before the onset of menstruation, increases in intensity gradually, is present throughout the menstrual period, and persists as pelvic soreness for a few days after the cessation of menses (Scommegna, 1981). Women who develop progressively more severe menstrual cramps in their late teens and early twenties, who are the daughters or sisters of women with endometriosis, and who have short menstrual cycles and heavy bleeding, probably should undergo a thorough diagnostic exam to see whether they, too, have the condition.

Determination of the cause of secondary dysmenorrhea is made by a physician after taking a careful history, performing a complete pelvic examination, and using other diagnostic techniques as necessary. For example, sonography, a technique that uses sound waves to picture pelvic organs, may be useful in establishing a diagnosis of fibroids. A surgical procedure in which a small incision is made in the abdominal wall at the navel and a long tubelike instrument with a light and viewing attachment is used to look inside the pelvis—laparoscopy—is used to diagnose endometriosis and other disorders involving the ovaries and fallopian tubes.

TREATMENT

Treatment is based on diagnosis, severity of the symptoms, risks associated with the therapy under consideration, and on the needs of the individual patient—her age, general health, and whether she wants more children. In mild cases of endometriosis in a patient who does not plan to become pregnant right away, observation and symptomatic treatment may be adequate. However, women with endometriosis need to be told that symptomatic treatment will not prevent the natural progression of the disease, and chances of conception diminish over time. Scommegna suggests that the natural progression of the disease may be prevented by the cyclic administration of strongly progestational oral contraceptives. "Such regimens, by limiting the degree of endometrial proliferation, may ameliorate dysmenorrhea, reduce retrograde menstrual flow, and should control further proliferation and spread of the endometriosis" (Scommegna, 1981, p. 140).

In more severe cases of endometriosis, there are two general approaches to treatment: medical and surgical. Medical treatment is based on the fact that endometriosis improves during pregnancy and menopause. Therefore, hormonal drugs are given that create hormonal states similar to pregnancy and menopause. During pregnancy the cyclic thickening and secretion of the endometrial tissue outside of the uterus stops, and the tissue atrophies. In order to create a pseudopregnancy, increasingly large doses of estrogen and progesterone are given. Ovulation is suppressed, and the normal endometrial cycle is abolished. With continued treatment, the endometrial glands become small, and the ectopic endometrium shrinks. Treatment is generally continued for 6-12 months (Scommegna, 1981, p. 144).

Improvement with pseudopregnancy regimens is notable: Between 60% and 94% of women treated this way respond favorably. Pregnancy rates after treatment depend upon the degree of severity of the endometriosis but are reported to be as high as 50%. However, many women have severe side effects, which include nausea, vomiting, weight gain, and breakthrough bleeding, and only about 50% complete the course of treatment. Recurrences in the first year are seen in about 17% of patients, and thereafter at a rate of 5% to 10% each year.

Endometriosis also regresses with menopause because of the shrinking of endometrial tissue that occurs when estrogen levels decline. Drugs are now available to create a pseudomenopause. Danazol, a synthetic male sex hormone, inhibits the release of gonadotropins and prevents ovulation. With Danazol treatment, menstruation stops, and there is a rapid atrophy of uterine and ectopic endometrium. Symptoms are relieved promptly, and there is an obvious decrease in the size of endometriotic lesions. Marked improvement has been reported in 70% to 94% of the women treated, with 80% showing an improvement in pelvic findings (Scommegna, 1981, p. 150).

Unfortunately, women taking this drug sometimes develop some of the symptoms associated with menopause, such as hot flashes, night sweats, and atrophic vaginitis. Other side effects include weight gain and acne and, more rarely, symptoms of virilization, such as facial hair and voice changes. Danazol should not be used during pregnancy or lactation, or if there is impaired liver, kidney, or heart function. Danazol treatment is generally well tolerated and has fewer side effects and contraindications than the estrogen-progestin medications.

Danazol is given in a daily dose of 800 mg (200 mg four times a day) for three to nine months. Menstruation returns four to six weeks after treatment is discontinued, and the posttreatment conception rate is about 75%. Unfortunately, in spite of the marked improvement in symptoms and significant increase in fertility, the recurrence rate three years after completion of treatment is about 40%. Some surgeons prescribe Danazol for six months prior to surgery because it makes excision of ovarian endometriosis easier and tends to reduce adhesions; others use it after surgery to shrink any residual endometriosis (Older, 1984, p. 91).

In February 1990, the Food and Drug Administration approved a new drug, nafarelin acetate (Synarel), for the treatment of endometriosis. It is a gonadotropin-releasing hormone agonist (one of several under current investigation) that, according to its proponents, represents an improvement over Danazol in safety and effectiveness. Like Danazol, it leads to a hypoestrogenic state, but without the androgenic side effects (Rosemary Reiss, personal communication).

Synarel is taken as a nasal spray twice daily. The course of treatment is generally limited to six months because clinical trials have shown a loss in bone mass during treatment. Once therapy stopped, bone mass returned to only slightly less than it was before treatment. Other side effects include hot flashes, vaginal dryness, decreased libido, and headaches. In a double-blind clinical trial, endometrial lesions were 80% improved after six weeks on the drug, and the number of women experiencing pain dropped from 40% to 5%. The drug was also associated with a pregnancy rate that increased from 7% to 39% after six months of therapy. Another gonadotropin-releasing agonist, goserelin (Zoladex) is being used in England and Germany, but is not yet available in the United States (Carpi, 1990).

Conservative surgical treatment is aimed at removing the endometriosis implants and leaving the pelvic organs as intact as possible, thus preserving fertility. Lesions are excised or cauterized. If pelvic organs have been twisted out of shape or if they abnormally adhere to each other, they are surgically separated and restored to their normal position. Results following conservative surgery have been variable. Most patients report improvement of pelvic pain, though dysmenorrhea may not be completely gone. Pregnancy rates following conservative surgery range from 38% to 88%, depending upon the severity of the endometriosis. Recurrences after surgery seem to be related to the severity of the disease.

Definitive surgery involves removal of the uterus, tubes, and both ovaries, in addition to resection of the endometriosis. Women with severe symptoms who have completed their families are candidates for this treatment. Although some physicians advocate preservation of the ovaries in younger women, this may lead to a recurrence of endometriosis, and the use of small amounts of estrogen to relieve symptoms of estrogen deficiency is preferable (Older, 1984, p. 147).

A great deal of progress has been made in the understanding and treatment of both primary and secondary dysmenorrhea in recent years. Women no longer need passively to accept menstrual pain as something they must learn to live with. Although there is no panacea that will cure all symptoms instantaneously, with appropriate medical care symptoms can be ameliorated or eliminated. Successful treatment depends on the correct diagnosis and tailoring therapy to the needs of each individual woman.

Note

1. Prostaglandins are hormonelike substances that cause muscle contraction, control the dilation and constriction of blood vessels, and are involved in a number of other body functions, including the release of sex hormones.

References

Bickers, W. (1960). Dysmenorrhea and menstrual disability. *Clinical Obstetrics and Gynecology, 3*, 233-240.

Budoff, P. W. (1980). *No more menstrual cramps and other good news.* New York: Penguin.

Budoff, P. W. (1981). Antiprostaglandins for primary dysmenorrhea. *Journal of the American Medical Association, 246*(22), 2576-2577.

Carpi, J. (1990, March 22). Synarel: Endometriosis Rx option. *Medical Tribune, 31*(6), 3.

Coppen, A., & Kessel, N. (1963). Menstruation and personality. *British Journal of Psychiatry, 109*, 711-721.

Dawood, M. Y. (1981a). Hormones, prostaglandins, and dysmenorrhea. In M. Y. Dawood (Ed.), *Dysmenorrhea* (pp. 21-52). Baltimore, MD: Williams & Wilkins.

Dawood, M. Y. (1981b). Overall approach to the management of dysmenorrhea. In M. Y. Dawood (Ed.), *Dysmenorrhea* (p. 276). Baltimore, MD: Williams & Wilkins.

Dingfelder, J. R. (1981). Primary dysmenorrhea treatment with prostaglandin inhibitors: A review. *American Journal of Obstetrics and Gynecology, 130*, 874-879.

Dysmenorrhea: New theory, new therapy. (1981). *Sexual Medicine Today, 5*(9), 6-14.

Endometriosis risk factors linked to menstrual cycles. (1986, April 11). *American Medical News*, 53.

Friederich, M. A. (1983). Dysmenorrhea. In S. Golub (Ed.), *Lifting the curse of menstruation* (pp. 91-106). New York: Haworth.

Fuchs, F. (1982). Dysmenorrhea and dyspareunia. In R. C. Friedman (Ed.), *Behavior and the menstrual cycle* (pp. 199-216). New York: Marcel Dekker.

Gannon, L. R. (1985). *Menstrual disorders and menopause*. New York: Praeger.

Garling, J., & Roberts, S. J. (1980). An investigation of cyclic distress among staff nurses. In A. J. Dan, E. A. Graham, & C. P. Beecher (Eds.), *The menstrual cycle* (Vol. 1, pp. 305-311). New York: Springer.

Golub, S. (1985). Menstrual cycle symptoms from a developmental perspective. In Z. DeFries, R. C. Friedman, & R. Corn (Eds.), *Sexuality: New perspectives*. Westport, CT: Greenwood.

Golub, S., & Catalano, J. (1983). Recollections of menarche, current menstrual attitudes, and perimenstrual symptoms. *Women & Health, 8*(1), 49-61.

Golub, S., & Harrington, D. M. (1981). Premenstrual and menstrual mood changes in adolescent women. *Journal of Personality and Social Psychology, 4*(5), 961-965.

Heczey, M. D. (1980). Effects of biofeedback and autogenic training on dysmenorrhea. In A. J. Dan, E. A. Graham, & C. P. Beecher (Eds.), *The menstrual cycle* (Vol. 1, pp. 283-291). New York: Springer.

The high cost of pain. (1985, December 2). *Newsweek*, p. 78.

Kessel, N., & Coppen, A. (1968). The prevalence of common menstrual symptoms. *The Lancet, 2*, 61-65.

Lamb, E. J. (1981). Clinical features of primary dysmenorrhea. In M. Y. Dawood (Ed.), *Dysmenorrhea* (pp. 107-129). Baltimore, MD: Williams & Wilkins.

Laros, Jr., R. K. (1981). Secondary dysmenorrhea (excluding endometriosis). In M. Y. Dawood (Ed.), *Dysmenorrhea* (pp. 155-164). Baltimore, MD.: Williams & Wilkins.

Lawlor, C., & Davis, A. (1981). Primary dysmenorrhea. *Journal of Adolescent Health Care, 1*, 208-212.

Lundstrom, V. (1981). Uterine activity during the normal cycle and dysmenorrhea. In M. Y. Dawood (Ed.), *Dysmenorrhea* (pp. 53-74). Baltimore, MD: Williams & Wilkins.

Moos, R. (1968). The development of a menstruation distress questionnaire. *Psychosomatic Medicine, 30*, 853-867.

Morrison, J. C., & Nicolls, E. T. (1981). Epidemiologic, social and economic aspects of dysmenorrhea. In M. Y. Dawood (Ed.), *Dysmenorrhea* (pp. 95-106). Baltimore, MD: Williams & Wilkins.

Older, J. (1984). *Endometriosis*. New York: Charles Scribner's Sons.

Paige, K. E. (1973). Women learn to sing the menstrual blues. *Psychology Today, 7*
    41-46.

Physicians' Desk Reference. (1986). Oradell, NJ: Medical Economics Co.

Pickles, V. R., Hall, W. J., Best, F. A., & Smith, G. N. (1965). Prostaglandins in
    endometrium and menstrual fluid from normal and dysmenorrhoeic subjects.
    Journal of Obstetrics and Gynaecology, 72, 185-192.

Scommegna, A. (1981). Secondary dysmenorrhea: Endometriosis. In M. Y. Dawood
    (Ed.), *Dysmenorrhea* (pp. 131-154). Baltimore, MD: Williams & Wilkins.

Snowden, R., & Christian, B. (Eds.). (1983). *Patterns and perceptions of menstruation.*
    New York: St. Martin's Press.

Stolzman, S. M. (1983). *Menstrual attitudes, beliefs, and symptom experiences of adoles-
    cent females, their peers, and their mothers.* Paper presented at the meeting of the
    Society for Menstrual Cycle Research, San Francisco.

Svennerud, S. (1959). Dysmenorrhea and absenteeism, some gynaecologic and
    medico-social aspects. *Acta Obstetrica et Gynecologica Scandinavica, 164*, 638-
    640.

Whitehead, W. E., Busch, C. M., Heller, B. R., & Costa, Jr., P. T. (1986). Social learning
    influences on menstrual symptoms and illness behavior. *Health Psychology,
    5*(1), 13-23.

Widholm, O., & Kantero, R. L. (1971). Menstrual patterns of adolescent girls accord-
    ing to chronological and gynecological ages. *Acta Obstetrica et Gynecologica
    Scandinavica, 50*(14), 19-29.

Woods, N. F., Most, A., & Dery, G. K. (1982). Prevalence of perimenstrual symptoms.
    American Journal of Public Health, 72(11), 1257-1264.

Ylikorlkala, O., & Dawood, M. Y. (1978). New concepts in dysmenorrhea. *American
    Journal of Obstetrics and Gynecology, 130*, 833-847.

Zborowski, M. (1969). *People in pain.* San Francisco: Jossey-Boss.

8

Premenstrual Symptoms
and Premenstrual Syndrome

Defining the Problem: Differentiating Between
Symptoms and Syndrome

According to *Webster's New Collegiate Dictionary*, a syndrome is "a group of signs and symptoms that occur together and characterize a particular abnormality." Using this definition, premenstrual syndrome does not exist. To date no abnormality has been found, though many have been postulated. Nevertheless, over the last 10 years premenstrual syndrome (PMS) has become a familiar and controversial topic, both to professionals and to lay people. The syndrome has been used as a legal defense in the United States and Great Britain, and efforts to classify PMS as a psychiatric disorder have been fraught with controversy.

The problem of definition haunts researchers studying PMS. Because the number and variety of symptoms included in the syndrome vary widely from one study to another, from one woman to another, and within the same woman from one cycle to another, it is difficult to draw definitive conclusions when reviewing the research that has been done. At best, PMS can be characterized as a group of psychological and somatic symptoms that are limited to the week

181

TABLE 8.1 Common Premenstrual Symptoms

Physical Symptoms	Psychological Symptoms
Pain	Negative Affect
Abdominal cramps	Tension
Backache	Irritability
Headache	Anger
Muscle stiffness	Depression
Breast tenderness	Anxiety
Water Retention	Mood swings
Weight gain	Crying
Bloating	Lethargy
Swollen ankles or fingers	Behavioral Change
Other	Lowered school or work performance
Fatigue	Altered daily routine, i.e., take naps
Skin disorders	Avoidance of social contact
Decreased coordination	Food cravings or changes in eating behavior
Increased energy	Changes in sexual interest or behavior
	Sleep disturbance

preceding menstruation and are relieved by the onset of menses. The cyclical nature of the symptoms is essential to a diagnosis of PMS. Physical complaints include headache, backache, painful breasts, and symptoms of water retention. Psychological complaints include depression, anxiety, irritability, lethargy, and aggressiveness (see Table 8.1 for an extensive list of symptoms) (Abplanalp, 1983; Dalton, 1964; Haskett, Steiner, Osmun, & Carroll, 1980).

In 1982 the Food and Drug Administration Advisory Review Panel on Miscellaneous Over the Counter Internal Drug Products adopted the following definition of PMS:

> A recurrent symptom complex that begins during the week prior to menstruation and usually disappears soon after the onset of the menstrual flow. This symptom complex consists predominantly of edema, lower abdominal pain (including cramps), breast tenderness, headache, abdominal bloating, fatigue, and the feelings of depression, irritability, tension and anxiety. (Food and Drug Administration, 1982)

The definition was further refined by a 1983 National Institute of Mental Health review conference where some specific requirements were added. The symptoms must be recurrent, usually occurring in two of three cycles, and there must be a symptom-free period followed by a premenstrual worsening of symptoms. However, in order to be useful to both researchers and clinicians, a definition must include, not only symptoms, but which symptoms, how many, some indication of their severity, and confirmation of their cyclicity.

Generally, menstruating women notice some emotional, physical, or behavioral symptoms in the week before menstruation. In about 3% to 5% of women the symptoms are so severe that they interfere with work or interpersonal relationships. Women are mainly disturbed by the mood symptoms. Depression is the most frequent complaint, with lethargy, sleep disturbance, craving for carbohydrates, and emotional lability also high on the list. Although pain and edema are bothersome, most often women who seek treatment do so because they are having problems with relationships or work.

Some PMS researchers would argue that there is not one premenstrual syndrome, but rather several different subtypes of the disorder characterized by different clusters of symptoms. Jean Endicott (quoted in Wray, 1982) says, "Some women are anxious and agitated. Some are angry. Some are lethargic and overeat, while others have insomnia and don't eat. It's highly unlikely that the same biological variables are involved in hypersomnia and insomnia." Thus the plural term, premenstrual syndromes, is sometimes used now.

In an attempt to resolve some of the problems in defining PMS for both research and clinical purposes, the National Institute of Mental Health established a commission in 1985 to develop a diagnostic category so that PMS could be included in the DSM-III-R, the diagnostic manual of the American Psychiatric Association, which is a widely used resource for mental-health practitioners. The purpose was to establish a set of operational criteria so that research findings from different studies could be compared with each other, and to facilitate communication between researchers and clinicians. PMS was given a new name: late luteal phase dysphoric disorder (LLPDD). However, there has been considerable disagreement about the inclusion of PMS by any name as a mental disorder. Proponents believe that inclusion will improve the treatment women receive for premenstrual problems. Opponents point out that the label chosen is not neutral: It suggests a causative link between the menstrual cycle and a disturbance in mood and behavior. Controversy is focused on the sex-specific nature of this diagnosis. Some feminist researchers and clinicians are concerned about the risk of stigmatizing women for mood changes associated with a normal biological process. Further, they argue, there is a lack of sufficient research at this time to warrant definition of PMS as a psychiatric disorder (Blumenthal & Nadelson, 1988). Gallant and Hamilton (1988) go even further. They contend that the labeling can affect scientific thinking: Beliefs about the impact of menstruation can bias scientific inquiry by restricting the ways in which problems are conceptualized. Because confirmation of the diagnosis at this time requires gathering only self-report data, it is unreliable. Research indicates that women's perceptions of their premenstrual behavior as being impaired are generally not validated when objective measures are used. Some other method, such as reports from significant others or behavioral measures, are necessary if the diagnosis is to be considered valid. The controversy has been resolved for the time being by including the disorder in the Appendix section of the DSM-III-R. The rationale here is that the diagnostic criteria can be used by both clinicians and researchers while more research evidence is collected either to validate or to negate this diagnosis.

Because there is no generally accepted definition of premenstrual syndrome, efforts to compare published data in order to determine the incidence or prevalence of premenstrual problems have been unrewarding. Incidence rates ranging from 20% to 95% have been reported among normal women (Coppen & Kessel, 1963; Ferguson & Vermillion, 1957; Moos, 1968; Paulson, 1957; Pennington, 1957; Sutherland & Stewart, 1965). In a summary of U.S. and European studies of the prevalence of premenstrual symptoms among adult women, Woods and her colleagues found the incidence of symptoms to range from a low of 4% for fatigue to a high of 70% for irritability (Woods, Most, & Dery, 1982). These authors also found that their estimates for many symptoms closely resembled those from other studies. However, when they restricted their attention to severe symptoms, as opposed to mild or moderate ones, their prevalence estimates were considerably lower. Only 2% to 8% of women found their symptoms to be severe or disabling. These statistics are comparable to those found in a French postal study of 2,501 women that was conducted with the help of the Sofres Medical, the medical branch of a national opinion poll company. Although 38% of the French women sampled had premenstrual symptoms each month, and only 14% never had symptoms, only 4% to 9% described themselves as "troubled very much" by the various symptoms (see Table 8.1; van Keep & Lehert, 1981). Similarly, Rose and Abplanalp (1983) have estimated that no more than 2% to 5% of women need medical attention for PMS. In a unique study exploring the possibility of racial differences in premenstrual symptoms, researchers found no difference in the prevalence or severity of premenstrual symptoms among the 321 Black women and 462 White women studied, except for a higher prevalence of food cravings among Blacks (Stout, Grady, Steege, Blazer, George, & Melville, 1986). Similarly, in a study of PMS and socioeconomic status, Gise and her colleagues found no differences in severity of premenstrual symptoms among high and low socioeconomic status women seeking treatment for PMS. However, depression and a history of sexual abuse were more prevalent in the women of low socioeconomic status (Gise, Paddison, Lebovits, & Strain, 1989). Thus it seems that a great many women, probably a majority, experience one or more premenstrual symptoms at different times in their lives. However, relatively few women are incapacitated by their symptoms.

Making the Diagnosis

Because of the widespread publicity given to PMS by the lay press and the media in recent years, the diagnosis of premenstrual syndrome is often made by patients themselves. Women come to their physicians or psychotherapists saying, "I have PMS." It is then up to the health professional to evaluate whether the patient does indeed experience cyclic symptoms, how severe they are, and whether they are related to other disorders, such as depression, dysmenorrhea, an endocrine disturbance, or something else.

The evaluation of PMS generally includes a psychiatric assessment, full medical history, and a physical examination, including a thorough gynecological examination. Psychological testing, laboratory tests, and a nutritional appraisal may be done as well. The patient's history should include information about when the symptoms began, for premenstrual tension is more likely to start after pregnancy, during or after taking contraceptive pills, following tubal ligation, or after a period of amenorrhea. Dalton has also noted that PMS is more likely to occur in women with a history of pre-eclampsia (a toxemia of late pregnancy that is characterized by hypertension and edema)

Premenstrual symptoms are many and varied; some of the more common ones are listed in the chart below. Very few women suffer from *all* of the symtoms and their severity can vary from month to month.

The key to discovering whether you have PMS is to identify your symptoms and determine *when* they occur. If your symptoms appear in the week or two before your menstrual period, and disappear during or after your period, then you may well have PMS. However, if your symptoms don't follow any pattern, they might be caused by some other condition. This is why it's important to keep a record of your symptoms for several months so that you will know whether your symptoms are connected with your menstrual cycle.

3-MONTH SYMPTOM DIARY

1			
2			
3			
4			
5			
6			
7			
8			
9			
10			
11			
12			
13			
14			
15			
16			
17			
18			
19			
20			
21			
22			
23			
24			
25			
26			
27			
28			
29			
30			
31			

SOME COMMON PMS SYMPTOMS This list includes the most common symptoms. It is not complete or comprehensive, since many other symptoms have been reported by women. If you experience symptoms other than the ones listed here, add them in the blank spaces.

CODE	SYMPTOM	CODE	SYMPTOMS
T	Tension	BT	Breast tenderness
I	Irritability	WG	Weight gain
D	Depression	S	Swelling of joints
A	Anxiety		(fingers, ankles)
F	Fatigue	B	Bloating
DC	Difficulty in concentrating	AH	Abdominal heaviness
AC	Abdominal cramps		
H	Headache		
BA	Backache		
MS	Muscle spasms		

Charting Your Symptoms

The best way to determine whether you are experiencing PMS is to record your symptoms on a calendar. Then you can quickly see whether they are related to your menstrual cycle. Follow these steps.

Step 1: Identify your symptoms. Check the list above and underline symptoms you have experienced most frequently. If you frequently experience one or more symptoms other than those listed, write them in the blank spaces provided and fill in a code letter for each one. (Be sure not to use letters which are already being used for another symptom, or "M" which you will be using to record your menstrual period.)

Step 2: Keep a daily record of your symptoms. Use the code for each symptom. On the date you experience the symptom, write the letter or letters in the corresponding box on the calendar. It's important to record your symptoms each day, in order to make your chart as reliable as possible. (Try to set aside a specific time of day to do this.) If you wait a few days and then try to remember how you felt, you may end up minimizing or perhaps over-emphasizing the severity of your symptoms. Use a capital letter for severe symptoms and a small letter for milder ones. Write "M" for each day of your menstrual flow.

Figure 8.1. Calendar for Recording Premenstrual Symptoms
Source: Consumer Products Division, Chattem, Inc. Reprinted with permission.

or postnatal depression. Further, women with PMS are less tolerant of oral contraceptives, often experiencing such side effects as weight gain, depression, and headaches.

In order to diagnose PMS, patients are instructed to keep a symptom diary for three months before treatment is begun. Symptoms are noted daily, preferably at the same time each day, in order to make the calendar as reliable as possible. A frequently used calendar and coding system are shown in Figure 8.1. A reliable three-month calendar makes it easy to identify a premenstrual pattern of symptoms, if such a pattern is present.

Recently researchers have begun to use visual analog scales to assess even more subtle variations in mood (Rubinow, Roy-Byrne, Hoban, Gold, & Post, 1984). Patients are asked to rate their mood (depression and anxiety) on 100 mm line visual analogue scales in the morning and evening for three months. Using this technique, Rubinow and his colleagues found that only 8 of the 20 women studied who had presented with self-diagnosed premenstrual syndrome actually had a mean depression rating the week before menstruation that was 30% higher than during the week after menstruation (Rubinow, Roy-Byrne, Hoban, Gold, & Post, 1984, pp. 685-686).

The Rubinow study also confirmed the importance of expectations in the attribution of menstrual symptoms. The figures show that several of the women had cyclical changes in mood that were unrelated to menstruation. And, as is the case with other stereotypes where we remember those characteristics that fit our stereotypic beliefs but forget those that do not fit, some of these women remembered the feelings of depression and anxiety that they experienced premenstrually but ignored those occurring at other times of the month. Thus their beliefs about menstruation and their expectations regarding the generality and severity of symptoms associated with the menstrual cycle served to bias the way in which they interpreted their symptoms (Ruble & Brooks-Gunn, 1979).

Doctors as well as patients may be guilty of this bias. In a slice-of-life dramatic bit, Lily Tomlin visits the doctor:

At the Doctor's
    You're sure, Doctor?
    Pre*men*strual syndrome?
    I mean, I'm getting divorced.
    My mother's getting divorced.
    I'm raising twin boys.
    I have a lot of job pressure—
    I've got to find one.
    The ERA didn't pass,
    not long ago I lost a very dear friend, and . . . and
    my husband is involved . . .
    not just involved, but in love, I'm afraid . . . with
    this woman . . .
    who's quite a bit younger than I am.

And you *think* it's my *period*
and *not* my life? (Wagner, 1986)

Who Gets Premenstrual Syndrome?

There seems to be a relationship between several different variables and PMS. Age, genetic factors, pregnancy and problems during pregnancy, the use of oral contraceptives, stress, and a previous history of depression have all been implicated. Age, for example, has been identified by many investigators. Lloyd (1963) was the first to write about it, referring to premenstrual symptoms of irritability and depression as the "mid-thirties syndrome" and pointing out that the modal age seems to lie around the 35th year. Now there is both clinical and research support for this observation. Clinically, Dalton (1964) has noted an increase in the incidence of PMS with increasing age in both childless and parous women. She reports a peak incidence of about 30% among women between the ages of 35 and 44, with which several researchers concur. In a study comparing the physical and psychological symptom scores of high-school students (15-16 years of age) with those of a group of adult women (average age 37 years), Golub and Harrington (1981) found that the younger women experienced more symptoms during the menstrual phase of the cycle, whereas the older women had more premenstrual symptoms. Similarly, Moos (1968), in his study of 700 women, compared subjects under 21 with those over 31 and found that the older women were significantly more likely to complain of symptoms in the premenstrual phase of the cycle. Rees (1953) found an incidence of moderate premenstrual tension—about 25%—among women between the ages of 15 and 24, with the incidence rising to 31% in the 25- to 34-year-old age group, and Rees observed that severe premenstrual tension was considerably more likely to be found among women over the age of 24. In a study of 748 Finnish students, Timonen and Procope (1973) noted increased premenstrual depression among subjects over the age of 26, and premenstrual headaches and abdominal swelling were likewise found to increase with age. In his sample of women ranging in age from 15 to 45, Kramp (1968) found that 50% suffered with premenstrual symptoms severe enough to warrant consulting a physician or taking a drug. There was a peak incidence of about 23%

among women between the ages of 30 and 39 years, and another peak of about 20% in those aged 20 to 24. Kramp also noted an incidence of 30% among a group of psychiatric patients between the ages of 35 and 39. He concluded that PMS is most common in the 30- to 40-year-age group.

Additional support for the relationship between age and PMS comes from a study of mothers and daughters in which a higher incidence of premenstrual symptoms was found in the mothers (76%) than the daughters (67%) (Widholm & Kantero, 1971). And more recently, Rivera-Tovar and Frank (1990) compared the severity of symptoms of two groups of women who met the criteria for Late Luteal Phase Disorder (undergraduate students and women seeking treatment for PMS). Significant differences were found in the ages of the two groups. The students' symptoms were somewhat less severe, with significantly fewer complaints of fatigue and impaired concentration.

Rouse (1978) looked at the influence of oral contraceptives and age on premenstrual symptoms. He used the Menstrual Distress Questionnaire to compare the symptoms of 392 British women attending family-planning clinics. Subjects were divided into three age groups: over 30, between 20 and 30, and below 20 years of age. In addition, each group was subdivided into users and nonusers of oral contraceptives. As in other studies, Rouse found that women who were not taking oral contraceptives complained of more menstrual and premenstrual symptoms. In addition, women over 30 were more likely to complain of symptoms in the premenstruum and menstruum. Andersch and Hahn (1981) also found a significantly higher incidence of premenstrual symptoms among nonusers of oral contraceptives over the age of 24, with a tendency for mood symptoms to be more severe in the older age group. Also, some women were found to experience severe PMS after they stopped taking birth-control pills.

A study by Metcalf and Mackenzie (1980) offers one possible explanation for the age-related difference in symptoms. They note that although only 62% of women between the ages of 20 and 24 ovulate in every cycle, about 91% of women between the ages of 30 and 39 ovulate regularly. Because anovulatory cycles lack the pre- and post-ovulatory variations in estrogen and progesterone, the age difference in the incidence of ovulation may explain the age difference in premenstrual symptom severity.

However, age-related social and psychological factors cannot be ruled out. Women in their thirties are more likely to be married and caring for small children than are younger women. These are often difficult years for women, who are stressed by the demands of child care, housework, and work outside of the home. They may be short of sleep, tired, and irritable and therefore more vulnerable to shifts in mood occurring during the premenstruum.

Nor can genetic factors or pregnancy be ignored. In a study of women in a clinic group of PMS patients, 30% had a sister or mother with PMS, and 45% claimed PMS began shortly after pregnancy (Sanders, Warner, Backstrom, & Bancroft, 1983). Most recently, Wilson and her colleagues compared two groups of mothers and their adolescent daughters (with or without PMS). The PMS mothers and daughters had similar premenstrual symptoms, but the non-PMS mother-daughter dyads did not. Wilson goes on to demonstrate that menstrual attitudes do not appear to be a factor in the genesis of PMS. While mothers with PMS viewed menstruation as debilitating and bothersome, daughters with PMS did not (Wilson, Turner, & Keye, 1991).

There is some evidence that stress increases menstrual-cycle symptoms. Several researchers have found a relationship between negative life events, such as work pressures, family problems, or other hassles of everyday life, and an exacerbation of psychological symptoms, specifically tension, irritability, depression, and feelings of being out of control (Maddocks & Reid, 1985; Wilcoxon, Schrader, & Sherif, 1976; Woods, Lentz, Mitchell, & Taylor, 1989). Although we cannot say that stress causes premenstrual symptoms, it is likely that it is a contributing factor, and Maddocks et al. suggests that the relationship is probably a circular one, with premenstrual symptoms enhancing feelings of stress. The scenario is something like this: Marital or work problems lead to heightened tension; these feelings are compounded by premenstrual mood changes, resulting in higher levels of anxiety and depression, which in turn increase the likelihood of further deterioration in marital or work relationships. Unfortunately, many women focus on PMS as the critical issue, instead of dealing with their other problems or calling upon other coping mechanisms.

The link between PMS and depression is probably the most important one to be considered in addressing the question of who gets PMS. Halbreich and Endicott (1985) have noted that about two-thirds of women with a history of major affective disorder (for instance, depression) experience significant premenstrual dysphoria, and most women with marked premenstrual depression have a history of psychiatric illness. Premenstrual dysphoria is also associated with increased risk of future major depressive disorder. In two studies of college students, those with "premenstrual affective syndrome" were more likely to be diagnosed as having a depressive disorder during a four-year follow-up. Similarly, in a study of patients with panic attacks, more than half of female agoraphobics experienced premenstrual exacerbation of their anxiety symptoms (Breier, Charney, & Heninger, 1986). The implications of these findings are clear. Clinicians need to be alert to the possibility of menstrual-cycle-related changes in mood. Most women have premenstrual worsening of their symptoms if they are already experiencing a depressive syndrome. If these women are being treated with medication for chronic depression or anxiety, awareness of cycle phase will prevent the clinician from thinking that the medicine is not working and perhaps changing medication prematurely. Conversely, attention to cycle phase may lead to a planned increase in medication during the premenstrual phase of the cycle if deemed necessary.

Etiology

The causes of premenstrual syndrome are not known. Some women react to menstrual-cycle changes, while others do not. Although many theories have been proposed, no one explanation has found consistent research support. Nevertheless, it is useful to review the most salient theories, for they do influence treatment.

Ovarian Hormones. Katharina Dalton, a British physician who has been studying and treating PMS since the late 1940s, is the major proponent of the theory that PMS is caused by imbalances in the ratio of estrogen to progesterone after ovulation and that it is a deficiency of progesterone that causes symptoms of anxiety, water retention, and breast tenderness (Dalton, 1964).

There are alterations in the progesterone and estradiol levels of some—but not all—PMS patients. These patients have lower progesterone to estradiol ratios during the last 7 to 10 days of the menstrual cycle. Because progesterone is believed to be tranquilizing and estrogen conversely to increase nervous activity, a lowering of the progesterone-to-estradiol ratio could lead to the increase in tension and irritability seen premenstrually (Day & Taylor, 1981).

Rausch and Janowsky (1982) have also suggested that dysphoric emotional symptoms may be related to decreasing levels of progesterone. They note that symptoms begin in the luteal phase and become more intense as progesterone levels drop from their peak to their low premenstrual level. A similar drop in progesterone level accompanies the well-known postpartum blues; and depressive symptoms have also been reported after withdrawal of exogenous progesterone treatment. Alternatively, Rausch and Janowsky suggest that there is considerable evidence to support the theory that the estrogen-progesterone ratio is the cause of premenstrual tension. They cite studies of oral contraceptives with varying estrogen-progesterone ratios in which it was found that women with a history of premenstrual irritability who took progesterone-dominant pills had lower incidences of adverse mental changes than those who took estrogen-dominant pills. Although other studies of oral contraceptives cite an increased incidence of depressive symptoms, these differences may be due to similar treatment of women with different subgroups of symptoms. Stricter diagnostic criteria would clarify this problem.

Most researchers are not convinced. Reid and Yen (1980) note that the data supporting the hypothesis of an excess of estrogen or a deficiency of progesterone are limited and often contradictory. For example, O'Brien and his colleagues measured plasma progesterone concentrations and other electrolytes and found higher postovulatory progesterone levels in a group of women with PMS. They concluded that progesterone deficiency is not the cause of PMS and suggested that treatment with progesterone does not make sense unless a deficiency is found (O'Brien, Selby, & Symonds, 1980). Other researchers have likewise been unable to replicate evidence of relative progesterone deficiency in PMS. Sanders and his colleagues note that the fall in plasma-hormone concentration that has been suggested as a cause of the negative mood change does not account for PMS, for the negative symptoms "are well established before the hormone fall begins" (Sanders, Warner, Backstrom, & Bancroft, 1983). However, Dalton (1987) points out that our techniques of measuring progesterone by radioimmunoassay only estimate total progesterone levels. They do not permit us to know what the free levels of the hormone are, yet it is these free levels that may be significant in precipitating symptoms. Thus, this is a tenable (though weak) hypothesis, whose validation awaits further advances in hormone measurement techniques and better-designed treatment studies.

The response of premenstrual symptoms to progestin therapy has been variable and mostly disappointing. Until recently there were no double-blind controlled studies demonstrating the efficacy of progestins in PMS. However, in June 1985, Dennerstein and her colleagues published the results of a double-blind, randomized, two-month trial of oral progesterone in the treatment of PMS. They reported an overall beneficial effect on water retention and mood symptoms (Dennerstein, Spencer-Gardner, Gotts, Brown, Smith, & Burrows, 1985). Dennerstein is careful to state that although the study indicates a beneficial effect of progesterone, it does not necessarily mean that a progesterone deficiency is the cause of PMS, and in fact, several other studies in recent years have not substantiated the efficacy of progesterone (Rubinow, 1991).

Hormones Related to Water and Electrolyte Balance. Symptoms such as bloating, breast changes, and headache have been attributed to premenstrual fluid retention. Breast volume gradually increases just before ovulation and reaches a maximum on the first day of menstruation. Estrogen is reported to cause a release of histamine from breast tissue, which is thought to be responsible for breast edema and tenderness. Headache is thought to be the result of increased intracranial pressure.

In a careful study of mood, weight, and urinary potassium and sodium levels, Janowsky and his colleagues found a gradual increase in negative affect, weight, and the potassium/sodium ratio during the luteal, premenstrual, and early menstrual phases of the cycle (Janowsky, Berens, & Davis, 1973). The shift in potassium/sodium ratio, with its concomitant increase in sodium retention, may explain the water-retention symptoms.

Although some researchers speculate about some defect in the renin-angiotensin-aldosterone system as the cause of PMS, the evidence here, too, is contradictory. Reid and Yen (1981) summarize it as follows:

> The poor correlation between weight gain and symptomatology and the frequent failure of symptoms to improve with diuresis alone

suggest that symptoms such as headache, abdominal bloating, and breast tenderness may be the result of localized processes at these sites.

Some researchers believe that aldosterone may be the cause of the water and sodium retention seen in the premenstrual syndrome. Aldosterone, the main mineralo-corticoid hormone secreted by the adrenal cortex, regulates the volume of extra-vascular and intra-vascular fluid by regulating renal sodium excretion or reabsorption. Progesterone acts as an antagonist to aldosterone and thus influences urinary sodium excretion. Dalton (1964) has suggested that the water and sodium retention in PMS could be caused by an excess of aldosterone with insufficient progesterone to act as an aldosterone antagonist.

Prolactin, a hormone secreted by the anterior pituitary gland, has also been proposed as a cause of premenstrual syndrome. It stimulates lactation, plays a role in controlling ovarian hormones, and is known to be associated with water retention. Prolactin levels fluctuate throughout the menstrual cycle, with peaks occurring at ovulation and again in the mid- and late luteal phases of the cycle, when women experience symptoms of PMS. At least one study reported higher levels of prolactin among PMS patients than among normal controls (Rausch & Janowsky, 1982). Prolactin levels are also high immediately after childbirth. However, prolactin levels are not as high among women with PMS as those found in pathological states of hyper-prolactinemia—which are not characterized by PMS symptoms. Although some studies report relief of symptoms with bromocriptine, a drug that inhibits the release of prolactin, the data here are incomplete and contradictory, and there is no good evidence to support bromocriptine's usefulness in the treatment of PMS.

The Neurotransmitters. Serotonin, norepinephrine, and dopamine have been implicated both in psychiatric disorders and in the regulation of salt and water balance. There is a great deal of experimental evidence that ovarian hormones and the neurohormones exhibit overlapping functions in regulating ovulation and have other overlapping behavioral effects. For example, animal studies indicate that estrogen induces running behavior in rats, as do some of the anti-depressant medications, and progesterone has a sedative effect. However, although fluctuating levels of estrogen and progesterone do influence neurotransmitters in the brain, it is still not known how specific neurotransmitters affect emotions. Also, because of the close interaction between the ovarian hormones and neurotransmitters, it is not known which is the primary determinant of the mood and other changes: Are the estrogen and progesterone influencing symptoms directly or indirectly by affecting neurohormones?

Estrogen and progesterone also affect circadian rhythms, and one study suggests that women with PMS may have a disturbance of their biological clocks. Parry and her colleagues at the University of California, San Diego, found a significant reduction in the duration and amount of melatonin secretion among PMS patients as compared with a matched group of normal control subjects. Melatonin is a hormone that varies with the light-dark cycle and appears to be a marker of circadian rhythms; it is secreted at night by the pineal gland. In addition to abnormalities in melatonin secretion, these authors found that like some other groups of depressed patients, women with PMS respond favorably to phototherapy, that is, treatment with bright light, particularly in the evening, and to late-night sleep deprivation (Parry, Berga, Kripke, Klauber, Laughlin, Yen, & Gillin, 1990).

Reid and Yen (1981) have postulated that PMS is the result of an aberrant release of, or sensitivity to, hypothalamic hormones, specifically beta-endorphin and alpha-melanocyte-stimulating hormone. Endorphins are widely distributed throughout the body and appear to function as neurotransmitters or neuromodulators. They regulate the release of various other hormones from the pituitary and elsewhere and have been implicated in the release of luteinizing hormone, follicle-stimulating hormone, vasopressin, and insulin. Reid and Yen note that differing levels of gonadal steroids from month to month and from person to person may account for the very heterogeneous symptoms seen. The endorphins are located within the brain and involve both the anterior and intermediate lobes of the pituitary. Hence, when their normal balance is disturbed, mood, appetite, fluid retention, breast pain, behavioral changes, and many of the other symptoms seen in PMS may occur.

Prostaglandins. These naturally occurring substances are synthesized from unsaturated fatty acids present in the body; they function primarily as regulators of smooth muscles. Fluctuations in prostaglandin levels, particularly an excess of Prostaglandin F, are known to cause dysmenorrhea. The uterus contracts too much, squeezing so hard that it compresses uterine blood vessels and cuts off the blood supply, thus causing pain and cramps. The role of prostaglandins in PMS is less clear. It is possible that they influence neurotransmitters, which in turn affect mood. The prostaglandins themselves may be directly involved in the production of physical symptoms such as pain, tenderness, and nausea (Budoff, 1980).

Nutritional Factors. Various vitamins and minerals have also been accused of causing or contributing to PMS. A nutritional deficiency of magnesium has been postulated as a cause of premenstrual symptoms. Abraham (1982) reports one study in which patients were given 4.5 g to 6 g of magnesium nitrate daily for one week premenstrually and two days menstrually with excellent response for nervous tension, breast pain, and water retention symptoms. Other researchers have speculated about the relationship between estrogen and vitamin B_6. It is thought that estrogen may lead to a deficiency of B_6 by altering tissue distribution and perhaps enhancing the body's need for B_6. Because this vitamin is necessary in the biosynthesis of the neurohormones dopamine and serotonin, aberrant metabolism of these brain monoamines has been considered as a possible cause of PMS as well as depression in users of oral contraceptives. Significant clinical improvement has been seen after vitamin B_6 administration to oral-contraceptive users with depression, and some researchers and clinicians have reported a good response to treatment of PMS with B_6. Whether or not this is a placebo effect is not known. However, five out of seven studies have shown that vitamin B_6 may be superior to a placebo (*Psychiatric News*, 1987).

Several studies in which large doses of vitamin A were used successfully to treat PMS have also appeared in the literature. Vitamin A is thought to alleviate PMS by opposing hyperfunction of the thyroid or by exerting a direct diuretic or antiestrogen effect.

However, none of these hypotheses has been proven to date, and a vitamin-deficiency theory for the etiology of PMS appears unlikely until there is further clarification of the role of vitamins in hormone metabolism. An Australian study supports the view that vitamin deficiencies do not cause PMS. Women suffering from premenstrual syndrome were not deficient in magnesium, zinc, vitamin A, vitamin E, or vitamin B_6 according to researchers at the University of Sydney. Moreover, women who had psychological symptoms had as much of these nutrients in their blood as a group that was symptom free (*Nutrition Action Healthletter*, 1989)

Psychological Factors. Is PMS a psychosomatic disorder? Personality disturbances, negative attitudes toward menstruation, difficulty in accepting one's role as a woman, marital discord, conscious or unconscious conflicts, and other life stresses have all been postulated as possible causes of PMS (Coppen & Kessel, 1963; Paulson, 1961; Rees, 1953). Some researchers have theorized or found a relationship between PMS and adverse menarcheal experiences—fear upon discovering menstruation or a lack of preparedness (Shainess, 1961). However, recent studies have found no relationship between early experiences with menstruation and the later development of symptoms (Golub & Catalano, 1983; Woods, Dery, & Most, 1983). Nor are women who experience PMS necessarily more anxious or neurotic than women who do not, though here, too, the data are contradictory (Clare, 1979; Golub, 1976). Perhaps the strongest evidence that premenstrual symptoms occur in "normal" as well as neurotic women is the universality of the symptoms. Recall that in the World Health Organization study the majority of women in all 10 countries studied reported some physical discomfort around the time of menstruation. The most common symptoms reported were back and abdominal pain, followed by headache, breast discomfort, and limb and abdominal swelling. Women in all the countries studied experienced some negative mood in conjunction with menstruation, specifically irritability, lethargy, and depression. However, fewer women were aware of mood changes than perceived physical discomfort (Snowden & Christian, 1983). As for accepting one's role as a woman, a recent study found, not only that most of the women who were complaining of premenstrual symptoms had normal scores on a standardized personality test (the Minnesota Multiphasic Personality Inventory, MMPI), but also that they strongly endorsed the feminine role. The finding that almost half of these subjects reported marital distress is provocative (Stout & Steege, 1985). It is consistent with Coppen and Kessel's (1963) report of a greater prevalence and severity of PMS symptoms in married as opposed to single women and with my hypothesis that the pressures of child rearing contribute as well.

Research by Gallant (1991) points in a new direction. She found that some women report their premenstrual experiences as severely distressing while others who experience similar changes in mood and physical symptoms do not. Why the difference? The women who reported severe symptoms had lower self-esteem, more stress in their lives, more angry feelings and more guilt about feeling angry, and less effective coping skills. This clearly has implications for the psychological treatment of women who seek therapy for PMS.

Treatment

In view of the lack of a consistent definition of PMS or any satisfactory explanation of its cause(s), it is not surprising that a wide variety of different treatments has been proposed over the years. Abplanalp (1983) notes that PMS has been treated with oral contraceptives, estrogen alone, natural progesterone, synthetic progestogens, minor tranquilizers, nutritional supplements (pyridoxine), minerals (magnesium and calcium), lithium, diuretics, bromocriptine, exercise, and psychotherapy. Yet, very few studies of treatment efficacy have involved double-blind evaluations of the various treatment agents, and thus it is not known which are truly effective. For example, uncontrolled studies and reports from some clinics suggest that progesterone is helpful. Yet in a double-blind controlled study of the efficacy of progesterone in the treatment of PMS, Sampson (1979) found that whether patients received progesterone or a placebo, 60% were helped—that is, a placebo was at least as effective as progesterone in this study. In a later paper, Sampson (1981) concludes that although reports from clinics and uncontrolled studies suggest that progesterone is helpful in PMS, when the treatment is given in controlled double-blind studies, a high placebo effect is usually found.

Although there is no universally agreed upon program for the treatment of PMS, a regimen proposed by several clinicians for helping women with symptoms is generally accepted (Abraham, 1982; Budoff, 1980; Harrison, 1982; Herz, 1983; Osofsky, Keppel, & Kuczmierczyk, 1988). This includes careful evaluation of both the somatic symptoms and the psychological status of the patient, for intrapsychic and environmental factors such as stress may play a role. Then an individualized treatment program that addresses both specific symptoms and life-style changes and aims at alleviating intra- and interpersonal stress is recommended. Herz (1983) advocates a biopsychosocial approach, beginning with daily records of basal temperature, weight, and symptoms over two to three cycles. Dietary change is advised:

1. No caffeinated beverages
2. No sugar
3. Frequent small meals comprised of high protein, high-complex carbohydrate, low-fat foods
4. Reduced sodium intake

People are not aware of how much caffeine they consume. It is present, not only in coffee and tea, but also in many soft drinks and medications (pain relievers, cold remedies, weight-loss drugs). Most people tolerate caffeine, but some are sensitive to caffeinated beverages: They develop insomnia, feel jittery, or get palpitations or tremors. Now there are two new studies confirming a link between caffeine consumption and perimenstrual weight gain and swelling that lend further support to the efficacy of reducing or eliminating caffeinated beverages from the diet (Monagle, Dan, & Krogh, 1991; Rittenhouse & Lee, 1991). These researchers also found that the number of cigarettes smoked daily was significantly correlated with premenstrual water retention (swelling, painful breasts, and weight gain). A word of caution: Abrupt elimination of caffeine from the diet may lead to withdrawal symptoms such as headache, lethargy, fatigue, muscle stiffness, and pain. These symptoms generally decrease progressively over the course of a week. So the best way to give up caffeine is to taper off gradually (Blakeslee, 1991).

Premenstrual chocolate craving and sweets binges are well documented in the folklore. An association has been described between depression and excessive carbohydrate intake among some patients with depression or Seasonal Affective Disorder (depression related to diminished exposure to sunlight in winter). New research now lends validity to the efficacy of making some dietary changes. In a study of diet and PMS at MIT's Laboratory of Neuroendocrine Regulation and Clinical Research, scientists found that PMS patients consumed significantly more calories, carbohydrates, and fat during the luteal phase than they did in the follicular phase. Control subjects exhibited no such variations. These researchers then decided to assess the patients' moods after they were given high carbohydrate meals. Sure enough, depression, tension, anger, sadness, and fatigue scores improved significantly. Janet Wurtman notes that the synthesis of

serotonin, a neurotransmitter involved in regulating mood and appetite, is increased following carbohydrate intake. She concludes that
women suffering from PMS may consume large amounts of carbohydrate in an attempt to improve their mood, and she suggests that
frequent meals and increased intake of complex carbohydrates such
as vegetables, pasta, rice, and popcorn will lead to mood improvement (Brzezinski, Wurtman, Laferrere, Gleason, & Wurtman, 1989).

In addition to dietary change, some clinicians suggest vitamin and
mineral supplements. For example, Herz (1983) recommends 100 mg
each of magnesium and vitamin B_6 twice a day during the second half
of the cycle. Abraham (1982) also advocates a therapeutic trial of
B-complex vitamins. And Dalton (1987) suggests a four-week therapeutic trial of 50 mg B_6 three times a day. However, as noted earlier,
PMS is probably not the result of a vitamin or mineral deficiency, and
taking vitamin B_6 is not without risk. An excess can cause nervous-
system disorders. Symptoms range from numbness of the hands and
feet to tingling sensations and impaired muscle coordination. Gareth
J. Parry, a researcher at the University of California School of Medicine
in San Francisco, cautions against taking more than 100 mg a day
(*Tufts University Diet . . .* , 1986). Vitamins or minerals taken in doses
higher than the recommended daily allowance act like drugs and
should be thought of as such.

Daily exercise is proposed as an effective way for a woman to
alleviate tension and increase her sense of control over her life. But
exercise does more for premenstrual symptoms than just relieve
stress. There is research evidence that regular exercise actually reduces symptoms. Prior and her associates (Prior, Vigna, Sciarretta,
Alojado, & Schulzer, 1987) engaged eight sedentary women and a
group of seven women runners who were training for a marathon in
a six-month exercise training program. The sedentary women, the
marathon-training women, and a comparison group of six normally
active women completed daily and monthly questionnaires regarding menstrual symptoms. The women who were training experienced
significant decreases in several premenstrual symptoms, specifically:
global complaints, personal stress, breast tenderness, and fluid retention. There were no significant changes in depressive symptoms or
anxiety, though both were reduced. Most interesting was the fact that
there were no changes in the nontraining group.

Other stress-reducing techniques, such as relaxation exercises,
yoga, meditation, and music, are prescribed for symptoms of tension

and anxiety. Time management readings or workshops provide guidelines and the impetus for women to reorganize their schedules to find time for exercise, rest, and play.

Psychotherapy can be helpful in enabling a woman to explore her attitudes and expectations regarding menstruation as well as more specific problems in her life, with an eye to making whatever changes will enable her to manage more comfortably. In recognizing and accepting premenstrual mood swings, for example, a woman can learn to nurture herself when she needs it. If psychological symptoms are severe, therapeutic doses of tranquilizers may be prescribed. Some caution is advised in seeking a therapist. In a study of psychotherapists' responses to the topic of menstruation in psychotherapy, Rhinehart (1989) found that menstruation was discussed by about 45% of the female therapists surveyed and only 15% of the male therapists. Not everyone—not even all psychotherapists—is comfortable talking about menstruation. Generally, male therapists reported more discomfort discussing menstruation with their female clients than did female therapists.

Other symptom-specific treatments include diuretics for water retention and analgesics for pain. Budoff (1980) specifically recommends Dyrenium because it fosters sodium and water loss without lowering potassium levels as the other antihypertensive diuretics do. Analgesics may be used in the treatment of abdominal, back, or breast pain, and propanolol or ergotamine may be useful in the treatment of menstrual migraine.

Research aimed at discovering the etiology of PMS continues. However, until one or more specific causal agents are found, acknowledging the validity of the symptoms (Yes, I know you really feel "blah") and providing specific suggestions such as those outlined above represent the treatment of choice for premenstrual syndrome. In fact, dietary change, exercise, and supportive psychotherapy often substantially ameliorate symptoms.

This chapter would not be complete without a discussion of the use of progesterone in the treatment of PMS. Despite the controversy about its efficacy, progesterone is being used in several PMS centers in the United States and has been used by Dalton in England for the last 20 years. Dalton (1987) has stressed the importance of using natural progesterone rather than synthetic progestogens in the treatment of PMS, for they lower rather than raise plasma progesterone levels. She also notes other difficulties with the synthetic progestogens: "The effect of natural progesterone is to cause prolifer-ation of the endometrium whereas the synthetic progestogens cause an initial proliferation followed by atrophy of the endometrium. Progesterone is not estrogenic, anabolic, nor androgenic whereas some progestogens have these qualities" (Dalton, 1982, p. 237). Syn-thetic progesterone taken as pills can also have such side effects as weight gain and phlebitis.

Generally, women receiving progesterone treatment for PMS are given 200 mg or 400 mg progesterone suppositories to be used once or twice daily. However, doses up to 400 mg every four hours may be needed, and dosage must be tailored to the individual patient. When given by suppository, progesterone raises blood progesterone levels within one hour of administration, and the effect lasts for 12 to 24 hours. Thus Dalton stresses that progesterone must be given in effec-tive doses and at least once a day, but sometimes twice daily. Although progesterone suppositories are readily available in Britain, the use of progesterone for the treatment of PMS has not yet been approved in the United States by the FDA. (The only approved uses to date are for treating cessation of menstrual flow and abnormal uterine bleeding due to hormonal imbalance.) Therefore, vaginal or rectal progester-one suppositories currently being used are prepared by pharmacists specifically for individual patients. There are side effects. Vaginal and rectal swelling is common. Some women bleed throughout the cycle, while others do not menstruate at all. Animal studies have shown increased rates of breast tumors and cervical cancer.

Keeping in mind the relationship between PMS and depression, those women who do not respond to the usual regimen of education, support, stress-reduction, and nutritional information may benefit from targeting specific symptoms. Because of the sedative properties of progesterone, some researchers suggest that it be given only to patients with symptoms of anxiety and irritability. They add that it should be used with caution or in lower doses among women with primary symptoms of depression because of its possibly depressive side effects (Osofsky, Keppel, & Kuczmierczyk, 1988). Other psycho-pharmacological agents, that is, antidepressants, amphetamines, or lithium, are effective in treating depression.

Among the most recent studies, Freeman and her colleagues (Free-man, Rickels, Sondheimer, & Polansky, 1990) report in the *Journal of the American Medical Association* that progesterone has, once again, been found to be ineffective as a treatment for premenstrual syndrome. In a well-designed, placebo-controlled, double-blind cross-over study of 168 women who were given progesterone by suppository in doses of 400 mg and 800 mg or a placebo, no symptom cluster or individual symptom differed significantly between progesterone and placebo. No significant effect for increased progesterone dose was found. PMS symptoms decreased with both progesterone and placebo treatments when the number of suppositories was increased. Parity did not affect treatment response. The subjects, all of whom had moderate to severe premenstrual symptoms and low or absent postmenstrual symptoms, met the National Institute of Mental Health guidelines for PMS. As in other studies, where the prevalence of history of major depression is reported to be 30% to 76%, 56% of the women studied had a history of major depressive disorder. In keeping with the description of PMS as a "midthirties syndrome," it is notable that the mean age of the subjects was 34 years. The authors conclude that "evidence from this study that progesterone suppositories have no clinically significant therapeutic effect greater than that of placebo for premenstrual symptoms should turn investigation to other treatments for this distressing disorder affecting the lives of many women" (Freeman et al., 1990).

The Politics of PMS

PMS confronts feminist researchers and clinicians with a dilemma. The desire to help those with premenstrual syndrome conflicts with concern that PMS may be used as an excuse to exclude women from certain experiences, occupations, or opportunities for achievement. Women have worked hard to be recognized as competent, rational, reliable, and productive. We do not want to lose that recognition. When premenstrual symptoms are labeled premenstrual syndrome (PMS) and PMS is seen as a common disorder—or even worse as a legal defense—it impugns the rationality of women's behavior in general.

Laws (1983) has argued that premenstrual tension (Laws' term for PMS) is a political construct. The way we define illness does not depend only on the presence or seriousness of symptoms. Other factors come into play. Cultural definitions and the medical establishment may decide that premenstrual tension is or is not a sign of illness.

The media play an important role in providing women with health-related information, but when it comes to PMS, they are not doing a very good job. After analyzing 78 articles in the popular press, Chrisler and Levy (1990) confirmed that the general description given of PMS is negative, confusing, and often inaccurate. Unfortunately, menstrual cycle symptoms are generally portrayed in stereotypic ways, with the premenstrual woman being depicted as cranky and irritable. Never mind that men are often cranky and irritable too. While women's moods may vary cyclically, there is no evidence that women are more prone to anger than men. In fact, the opposite is probably true. Witness the far higher rates of crime and accidents among men. Some have suggested that the worst part of being premenstrual is that that is when women are most like men. Thus it is hard to deny that menstruation is more than a biological phenomenon, it is a cultural event, and as such it is directly related to the place of women in society. As Gloria Steinem (1978) has so aptly pointed out in her spoof "If Men Could Menstruate," menstruation is surrounded by negatives because those who menstruate belong to a subordinate class.

The symptoms that concern women most are depression, anxiety, and anger. These do not jibe with our image of the ideal woman as nice, kind, and caring toward others. If we label the feelings we have premenstrually as signs of illness, they provide us with an excuse for behaving in ways that at other times are unacceptable to us. Thus one can retain the feeling that one is a good woman and blame unacceptable parts of one's personality on hormones being out of whack. Rather than accepting the cyclic changes as the norm, some baseline from which we are not expected to deviate becomes the norm. And when we do have mood changes or get angry, it is labeled illness. Rome (1983) has pointed out that this process invalidates women's right to feel angry. She says, "Calling these times of rage symptoms of disease is a handy way of not looking at what women are upset about and why." Women's complaints are explained away as just being "that time of the month" and are not taken seriously.

Medicine's view of menstruation has changed over the years in a manner that has nothing to do with scientific knowledge. Almost nothing was known about menstruation in the eighteenth century, yet

•hysicians at that time saw menstruation as a normal function. In ontrast, doctors in the late nineteenth century labeled menstruation form of illness. Louise Lander (1988), a lawyer and writer interested n the politics of health, calls this "the zig-zag effect" and attributes t to the influence of social forces on medical doctrine. Middle-class vomen were important to the economy in the eighteenth century, and hey are today as well. However, because menstruation represents reedom from the burdens of pregnancy, nursing, and the constant are of small children and because this reproductive freedom im->inges on the male world of work—women threaten men's jobs— menstrual cyclicity will be used to keep women in their place (Lander, 988).

In England, in the early 1980s, supported by testimony from Kath-rine Dalton, a British physician, PMS was used successfully as a nitigating factor in the sentencing of a woman convicted of a crime, illowing her to be placed on probation. However, two attempts imilarly to use PMS as a defense or mitigating factor in the United States have failed. In 1982 Shirley Santos, a 24-year-old mother of six, vas arrested for striking her 4-year-old child. Defense counsel moved o dismiss charges against the defendant on the grounds that she was uffering from premenstrual syndrome at the time of the assault. After oral arguments the motion for dismissal was denied, and the defen-dant subsequently withdrew her defense, admitted responsibility for ner actions, and pleaded guilty. Santos was sentenced to a 1-year conditional discharge, requiring her to undergo psychological evalu-ation and vocational counseling. In 1983, the defendant in another case tried to have a judgment dismissed that she owed the plaintiff expenses for his medical bills: She claimed that she was suffering from premenstrual syndrome when she stabbed him. The judge's memo-randum referred to the fact that PMS is not listed in the *Diagnostic and Statistical Manual* (DSM-III) and that PMS was not recognized as a mental illness, mental disorder, or personality disorder. He went on to say that the impact of PMS on human behavior is still the subject of medical debate and "its acceptance as an explanation for improper conduct has not yet been established either medically or legally" (Lander, 1988).

Elissa Benedek, Director of Research and Training at the Center for Forensic Psychiatry in Ann Arbor, Michigan, reviewed the use of PMS as a legal defense in the United States. She cautions that:

If PMS is used extensively as a defense, it may have successful consequences for a small percentage of criminals but subsequent consequences for women in general. One must be wary of any theory that adds to the public perception and scientific perception that women are not in control at least once a month. (Benedek, 1988)

Benedek concludes that the PMS defense has been unsuccessful here and considers its future success unlikely. All women must be alert to any suggestion that women go crazy every month. Particularly because there is no evidence that women lose control of themselves premenstrually. Women's biology is not responsible for what women do, and they should not be relieved of responsibility for their behavior during any phase of the menstrual cycle.

Mulligan (1983) suggests a compromise. She argues in favor of the use of a PMS defense to help women who suffer from the "worst effects of the syndrome." She suggests that

PMS could be a humanizing factor which would allow the judge to give a more suitable sentence, not because this defendant belongs to a class of women who have PMS, all of whom are violent and crazy, but because this individual has a recognized condition that is causing her to behave in a manner deemed unacceptable.

The decision as to guilt or innocence would not be affected by this but the punishment would. It would be used as a mitigating factor in much the same way as an illness or lack of a criminal record might be. Mulligan sees this as a reasonable solution, balancing the needs of the individual woman defendant and the community of women in general.

References

Abplanalp, J. M. (1983). Premenstrual syndrome: A selective review. In S. Golub (Ed.), *Lifting the curse of menstruation* (pp. 107-123). New York: Haworth.

Abraham, G. E. (1982). The nutritionist's approach. In C. Debrovner (Ed.), *Premenstrual tension* (pp. 71-93). New York: Human Sciences Press.

Andersch, B., & Hahn, L. (1981). Premenstrual complaints, II: Influence of oral contraceptives. *Acta Obstetrica et Gynecologica Scandinavica, 60*, 579-583.

Benedek, E. P. (1988). Premenstrual syndrome: A view from the bench. *Journal of Clinical Psychiatry, 49*(12), 498-502.

Blakeslee, S. (1991, August 7). The secrets of caffeine, America's favorite drug. *The New York Times*, C1, 11.

Blumenthal, S. J., & Nadelson, C. C. (1988). Mood changes associated with reproductive life events: An overview of research and treatment strategies. *Journal of Clinical Psychiatry, 49*(12), 466-468.

Breier, A., Charney, D. S., & Heninger, G. R. (1986). Agoraphobia with panic attacks. *Archives of General Psychiatry, 43*, 1029-1036.

Brzezinski, A., Wurtman, J. R., Laferrere, B., Gleason, R., & Wurtman, R. J. (1989). *Nutrient intake improves mood in premenstrual syndrome*. Paper presented at the meeting of the Society for Menstrual Cycle Research, Salt Lake City, UT.

Budoff, P. W. (1980). *No more menstrual cramps and other good news*. New York: Penguin.

Chrisler, J., & Levy, K. (1990). The media construct a menstrual monster: A content analysis of PMS articles in the popular press. *Women & Health, 16*(2), 89-104.

Clare, A. W. (1979). The treatment of premenstrual symptoms. *British Journal of Psychiatry, 135*, 576-579.

Coppen, A., & Kessel, N. (1963). Menstruation and personality. *British Journal of Psychiatry, 109*, 711-721.

Dalton, K. (1964). *The premenstrual syndrome*. Springfield, IL: Charles C Thomas.

Dalton, K. (1987). *Once a month*. Claremont, CA: Hunter House.

Day, J. B., & Taylor, R. W. (1981). Aetiology of premenstrual syndrome. In P. A. van Keep & W. H. Utian (Eds.), *The premenstrual syndrome* (pp. 11-29). Lancaster, England: MTP Press.

Dennerstein, L., Spencer-Gardner, C., Gotts, G., Brown, J. B., Smith, M. A., Burrows, G. D. (1985). Progesterone and premenstrual syndrome: A double blind crossover trial. *British Medical Journal, 290*, 1617-1621.

Ferguson, J. H., & Vermillion, M. B. (1957). Premenstrual tension: Two surveys of its prevalence and a description of the syndrome. *Obstetrics and Gynecology, 9*, 615-619.

Food and Drug Administration. (1982, December 7). Orally administered menstrual drug products for over the counter human use: Establishment of a monograph. *Federal Register, 47*, 199.

Freeman, E., Rickels, K., Sondheimer, S. J., & Polansky, M. (1990, July 18). Ineffectiveness of progesterone suppository treatment for premenstrual syndrome. *Journal of the American Medical Association, 264*(3), 349-353.

Gallant, S. (1991). *The role of psychological factors in the experience of premenstrual symptoms*. Paper presented at the meeting of the Society for Menstrual Cycle Research, Seattle, WA.

Gallant, S. J., & Hamilton, J. A. (1988). Controversy over a diagnosis of premenstrual dysphoria. *The Health Psychologist, 10*(2), 7-8.

Gise, L. H., Paddison, P. L., Lebovits, A. H., & Strain, J. J. (1989). *PMS and socioeconomic status*. Paper presented at the meeting of the Society for Menstrual Cycle Research, Salt Lake City, UT.

Golub, S. (1976). The magnitude of premenstrual anxiety and depression. *Psychosomatic Medicine, 38*, 4-12.

Golub, S., & Catalano, J. (1983). Recollections of menarche and women's subsequent experiences with menstruation. *Women & Health, 8*(1), 49-61.

Golub, S., & Harrington, D. M. (1981). Premenstrual and menstrual mood changes in adolescent women. *Journal of Personality and Social Psychology, 5*, 961-965.

Halbreich, U., & Endicott, J. (1985). Relationship of dysphoric premenstrual changes to depressive disorders. *Acta Psychiatrica Scandinavica, 71*, 331-338.

Harrison, M. (1982). *Self-help for premenstrual syndrome.* New York: Random House.

Haskett, R. F., Steiner, M., Osmun, J. N., & Carroll, B. J. (1980). Severe premenstrual tension: Delineation of the syndrome. *Biological Psychiatry, 15*(1), 121-139.

Herz, E. K. (1983). *Menstrual changes: Medical evaluation and treatment.* Paper presented at the meeting of the American Psychiatric Association, New York.

Janowsky, D. S., Berens, S. C., & Davis, J. M. (1973). Correlations between mood, weight and electrolytes during the menstrual cycle: A renin-angiotensin-aldosterone hypothesis of premenstrual tension. *Psychosomatic Medicine, 35*, 143-154.

Kramp, J. L. (1968). Studies of the premenstrual syndrome in relation to psychiatry. *Acta Psychiatrica Scandinavica, 203*, 261-267.

Lander, L. (1988). *Images of bleeding.* New York: Orlando Press.

Laws, S. (1983). The sexual politics of pre-menstrual tension. *Women's Studies International Forum, 6*(1), 19-31.

Lloyd, T. S. (1963). The mid-thirties syndrome. *Virginia Medical Monthly, 90*, 51.

Maddocks, S. E., & Reid, R. L. (1985). *The role of negative life stress and premenstrual syndrome: Some preliminary findings.* Paper presented at the conference of the Society for Menstrual Cycle Research, Galveston, TX.

Metcalf, M. G., & Mackenzie, J. A. (1980). Incidence of ovulation in young women. *Journal of Biosocial Science, 12*, 345-352.

Monagle, L., Dan, A., & Krogh, V. (1991). *Smoking, alcohol, caffeine consumption, and menstrual symptoms in a Southern Italian population.* Paper presented at the meeting of the Society for Menstrual Cycle Research, Seattle, WA.

Moos, R. H. (1968). The development of a menstrual distress questionnaire. *Psychosomatic Medicine, 30*, 853-867.

Mulligan, N. (1983). Premenstrual syndrome. *Harvard Women's Law Journal, 6*(1), 219-227.

Nutrition Action Healthletter. (1989, June). p. 4.

O'Brien, P. M. S., Selby, C., & Symonds, E. M. (1980). Progesterone, fluid, and electrolytes in premenstrual syndrome. *British Medical Journal, 87* 1161-1163.

Osofsky, H. J., Keppel, W., & Kuczmierczyk, A. R. (1988). Evaluation and management of premenstrual syndrome in clinical psychiatric practice. *Journal of Clinical Psychiatry, 49*(12), 494-498.

Parry, B. L., Berga, S. L., Kripke, D. F., Klauber, M. R., Laughlin, G. A., Yen, S. S. C., & Gillin, C. (1990). Altered waveform of plasma nocturnal melatonin secretion in premenstrual depression. *Archives of General Psychiatry, 47*, 1139-1146.

Paulson, M. J. (1957). Psychological concomitants of premenstrual tension. *American Journal of Obstetrics and Gynecology, 81*, 733-738.

Paulson, M. J. (1961). Psychological concomitants of premenstrual tensions. *American Journal of Obstetrics and Gynecology, 81* 733-738.

Pennington, W. M. (1957). Meprobamate in premenstrual tension. *Journal of the American Medical Association, 164*, 638-640.

Prior, J. C., Vigna, Y., Sciarretta, D., Alojado, N., & Schulzer, M. (1987). Conditioning exercise decreases premenstrual symptoms: A prospective, controlled 6-month trial. *Fertility and Sterility, 47*(3), 402-408.

Psychiatric News. (1987, November 6). p. 23.

Rausch, J. L., & Janowsky, D. W. (1982). Premenstrual tension: Etiology. In R. C. Friedman (Ed.), *Behavior and the menstrual cycle* (pp. 397-427). New York: Marcel Dekker.

Rees, L. (1953). Psychosomatic aspects of the premenstrual tension syndrome. *British Medical Journal, 99*, 62-73.

Reid, R. L., & Yen, S. S. C. (1981). Premenstrual syndrome. *American Journal of Obstetrics and Gynecology, 139*, 85-104.

Rhinehart, E. D. (1989). *Psychotherapists' responses to the topic of menstruation in psychotherapy.* Paper presented at the meeting of the Society for Menstrual Cycle Research, Salt Lake City, UT.

Rittenhouse, C. A., & Lee, K. A. (1991). *Biopsychosocial factors that influence the experience of perimenstrual weight gain.* Paper presented at the meeting of the Society for Menstrual Cycle Research, Seattle, WA.

Rivera-Tovar, A. D., & Frank, E. (1990). Late luteal phase dysphoric disorder in young women. *American Journal of Psychiatry, 147*, 1634-1636.

Rome, E. (1983). *Premenstrual syndrome examined through a feminist lens.* Paper presented at the meeting of the Society for Menstrual Cycle Research, San Francisco, CA.

Rose, R. M., & Abplanalp, J. M. (1983). The premenstrual syndrome. *Hospital Practice*, 129-141.

Rouse, P. (1978). Premenstrual tension: A study using the Moos menstrual questionnaire. *Journal of Psychosomatic Research, 22*, 215-222.

Rubinow, D. (1991). *Models of PMS.* Paper presented at the meeting of the Society for Menstrual Cycle Research, Seattle, WA.

Rubinow, D. R., Roy-Byrne, P., Hoban, M. C., Gold, P. W., & Post, R. M. (1984). Prospective assessment of menstrually related mood disorders. *American Journal of Psychiatry, 141*(5), 684-686.

Ruble, D. N., & Brooks-Gunn, J. (1979). Menstrual symptoms: A social cognition analysis. *Journal of Behavioral Medicine, 2*(2), 171-194.

Sampson, G. A. (1979). Premenstrual syndrome: A double-blind controlled trial of progesterone and placebo. *British Journal of Psychiatry, 135*, 209-215.

Sampson, G. A. (1981). An appraisal of the role of progesterone in the therapy of premenstrual syndrome. In P. A. van Keep and W. H. Utian (Eds.), *The premenstrual syndrome* (pp. 51-69). Lancaster, UK: MTP Press.

Sanders, D., Warner, P., Backstrom, T., & Bancroft, J. (1983). Mood, sexuality, hormones and the menstrual cycle, I: Changes in mood and physical state: Description of subjects and method. *Psychosomatic Medicine, 45*(6), 487-501.

Shainess, N. (1961). A reevaluation of some aspects of femininity through a study of menstruation. *Comprehensive Psychiatry, 2*, 20-26.

Snowden, R., & Christian, B. (Eds.). (1983). *Patterns and perceptions of menstruation.* New York: St. Martin's Press.

Steinem, G. (1978, October). If men could menstruate. *Ms. Magazine*, 110.

Stout, A. L., Grady, T. A., Steege, J. F., Blazer, D. G., George, L. K., & Melville, M. L. (1986). Premenstrual symptoms in black and white community samples. *American Journal of Psychiatry, 143*(11), 1436-1439.

Stout, A. L., & Steege, J. F. (1985). Psychological assessment of women seeking treatment for premenstrual syndrome. *Journal of Psychosomatic Research, 29*(6), 621-629.

Sutherland, H., & Stewart, I. (1965). A critical analysis of the premenstrual syndrome. *Lancet, 1,* 1180-1183.

Timonen, S., & Procope, B. J. (1973). The premenstrual syndrome: Frequency and association of symptoms. *Annales Chirurgiae et Gynaecologiae Fenniae, 62,* 108-116.

Tufts University Diet and Nutrition Newsletter. (1986, February), 3(12), 7.

van Keep, P. A., & Lehert, P. (1981). The premenstrual syndrome—an epidemiological and statistical exercise. In P. A. van Keep & W. H. Utian (Eds.), *The premenstrual syndrome* (pp. 31-42). Lancaster, England: MTP Press.

Wagner, J. (1986). *The search for signs of intelligent life in the universe.*

Widholm, O., & Kantero, R. L. (1971). Menstrual patterns of adolescent girls according to chronological and gynecological ages. *Acta Obstetrica et Gynecologica Scandinavica, 50*(14), 19-29.

Wilcoxon, L. A., Schrader, S. L., & Sherif, C. W. (1976). Daily self-reports on activities, life events, moods, and somatic changes during the menstrual cycle. *Psychosomatic Medicine, 38*(6), 399-417.

Wilson, C. A., Turner, C. W., Keye, Jr., W. R. (1991). *Premenstrual symptoms in mother-adolescent daughter dyads, mothers diagnosed with or without premenstrual syndrome.* Paper presented at the meeting of the Society for Menstrual Cycle Research, Seattle, WA.

Woods, N. F., Dery, G. K., & Most, A. (1983). Recollections of menarche, current menstrual attitudes, and perimenstrual symptoms. In S. Golub (Ed.), *Menarche* (pp. 887-898). Lexington, MA: D. C. Heath.

Woods, N. F., Lentz, M. J., Mitchell, E. S., & Taylor, D. (1989). *Perimenstrual symptoms and the health seeking process.* Paper presented at the meeting of the Society for Menstrual Cycle Research, Salt Lake City, UT.

Woods, N. F., Most, A., & Dery, G. K. (1982). Prevalence of perimenstrual symptoms. *American Journal of Public Health, 72*(11), 1257-1264.

Wray, H. (1982). Premenstrual changes. *Science News, 122*(24), 380-381.

9

Menopause:
The Cessation of Menstrual Life

Unveiling the Mysteries:
What Happens and When

Many eminent women, Margaret Mead among them, see menopause as an energetic, creative time in a woman's life: A time when women are free to direct their attention toward activities other than home and family. Some see it as a time to make changes in their lives. Indeed, it is true that a number of women have made their greatest contributions after age 50 (Brody, 1981). Yet menopause is anticipated by most women with the same ambivalence that they have about the rest of menstrual life. "What a relief—no more mess and pain." But, at the same time some say, "I worry about getting wrinkled, growing fat, or going crazy," and "What is sex like after menopause?"

Years ago, menopause presented no problem for most women, for life expectancy did not extend beyond age 40. Today the average woman lives to age 78, some 28 years beyond her menopause. Thus there are now some 40 million women in the United States who are postmenopausal, and our numbers are growing (Markson, 1983; Budoff, 1983).

Menopause literally means cessation of the monthly rhythm of menstruation, an end to menstrual cycles. The more general term, climacteric, refers to the gradual changes that occur over a period of several years and mark the end of reproduction. The most widely used definition of menopause today is an absence of menstrual periods for one year (Voda & Eliasson, 1983). Menopause is the result of age-related changes in ovarian function, which gradually decreases. Female sex-hormone levels decline to a lower baseline level where they will remain stable for the rest of a woman's life. The ovaries gradually lose their ability to release a follicle (ovulation). At first, ovulation may stop but menstrual periods may continue. Beginning about age 43 (or approximately seven years before the last menstrual period), the length of the menstrual cycle and the bleeding patterns begin to change. These menstrual changes vary from woman to woman. Some women experience shorter cycles—menstruating every 20 days or so is not uncommon—others have longer cycles, menstruating less frequently. Some women experience no change in cycle length but find that their flow pattern has changed, either the number of days of bleeding or the amount of flow may diminish or increase. Shorter cycles of heavier bleeding or a short cycle followed by a long one are not uncommon. There is no predictable pattern: Cycles may vary and still be quite normal (Cutler, Garcia, & Edwards, 1983).

In the premenopausal woman experiencing regular menstrual cycles, estrogen, progesterone, and testosterone levels change from day to day in a predictable, rhythmic way. However, as a woman enters the menopausal transition years, the irregular patterns of the cycle reflect changes in the ovaries, specifically aging, reduction in size of the ovaries, and the concomitant decline in blood estrogen levels. Estradiol levels decrease from a premenopausal mean of 120 pg/ml to a postmenopausal mean of 13 pg/ml (Morokoff, 1988). These changes are gradual; they have no clearly marked beginning or end. The ovaries do not cease to produce hormones altogether, and they are not the only source of estrogen. The central area of the ovary is filled with cells that produce androgens, androstenedione, and testosterone (these are male sex hormones that women have, too, but in smaller quantities). Fat cells in the body take up the androstenedione and convert it to estrone—a weak estrogen. Estrone is further converted by the liver into estradiol. Both estrone and estradiol (two types of naturally occurring estrogen) are positively correlated with

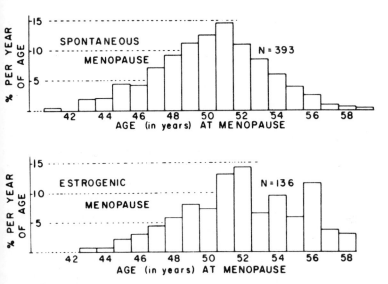

Figure 9.1. Frequency Distribution for Age at Menopause
Source: Treloar, A. E. (1982). Predicting the close of menstrual life. In A. M. Voda, M. Dinnerstein, & S. R. O'Donnell (Eds.), *Changing perspectives on menopause* (p. 297). Austin: University of Texas Press. Reprinted with permission.

weight in the postmenopausal woman. Thus women with more fat make more estrogen. The ovaries also continue to secrete testosterone after menopause. In addition, the adrenal glands produce a variety of hormones: cortisol, androgens, and small amounts of estrogen and progesterone.

Timing. At what age do women experience menopause? Treloar (1982) has studied lifelong menstrual histories of a large number of women. In a sample of 393 women, he found that menopause occurred in women between 41 to 59 years of age, with the most common age being 51 years. Women who use estrogen experience menopause about one-and-a-half years later (see Figure 9.1). Other researchers have likewise found 51 to be the typical age at menopause in industrialized societies (Asso, 1983). Contrary to popular beliefs, there is no relationship between age at menarche and age at menopause. Although age at menarche has declined steadily, presumably because of improved nutrition, age at menopause is not thought to have changed. As far back as the sixth century A.D. the cessation of menstruation was well documented as not occurring before the 35th year, "nor does it *usually* continue after the fiftieth year" (Utian, 1980; italics mine). In American women menopause typically occurs between 48 and 52 years of age. However, there are women who continue to menstruate until their late fifties.

Several things seem to affect the age at which menopause occurs. Smoking, and even having smoked in the past, is associated with earlier menopause. This may be directly due to the effects of nicotine on the neuroendocrine system, alteration of sex hormone metabolism with subsequent lower estrogen levels, or to the fact that smokers may be thinner than nonsmokers. Hill (1982) reports the results of one study in which more than half the postmenopausal women who were 45-49 years of age smoked cigarettes, while only 28% of those still menstruating smoked. Likewise, heavy smokers were more likely to be postmenopausal than were light smokers. A similar pattern was found among drinkers. Almost 80% of the postmenopausal women were drinkers as opposed to only 60% of the premenopausal women. More drinkers than abstainers were postmenopausal, and heavy drinkers—those who consumed more than 4 ounces of alcohol a week—were more likely to be menopausal than light drinkers. In fact, the relationship between cigarette smoking and drinking is significant. When these researchers looked at both cigarette and alcohol use, they found that more smokers were postmenopausal, regardless of whether they used alcohol; they concluded that the relationship between alcohol use and early menopause was due to the link between drinking and smoking rather than an independent effect of alcohol. Nevertheless, those women who both smoked and drank were four times more likely to be postmenopausal before age 50 than women who abstained from both.

Weight may play a role. There is some evidence that somewhat heavier women have a later menopause. Taller women, with height independent of weight, also seem to have a later menopause (Lindquist, 1979).

The reasons for the correlation of other factors—various life events—with age at menopause are poorly understood. For example, women who are currently married as opposed to those who are widowed, divorced, or unmarried have a later menopause, as do women who have never been pregnant. Conversely, having twins or working outside the home appear to be related to an earlier menopause. The role of lifelong nutrition, stress, illness, race, familial patterns, or geographical factors is not yet known (Asso, 1983, p. 103).

Cultural Influences on Attitudes and Symptoms

Until recently menopause, like menstruation in general, was not considered an appropriate topic of conversation, certainly not in mixed company. Women entering menopause were seen as diseased, hormone deficient, sexless, irritable, and depressed. Over the years physicians perpetuated negative attitudes about menopause. For example, in the midnineteenth century, in a chapter on the "Change of Life" in a book on diseases of the female, readers found the following description of the menopausal woman:

> Compelled to yield to the power of time, women now cease to exist for the species, and henceforward live only for themselves. Their features are stamped with the impress of age, and their genital organs are sealed with the signet of sterility. . . . It is the dictate of prudence to avoid all such circumstances as might tend to awaken any erotic thoughts in the mind and reanimate a sentiment that ought rather to become extinct . . . in fine, everything calculated to cause regret for charms that are lost, and enjoyments that are ended forever. (Utian, 1980, p. 13)

Unfortunately, this misogyny did not end in the nineteenth century. In the 1960s the author of a best-selling book wrote, "A large percentage of women who escape severe depression or melancholia acquire a vapid cow-like feeling called a negative state. . . . a strange endogenous misery" (Wilson, 1966). In *Everything You Always Wanted to Know About Sex*, Reuben (1969) called menopausal women, "a caricature of their younger selves at their emotional worst." Little wonder that negative attitudes toward menopausal women persist.

For far too long women at menopause have been viewed as passive victims of their changing hormones. Most books about menopause look at it from a medical perspective and tend to see it as a deficiency disease, focusing on dysfunction. Menopause is not a disease. It is a change that signals the end of menstrual cycles. Recognizing that sociocultural factors play an important role in women's response to menopause is important. Certainly women's menopausal experiences are influenced by the physiological changes going on in their bodies at this time, but they are shaped by the social changes going on in their lives too. And women differ in the ways in which they respond to these changes.

In a study of female attitudes toward menopause, Maoz and his colleagues (Maoz, Dowty, Antonovsky, & Wijsenbeek, 1970) found 10 themes reflecting what menopause means to the 55 women they sampled. Three were a reflection of a positive attitude or gain and seven of a negative reaction. The gains were: being free of menstruation, being free of pregnancy, and a nonspecific sense of liberation. The losses were: loss of fertility, loss of health, loss of femininity, onset of old age, danger of emotional disturbance, danger of somatic disturbance, and a general feeling that it has "come too soon." As was true of young girls' attitudes toward menarche, most of the women's attitudes toward menopause were mixtures of both negative and positive feelings. However, negative attitudes do not necessarily mean inadequate coping. As with menstruation, throughout their reproductive lives women may complain about its nuisance and symptoms, but for the most part they cope very well and carry on.

An interesting finding is that attitudes toward menopause become more positive with age. In a now classic study done in 1963 of 267 women between the ages of 21 and 65, Neugarten and her colleagues (Neugarten, Wood, Kraines, & Loomis, 1968) found consistent age differences. Although more than half of the women in all age groups agreed that menopause is unpleasant and women should expect some trouble during menopause, the two older age groups had other, more positive attitudes. Menopausal and postmenopausal women were significantly more likely to recognize a "recovery" and gains occurring after menopause. They saw the postmenopausal woman as "feeling better, more confident, calmer, freer than before," but the majority of younger women disagreed. Similarly, on questions regarding life change and control over symptoms, the middle-aged women agreed that menopause creates no major discontinuity in life and that women have a relative degree of control over their symptoms. Reproductive capacity was not a great concern. When asked what the worst thing about menopause was, the largest number said, "Not knowing what to expect." Next came "The discomfort and pain" and "It's a sign you are getting old." The finding that younger women have more negative attitudes toward menopause than women who were experiencing menstrual changes or were postmenopausal was recently replicated (Theisen, Mansfield, Voda, & Seery, 1991). Attitudes toward menopause appear to be related to age, physical health, emotional health, the menopausal stage, and the ease of talking to others about menopause.

The effect of the negative stereotyping mentioned earlier is seen in the menopausal women's response to "Women worry about losing their minds during the menopause." Half of the women in the 45- to 55-year-old age group agreed with this statement, a significantly greater percentage than the other groups. Yet psychiatric studies have shown that hospitalizations for depression and suicide do not occur more often at this time of life. No differences in depressive symptoms have been found between women of other age groups and women during the climacteric. Recent studies show that life stress, which is no more likely to occur at the time of menopause, has more influence than does menopause on both the psychological and somatic symptoms experienced by menopausal women (Asso, 1983, p; 123). Looking again at age differences, the younger women also tended to deny the importance of sex in the older women's lives. They were more likely to disagree with the statement that menopausal women may experience heightened interest in sex. Yet, most of the menopausal women maintained that there was no relationship between menopause and changes in sexual behavior. Of those who did indicate that there was likely to be some change, half believed that sex becomes less important, while the other half said that sex becomes more enjoyable and more important.

Overall, women consistently saw *themselves* more positively than they saw other women who were going through menopause. This was particularly clear when women were given a list of adjectives with the word "myself" at the top, and then another with the same adjectives but with the phrase "women in menopause" at the top (Neugarten, 1973).

Women seemed more willing to express negative and perhaps unacceptable attitudes when the questions were less personal. The impression one comes away with is that women's overall attitudes about menopause are complex and ambivalent, with many expressing the feeling that "It's not me who needs help, it's the other woman." Perhaps as women begin to talk more freely about their experiences with menopause, middle-aged or older women will be able to "separate the old wives' tales from that which is true of old wives" (Neugarten, 1973, p. 5).

In a fascinating piece of research designed to look at the interplay between culture and women's responses to menopause and middle age, Datan and her colleagues (Datan, Antonovsky, & Maoz, 1981) studied the middle age of women in five Israeli subcultures. Subjects were 1,200 women representing five different ethnic groups. They ranged from the very traditional Israel-born Moslem Arab woman, whose husband was chosen for her, who is illiterate, whose life has been devoted to childbearing, and who is devoutly religious; to the modern woman (Jewish immigrants from Western Europe) at the other end of the continuum, who chose her own husband, who had had at least a high-school education, who planned childbearing, who generally worked outside the home, and who had moved away from religious orthodoxy. The three groups in between were Turks, Persians, and North Africans.

This study clearly demonstrates that women's responses to menopause and middle age are shaped by the cultures in which they grew up. In all five subcultures menopause was viewed as a combination of gains and losses but the combination differed by subculture. Successful adaptation seems to require a fit between what the women expect their lives to be like and the opportunities available to them in reality. In other words, women's feelings of well-being were greatest when there was a good fit between their expectations and their actual lives. The most modern and the most traditional women were the happiest and had the fewest negative menopausal symptoms. The groups in the middle, neither traditional nor modern, experienced more somatic and psychological symptoms and had the most negative attitudes about menopause.

The finding that women in all five groups welcomed the cessation of fertility was surprising. This response seems to be based on where women are in their lives rather than satisfaction with family size. Remember that these women ranged from Arab women who had been almost continuously pregnant to European women who typically bore only one or two children. However, although two-thirds of the European women wanted larger families, they no longer wished to be capable of pregnancy. Apparently, as it is written in Ecclesiastes, "To every thing there is a season."

Datan's (Datan, Antonovsky, & Maoz, 1981) research indicates that the modern woman has fewer constraints and more opportunities to seek satisfaction outside the home, actively coping with changes in her life cycle. However, the certainty of the traditional woman's life, despite what outsiders may see as its limitations, provides traditional women with a central role in the household and the comfort of the familiar. Both the modern and the traditional women had high levels of psychological well-being. It was the women in the middle groups, caught in a time of rapid cultural change, who experienced most difficulty in adapting to menopause.

It is notable that women in all five subcultures, so different from each other, shared certain enduring human values. All valued "the companionship of a good marriage" and all "cherished their children, while seeking personal autonomy and the satisfaction of a job well done" (Datan, Antonovsky, & Maoz, 1981, p. 116).

In looking at women in other cultures, one is struck by the fact that they do not seem to have the same anxiety about aging that European and American women have, and they often have increased freedom. In some cultures, the end of the childbearing years frees women from the demands of child care and enables them to participate more freely in other community activities. Among the Yoruba of West Africa, only older women can travel and engage in trade. In societies that ascribe a dangerous sexuality to women, there are restrictions on women's movements; menopause removes this dangerous sexuality, and society lessens its restrictions on postmenopausal women. For example, when they become older, upper-class urban Bengali women, who are traditionally confined to purdah, are permitted to go on religious pilgrimages to distant places. Among the Winnebago, old women sit next to the men. They are considered the same as men because they have no menstrual flow. In some cultures older women have positions of considerable power and authority over the younger generation. In traditional India, China, and Japan, the work of the daughter-in-law reduces that of the older woman as married daughters move into the household of her husband's family. In Sudan, the older women achieve a status closely resembling that of men and are greatly respected by their sons. Similarly, older women are valued and given considerable political and domestic power by the Iroquois and Canadian Blackfoot tribes (Brown, 1982).

Flint (1982) hypothesized that menopausal symptoms are subject to cultural influences. In 1969 she went to India and studied the reproductive histories of a group of high-caste, well-nourished women. When these women were asked whether they had any problems associated with menopause, few women had any symptoms other than changes in their menstrual cycles. Those women who had not yet reached menopause said they were looking forward to it, and those who had stopped menstruating were positive about it. Compare this with studies in the United States and Britain where 10% of women complained of severe symptoms, 16% were completely free of symptoms, and about 74% experienced some discomfort. Flint (1982) proposes that the difference in symptoms is related to cultural differences in values and attitudes about menopause and to role changes that occur when women reach this reproductive landmark. With the attainment of menopause, the Indian women, who have been restricted in many of their activities because of their culture's taboos about menstrual blood and childbirth, are released from the restrictions of purdah, can come out of the women's quarters and talk with the men—behavior never possible for them before. Their status becomes more elevated when they reach menopause; they are rewarded for attaining menopause. There is no such reward for aging in the American culture. Unfortunately, Flint does not mention another possible explanation for the lack of symptoms among the Indian women, namely that they belong to a different gene pool—which does not deny the role of culture in affecting symptoms, but rather acknowledges the complex interplay of biological and sociocultural factors.

In order to tease out the impact of sociocultural factors in the way women respond to menopause, menopause must be viewed in the context of other life events. Several researchers have addressed this issue. In a study of 448 Swiss housewives between the ages of 41 and 60, researchers found a clear increase in symptoms around the time of menopause, with about half of the women sampled experiencing some climacteric symptoms. The researchers explored the role of social class and children in the home and found that among women whose children had left home, symptoms were worst at the time when children had just left, with a peak in the premenopausal group. Unfortunately, the "climacteric complaints" were not specified in this study, but simply described as 17 climacteric symptoms that were "the early signs of the failing ovary." Because feelings of anxiety and depression were often included in such lists in the past, it may be that these premenopausal women were experiencing sadness at separating from their children and the loss of their maternal role. The increase in symptoms may have nothing to do with menopause at all. Those who still had children at home reported greater satisfaction with their ives than did women whose children had left. Social class was relevant too. The impact of aging and menopause, as measured by climacteric complaints and reports of satisfaction with one's life, was found to be less severe in women of the higher social classes than in lower-class women. Although both groups experienced a menopausal peak in symptoms, there is a significantly greater postmenopausal recovery among the higher social classes (van Keep & Kellerhals, 1974).

In another study looking at the role of social class and employment, the International Health Foundation interviewed 922 Belgian women between the ages of 46 and 55 in their homes (Severne, 1982). A list of different vasomotor and nervous symptoms was presented to the women, including, among others: hot flashes, palpitations, dizziness, insomnia, irritability, and depressive moods. The findings are important. Hot flashes increased in the perimenopausal and postmenopausal periods for women in all the groups (Severne, 1982, p. 241). Other symptoms revealed a difference between socioeconomic groups and between women who worked and those who did not. In the lower socioeconomic group, housewives had more vasomotor symptoms (hot flashes, palpitations, dizziness, etc.) than did women with jobs. Women in the lower socioeconomic group also had more nervous symptoms, with those who were employed having the greatest number of complaints. In contrast, women in the higher socioeconomic group with jobs experienced almost no menopausal change in nervous symptoms. Perhaps the striking difference between lower- and higher-class working women is related to the greater stress experienced by the lower socioeconomic group, who are responsible for both household and job demands; they may be stressed by fatigue and a lack of work satisfaction, while the higher socioeconomic group is more likely to have help at home and more interesting work (Severne, 1982, p. 243).

In general, the Belgian women seemed to consider the climacteric a normal physical event but one that was also bothersome. For the upper socioeconomic group the effect of working outside the home is almost always favorable. For women in the lower socioeconomic group, having a job seems to add stress during the perimenopausal period. However, having a job in the postmenopause seems to be a positive factor in both groups, adding to the women's satisfaction with life (Severne, 1982, p. 245).

Returning to the United States, of the women from the Baltimore area that Emily Martin interviewed for her book, *The Woman in the Body*, most saw menopause positively and were pleased at not having the inconvenience of menstruation any more. They described meno pause as a part of everything else going on in their lives. But for some it was a landmark event that led them to take stock of their lives. One woman said, "I realized that, boy, I've reached another milestone. I I was going to do anything, I'd better do it." She decided to get a divorce (Martin, 1987). This is a time when some women feel strong and take new steps toward independence and power.

How to Handle the Hot Flash and Other Symptoms

A wide variety of symptoms is reported to be associated with the menopause. These include hot flashes or flushes, sweating, head-aches, fatigue, vertigo, aches and pains, tingling sensations, in-somnia, irritability, weight gain, palpitations, nervousness, and depression. However, there is little agreement about which of these symptoms are actually experienced by greater numbers of women during the menopause than at other times in a woman's life. In a careful review of the research literature, Woods (1982) found that hot flashes were the most widely cited symptom; between 43% and 93% of women reported hot flashes during the menopause or during the year or two after the last menstrual period. A smaller percentage of women reported sweats, which often accompany hot flashes. These symptoms were followed in frequency by complaints of insomnia, headaches, fatigue, vertigo, rheumatic pains, tingly sensations, and irritability. Thus there does seem to be a symptom complex—a group of symptoms that the perimenopausal woman perceives as being related. Nevertheless, it is important to note that in the studies re-viewed, between 16% and 38% of all the women were symptom free.

In a study of 638 British women, McKinlay and Jefferys (1974) found that certain symptoms clustered together. Hot flashes were associated with night sweats, which were in turn associated with insomnia and headaches. It is possible that these vascular symptoms are related, and that the fatigue and irritability experienced are con-comitants of the sleep disturbance.

THE HOT FLASH

A hot flash is a sudden sensation of intense heat, sometimes followed by a flushing of the skin (an observable change in skin color) and accompanied by profuse sweating. Hot flashes usually involve the head, neck, and upper body and are sometimes accompanied by palpitations, chills, and in some cases mood changes. Although reliable figures on the number of women who experience hot flashes are not available, estimates range from 10% to 80%, with 75% a commonly cited statistic. Cutler and her colleagues reported that 71% of her sample of 124 perimenopausal women experienced hot flashes (Cutler, Garcia, & McCoy, 1987). Most women can expect their hot flashes to last for about two years, but some women continue to have them much longer (Voda, 1982).

Some women experience flashes only once or twice (or less) in a 24-hour period, while others may have up to five to seven per hour. In various studies the duration of each hot flash ranges from less than a minute to as long as an hour; however, most hot flashes seem to last about three minutes. They usually start in the head or neck and spread down (see Figure 9.2a, b; Voda, 1982, 148-149).

All hot flashes are not the same. They may be mild, a warm feeling that lasts less than a minute or two; or they may be moderate, a warm to extremely warm feeling that lasts from one to five minutes and is accompanied by sweating and perhaps flushing; or they may be severe, an extremely hot feeling, lasting from 1 to 12 minutes, usually accompanied by sweating or flushing. Severe hot flashes are extremely uncomfortable and may require a disruption of normal activity in order to seek relief. Feelings of dizziness, chills, or chest pain may accompany severe flashes. Hot flashes may begin prior to menopause, and patterns are the same for women who have surgically induced menopause. Fortunately, most hot flashes are either mild (about 49%) or moderate (about 39%); only about 12% are severe. Their frequency and intensity diminish over time (Voda, 1983).

Stress is a common trigger for hot flashes, as are spicy foods, coffee, tea, and alcohol. In one study, the number of hot flashes varied with the weather, and many women report an increase in hot flashes during the summer months. However, Voda (1982, p. 154) did not find a significant relationship between the frequency of hot flashes and ambient temperature, but as ambient temperature increased, so did

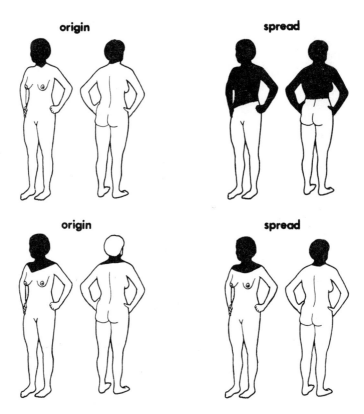

Figure 9.2a, b. The Hot Flash: Examples of Perceived Origin and Spread
in Two Different Women

Source: Voda, A. M. (1982). Menopausal hot flash. In A. M. Voda, M. Dinnerstain, & S. R.
O'Donnell (Eds.), *Changing perspectives on menopause* (p. 148). Austin: University of Texas Press.
Reprinted with permission.

the duration of the hot flash; perhaps women do not have more hot
flashes in hot weather, but the flashes that they do have last longer.

Women cope with hot flashes in a variety of ways. Some suck on
ice or drink cold liquids; others stand in front of an air conditioner or
refrigerator, remove clothing or bedding, open windows, fan themselves, wash with a cool cloth, or go swimming. Some use imagery:
Imagine yourself walking through the snow on a winter day or
swimming in a clear, icy lake. I have a hunch that those beautiful lace

and painted fans that Spanish women flash were designed by a menopausal woman.

Although the etiology of the hot flash is not yet known, it is apparently estrogen related. As estrogen levels drop, luteinizing-hormone levels in the blood rise, and a strong correlation has been found between pulsatile LH (luteinizing hormone) secretions and the menopausal flush. The relationship between LH and the flush indicates that both may be caused by the same mechanism. The neurons that secrete gonadotropin-releasing hormone (GnRH) are close to the thermoregulatory center in the brain. Therefore, some neurotransmitter signals may affect both GnRH release and the hot flash (Gannon, 1985). Archer (1982) notes that not all LH pulses are accompanied by a flush, but no flush was seen without an LH pulse. Therapy with exogenous estrogen alleviates these symptoms; however, if the estrogen is discontinued, the symptoms may return.

Thus far nothing has been said about the severity of menopausal symptoms. It is one thing to have hot flashes but quite another to be incapacitated by them. In a recent study of physicians, nurses, and menopausal or postmenopausal women, the women were found to rate their symptoms as significantly less frequent and less severe than did the doctors or nurses (Cowan, Warren, & Young, 1985). Polit and LaRocco (1980) note that only 10% of the patients interviewed in one study had symptoms that interfered with work. In their research, hot flashes were reported by 71% of the women, nervousness by 42%, weight gain by 36%, irritability by 35%, insomnia by 35%, depression by 34%, lack of energy by 32%, and headaches by 31%. However, 35% of the women described their symptoms as "somewhat mild," 20% described their symptoms as "somewhat severe," and only 3.7% felt that their symptoms were "extremely severe." Again, in this study, the number of symptoms reported was significantly greater in women with lower levels of education, and women employed outside the home reported fewer symptoms. One must be careful not to jump to the conclusion that working prevents menopausal symptoms. It may be that women who have satisfying work are in a better position to adapt to menopause; however, it is also possible that healthier women are more likely to be working at any age, menopausal or not. What is needed is longitudinal research, studies of women's physical and mental health over a number of years, to see if there really are changes attributable to whether or not a woman is experiencing discomfort at menopause.

PSYCHOLOGICAL SYMPTOMS

A number of psychological symptoms have been reported by menopausal women, for example, depression, irritability, and emotionality. Are these mood changes attributable to menopause, or are they secondary to other symptoms or to life stress? One strong indication that they are not caused by changing hormone levels is the fact that estrogen therapy is no more effective than a placebo in curing them; in contrast, hot flashes and vaginal discomfort are relieved by estrogen, but are not relieved by placebos. Thus, hormonal treatment is effective in relieving physical symptoms but not emotional ones. Several authors have suggested that the improvement in mood often seen after estrogen is given is attributable to the relief from hot flashes and the sleep disturbances that often accompany them.

What of the fear some women have of going crazy after menopause? Years ago there was a psychiatric diagnosis called "involutional melancholia." It referred to depression occurring around the time of menopause and served to perpetuate the myth that women were indeed more likely to become depressed at that time. If the menopause were a relevant cause of depressive illness, there should be a sharp peak in the incidence of depression among women between the ages of 45 and 55. However, review of research done in the last 20 years or so does not support the hypothesis that menopause is significantly related to depressive illness, and this diagnosis is no longer in use (Asso, 1980, p. 125; Winokur & Cadoret, 1975). The Massachusetts Women's Health Study (McKinlay, McKinlay, & Avis, 1989) of 2,500 Massachusetts women between the ages of 45 and 55 over a five-year period offers further confirmation: No relationship was found between natural menopause and depression. The vast majority of these women—85%—reported that they were never depressed. About 10% said that they were depressed occasionally, and 5% were persistently depressed. These figures are about the same as those found in the general population. Women who had had a hysterectomy showed twice as much depression as their peers, about 20%, but it was short-lived. When it did occur, depression was associated with multiple roles (spouse, mother, worker, and care-giver of elderly parent), concerns about the health of family members, and the demands of caring for them. Work once again was shown to have a positive effect on women's health—a phenomenon that has been dubbed the "healthy worker" effect. In sum, most women reported positive or neutral feelings concerning cessation of menstrual periods and no adverse impact on their health (McKinlay, McKinlay, & Avis, 1989).

This is not to say that menopausal psychological symptoms are unrelated to women's premenopausal level of adjustment. Research suggests that women who have low self-esteem and low life satisfaction earlier in their lives will have more difficulty with menopause. Polit and LaRocco (1980) found that the number of menopausal psychological symptoms women reported was significantly related to self-confidence and personal adjustment. What is not known is whether these women were depressed, irritable, nervous, etc., before they became menopausal, but there is some evidence that this is the case. McKinlay and her colleagues found that depressed women were twice as likely to report menopausal symptoms, such as hot flashes, sweats, or other problems, and were more likely to seek medical help (McKinlay, McKinlay, & Avis, 1989). Physicians who are seeing menopausal women need to be alert to the possibility that depression—as well as hot flashes—is a major cause for concern.

Stressful life events contribute to the incidence and severity of psychological and somatic symptoms during the menopausal years. This is a time when losses become salient: Children are leaving home, parents become sick and sometimes die, one's own health and that of friends or spouse may be threatened. In a study that focused on the relationship between stressful life events and symptoms, Cooke and Greene (1981) found that women between the ages of 35 and 54 experienced the most stress, and women who experienced less stress reported few symptoms. Longitudinal analysis of the McKinlay data mentioned earlier also revealed that stress in terms of family and friends being ill and causing demands and worry was associated with depression. Thus stress is a major factor contributing to the psychological and somatic symptoms of menopause.

On a more positive note, the majority of women report positive or neutral feelings about the cessation of menstruation.

BODY CHANGES AND OTHER SYMPTOMS

It is difficult to differentiate between the body changes that are a result of aging and those attributable to menopause. However, some changes are more clearly linked than others. For example, night sweats seem to be the nighttime equivalent of hot flashes. Women who experience them sometimes awaken hot and drenched with sweat. Cotton night clothes and bed linen are helpful, fostering evaporation and cooling. Like hot flashes, night sweats are relieved by estrogen therapy.

At menopause the skin loses some of its thickness and moisture and becomes more sensitive to the sun. There is also a progressive decrease in the density of scalp and body hair follicles. Breast tissue begins to lose some of its fullness in response to declining hormone levels. There may be a thinning of the lining of the urinary tract, leading to some loss of urinary control. And some women experience vaginal dryness with pain on intercourse.

Osteoporosis is a common problem for women—50% of women over 60 have it—and one of the causes appears to be declining estrogen levels. When estrogen levels fall, bones begin losing mass, becoming progressively thinner. This process begins in susceptible women at about age 35 and accelerates at menopause. Osteoporosis is more common in thin, fair-skinned, small-boned women who have not had children and less common in black women and women with larger bones. Smoking, heavy alcohol consumption, and a family history of osteoporosis add to the risk. Osteoporosis refers to increased porosity of the bone; the problem is that as porosity increases, fractures are more likely to occur.

The risks of getting osteoporosis can be reduced by maintaining adequate exercise and nutrition. Regular exercise promotes muscle tone and bone mass. Diet is also crucial. If there is not enough calcium in the diet, the calcium is taken from the bones. Dairy products are particularly high in calcium: three glasses of skim milk a day as part of a well-balanced diet will do the trick. However, some women do not tolerate milk products, and others avoid them as being too high in calories. Therefore, many gynecologists recommend that women begin taking supplementary calcium at about age 35 to be sure that they are consuming at least 1000 mg a day. After menopause women need 1,500 mg a day. Once the disease has been diagnosed, treatment consists of estrogen supplements, vitamin D (which promotes the uptake of calcium from the intestine into the blood), and calcium (Cutler, Garcia, & Edwards, 1983, pp. 81-105).

Sexuality and Menopause

Menopause does not mean the end of an active sex life, though some people fear that it does. Sex can be a lifelong pleasure. However, sexual interest is related to one's general feelings of health and well-being. If a woman is experiencing hot flashes and disturbed sleep, her interest in sex is likely to diminish, and if she is experiencing pain during intercourse, it is also likely that there will be a diminution in sexual desire, which in turn affects her partner's sexuality. In a recent study at Stanford University of menopausal women, 49% reported a decline in sexual activity since their menstrual cycles began to change, 38% reported no change, and 14% experienced an increase in activity. Changes in sexual behavior were related to a decline in personal interest. However, changes were also associated with difficulty in finding a suitable partner and with privacy problems resulting from a change in living arrangements. An increase in sexual activity was seen among women who had found a new love (Cutler, Garcia, & Edwards, 1983, p. 144).

Some changes in sexual behavior appear to be age related. Sex researchers since Kinsey have found a decade-by-decade decline in the frequency of marital intercourse, with rates declining from an average of three times a week for couples in their twenties, to once a week or less for couples after age 50 (Sarrel, 1988). What role can be ascribed to menopausal hormonal changes? Vaginal changes do accompany menopause. With the diminution of estrogen, the vagina loses some of its elasticity and becomes shorter and narrower. There is a diminution or absence of Bartholin's gland secretion. Vaginal walls become thinner and lose some of their ability to lubricate quickly, so that the vagina is less moist. The premenopausal woman takes from 6 to 20 seconds to lubricate when aroused, while the menopausal woman takes 1 to 3 minutes. If intercourse is attempted before the vagina is adequately lubricated, it may be painful. However, commercially available water-soluble lubricants such as K-Y Jelly, Ortho Personal Lubricant, or Lubrin can be used to facilitate intercourse. Alternatively, Replens, a vaginal gel, may be used to counter vaginal dryness. Estrogen therapy also improves vaginal lubrication. Estrogen creams in small doses (0.2 mg every or every other day) are very effective in the treatment of vaginal symptoms (Cutler et al., 1983, pp. 60-62).

Women sometimes experience burning when they urinate after intercourse. This may come from mechanical irritation of the urethra and the bladder as a result of the thrusting movement of the penis and is probably related to the thinning of the vaginal walls. With adequate lubrication, this is less likely to be troublesome.

For some women hormone replacement therapy may be the best solution. Among 80 postmenopausal women attending a menopause clinic at the Yale Mid-Life Study Center, almost half reported having intercourse only once a month or less, and 68% reported having a sexual problem. Among the problems reported were: decreased desire (77%), vaginal dryness (58%), painful intercourse (39%), decreased clitoral sensitivity (36%), decreased orgasmic intensity (35%), and decreased orgasmic frequency (29%). Hormone replacement therapy led to a good rate of improvement in a number of sexual measures (Sarrel, 1988, p. 7).

The impact of different combinations of hormones on sexual behavior and functioning has been the subject of study in recent years. These studies consistently find significant gynecologic improvements with the use of estrogen alone. Decreased vaginal dryness is often accompanied by reports of a decrease in painful intercourse, thus enabling women to resume their normal levels of sexual activity. The addition of progesterone, for which there are medical indications, does not seem to add any benefit from the standpoint of sexual functioning. If progestogen has any direct effect on sexuality, it is probably small in comparison to that of estrogen (Walling, Anderson, & Johnson, 1990).

Sherwin and Gelfand (1987) have suggested that androgen may offer a significant improvement in sexual responsiveness for women who are unresponsive to estrogen alone. In two studies of sexual functioning in women who had undergone hysterectomy, Sherwin found that women who received either androgen alone or androgen and estrogen in combination had significantly higher sexual desire scores during each of the treatment months than women in an estrogen-alone or placebo group. Sexual arousal scores were higher, and women in the androgen groups reported a greater number of sexual fantasies. Interestingly, outcome varied with the time since drug administration: higher levels of sexual behavior were reported when drug levels were high and lower levels when drug levels were low (Sherwin & Gelfand, 1987; Sherwin, Gelfand, & Brender, 1985).

The paucity of data available about what is the best type of androgen for treatment of postmenopausal symptoms, as well as what constitutes safe dosage and duration of treatment, makes it very important that androgen treatment of postmenopausal women be studied further.

Research supports the "use it or lose it" idea for women as well as for men. However, just why this is true is unclear. Sexually active women have less vaginal atrophy. Regular intercourse and masturbation are associated with normal vaginal pliability and function; abstinence is associated with progressive shrinkage (Leiblum, Bachmann, Kemmann, Colburn, & Swartzman, 1983). Masters and Johnson (1966) found that older women who continued to have sex once or twice a week also continued to lubricate rapidly when aroused. Thus regular sexual activity seems to promote the capacity for rapid vaginal lubrication. There is also some evidence that women approaching menopause who have regular weekly sexual intercourse have higher levels of estrogen and tend to be free of hot flashes or experience milder ones than women who abstain or have more sporadic sexual activity (McCoy, Cutler, Davidson, 1985). Of course the chicken and egg dilemma is relevant here. Does sexual activity enhance estrogen levels, or are women with higher estrogen levels more likely to seek sex?

Hormone Replacement Therapy: Pros and Cons

Vasomotor symptoms, hot flashes and night sweats, and atrophic vaginitis clearly respond to estrogen therapy. Secondary symptoms, such as insomnia or vaginal dryness, are also helped. There is little evidence that hormone therapy relieves psychological symptoms other than as they are related to physical distress. However, Utian (1980, pp. 121-146) does describes a "mental tonic effect" in postmenopausal women receiving exogenous estrogen therapy. Women given estrogen as opposed to a placebo seemed to have an improved feeling of well-being along with a reduction in other symptoms. Of course, estrogen therapy is also used in the prevention and treatment of osteoporosis.

Estrogen prescribed for the treatment of menopausal symptoms may be taken in pill form, as a wafer placed under the tongue, applied to the vagina in the form of a cream, or through the skin. The usual effective doses are:

Vaginally—0.2 mg of pure estradiol or 1.25 mg of conjugated estrogen cream

Orally —0.3 mg to 0.625 mg per day of conjugated estrogen for 25 days a month

Sublingually—0.5 mg every other day

Transdermally—0.05 mg to 0.1 mg of estradiol per day delivered at a controlled rate through the skin via a small patch (Budoff, 1983, pp. 28-31)

The aim is to use the lowest possible dose that provides relief of symptoms. Natural estrogens—those that are chemically identical to the ones made by the body—are preferable. They appear to be safer than synthetic estrogens, which differ chemically from the natural ones. Adverse side effects include: overstimulation of the liver; increases in blood pressure; and overstimulation of the endometrium (uterine lining), among others. Side effects are seen less often with lower dosages (Cutler et al., 1983, 106-121).

What are the risks? An increased risk of endometrial cancer is the key concern in using hormone replacement therapy for the treatment of menopausal symptoms. When estrogen replacement therapy (ERT) first came into use to counteract symptoms of menopause, estrogen was given alone. Then, in the 1970s, a series of studies revealed that women taking estrogen after menopause faced a significantly increased risk of uterine cancer. That risk has been countered by the use of progesterone. Progesterone helps prevent endometrial disease by stopping the endometrium from growing in response to estrogen and causing it to shed. Commonly given with estrogen as part of hormone replacement therapy, the usual dose is 5 mg of progesterone per day taken along with the estrogen for the last 10 days of a 25-day hormonal cycle, thus mimicking the natural menstrual cycle. When the hormones are discontinued, a menstrual-like flow often occurs. (These periods do not last forever. For women on long-term therapy, they stop after a few years when the endometrium no longer builds up a lining that must be sloughed off.) This regimen seems to work.

A recent Swedish study reported no increase in the risk of endometrial cancer in estrogen-progesterone users (Kiel, 1989).

Some endocrinologists also raise the question of increased risk of breast cancer among women who take estrogen after menopause. The National Cancer Institute is currently conducting a study of more than 6000 women to establish whether there is an increased risk and how great this risk is. Breast cancer experts note that estrogen can promote breast cancer. Girls who start to menstruate early and women who reach menopause late are known to have a greater risk. Many studies to date show no difference in breast-cancer rate between women who do and do not use estrogen replacement for a period of up to 15 years (Barrett-Connor, 1989). However, in a prospective study of ERT and the risk of breast cancer in a population of more than 23,000 postmenopausal women, Colditz and his colleagues (Colditz, Stampfer, Willett, Hennekens, Rosner, & Speizer, 1990) found a statistically significant increase in risk among current users. No effect was found for duration of use, and among former users, the risk declined with the passage of time since last use. After reviewing the data, these researchers conclude that the "magnitude of increased risk appears to be quite modest," but they suggest that the increased risk associated with taking hormones must be weighed against the beneficial effects of postmenopausal ERT on the risk of cardiovascular disease and hip fractures. A surprising link was found between taking hormones and drinking alcohol. Among women who did not consume alcohol the risk of breast cancer was not increased by current use of postmenopausal hormones. This finding is intriguing and warrants further study to see if it is due to chance or to a drug interaction that has important implications for users of estrogen.

In addition to alleviating hot flashes, ERT may offer some protection against cardiovascular disease. Hormone users have been reported to have significantly lower levels of plasma cholesterol (Barrett-Connor, Brown, Turner, Austin, & Criqui, 1979). Several studies indicate that women using estrogen have one-half to one-third the risk of dying of heart disease compared to women not taking estrogens, and in every age group the risk for women taking estrogen is one-third that of those not taking it (Barrett-Connor, 1989). One caveat: The studies cited were for estrogen alone, not estrogen opposed by progesterone. The consensus is that estrogen use is beneficial; however, progestins may offset the positive effects. The data simply are not in for the effect on heart disease of the currently used combined estrogen and progesterone hormone replacement therapy.

There is a study under way funded by the National Institutes of Health focusing on postmenopausal estrogen/progestogen intervention and cardiovascular disease risk factors, such as cholesterol levels, blood pressure, and blood clotting factors. Women will also be monitored for bone loss and endometrial changes. A sample of 840 women from different parts of the country will be randomly assigned to take either estrogen, a combination of estrogen and progestogen, or a placebo. At the end of the study, which is expected to last three years, sealed records listing which drug each woman took will be opened and researchers will determine the effects of the different treatments (National Women's Health Network, 1989).

Hormone replacement is most clearly indicated for women at serious risk for osteoporosis, a condition in which the bone becomes fragile and prone to fracture. Most women suffer some degree of bone loss, and 5% to 10% of women develop spinal fractures in the 25 years following menopause. If several spinal vertebrae are broken, there will be a significant loss of height and, possibly, the development of dowager's hump. Wrist, vertebral, and hip fractures affect as many as one-third of women by their midsixties. One-third of women who live to age 90 will have a hip fracture, and such fractures result in about a 12% reduction in life expectancy. In addition to shortening a woman's life, hip fractures cause significant morbidity. Only about half the women with fractured hips regain their mobility completely. Thus women who were functioning independently at home prior to the fracture often remain in long-term institutions for a year or more. Many require permanent long-term care facilities after the acute hospitalization. The protective effect of estrogens has been well established: ERT protects against bone loss and against fractures (Kiel, 1989, pp. 51-54; National Women's Health Network, 1989, p. 4).

Is the benefit worth the risk? That is the question each woman must answer in making a decision to use hormones. Here are the trade-offs:

Benefits:
  Prevention of osteoporosis and reduced risk of fractures
  Relief of vasomotor symptoms

    Prevention of pelvic tissue changes

    Possible reduction of heart disease

Risks:

    Possible increased risk of endometrial cancer

    Possible increased risk of breast cancer

    Possible increased risk of gallbladder problems

    Possible other drug side effects

In addition, some people cannot take estrogens. They are contraindicated for women with: breast cancer; uterine cancer or undiagnosed uterine bleeding; acute liver disease; vascular thrombosis or thrombophlebitis; and past history of high blood pressure, thrombophlebitis or thromboembolic disorders associated with previous use of estrogen.

Further, caution is indicated for women with the following conditions (they may use hormones but must be monitored closely with frequent check-ups): fibroid uterus (fibroids sometimes enlarge with estrogen); gallbladder disease; liver disease; severe hypertension; diabetes; a combination of several risk factors such as varicose veins, heavy smoking, and obesity (Utian, 1980, pp. 121-145).

There are alternative treatments for hot flashes for women who cannot use hormones. Clonidine, an antihypertensive drug that has been used in the prevention of migraine headaches because it decreases vascular reactivity, has been shown modestly to reduce the frequency, duration, and severity of hot flashes. Bellergal tablets, a combination of a sedative and two drugs that reduce autonomic nervous system activity, have been used for many years for relief of hot flashes (Utian, 1980, pp. 156-157). And oral progesterone alone may be used to treat severe hot flashes.

One further point should be made: The decision to take hormones need not be a lifetime commitment. Women may choose to use hormones to ease their transition from pre- to postmenopause and then, when the symptoms have improved, they may stop, gradually reducing the amount of hormone they are taking. Or, if the symptoms are primarily vaginal and/or urinary, vaginal estrogen cream used only for as long as it is needed may be an appropriate solution. Of course, any hormones must be taken under the supervision of a physician.

The Need to Talk

According to Weideger (1976), "menstruation and menopause are a dirty deal." Certainly there is little applause in our culture at the onset of fertility. Menstruation per se is perceived as a nuisance at best and at worst as being fraught with pain and other discomforts. Two-thirds of women would cheerfully do away with menstrual periods if that could be done safely and without sacrificing fertility. If periods are such an inconvenience, why do women not welcome menopause? The primary reason seems to be fear: fear of aging, fear of loss of sexuality, fear of getting depressed, and fear of loss of health. The truth is that menopause is a tangible sign of aging, but with it or without it, if we are lucky, we age. The truth is that declining estrogen levels affect female genitals. But research also shows that sex is good for menopausal women, and women should be encouraged to be sexually active if they are so inclined. Although more than half of women apparently have hot flashes at some time, only 10% experience severe symptoms related to the menopause. To date, it cannot be predicted who those women will be. Hormone treatment—a combination of estrogen and progesterone—appears to be reasonably safe for many women and offers help for women with severe symptoms. Health concerns other than hot flashes and genital changes have not been proven to be menopause related. So, maybe on balance menopause is not so bad. What seems clear from reviewing the literature and talking with menopausal women is the need for more facts and more sharing of experiences. In 1990, Mansfield and Voda (1991) asked 515 women between the ages of 35 and 55 where they obtained most of their information about menopause. Most respondents cited magazines, popular books, television, and family and friends. A large number knew nothing about their mothers' experience. Physicians and other health providers were infrequently mentioned. Clearly, this is an area where workshops and discussion groups would be a welcome addition to the reading material currently available.

References

Archer, D. F. (1982). Biochemical findings and medical management of the menopause. In A. M. Voda, M. Dinnerstein, & S. R. O'Donnell (Eds.), *Changing perspectives on menopause* (pp. 39-48). Austin: University of Texas Press.

Asso, D. (1983). *The real menstrual cycle*. New York: John Wiley.

Barrett-Connor, E. (1989). *Long term estrogen replacement therapy: What we know and what we need to know.* Paper presented at the meeting of the Society for Menstrual Cycle Research, Salt Lake City, UT.

Barrett-Connor, E., Brown, V., Turner, J., Austin, M., & Criqui, M. H. (1979). Heart disease risk factors and hormone use in postmenopausal women. *Journal of the American Medical Association, 241,* 2167-2169.

Brody, J. E. (1981, July 29). Personal health. *The New York Times,* C17.

Brown, J. K. (1982). A cross-cultural exploration of the end of the childbearing years. In A. M. Voda, M. Dinnerstein, & S. R. O'Donnell (Eds.), *Changing perspectives on menopause* (pp. 51-99). Austin: University of Texas Press.

Budoff, P. W. (1983). *No more hot flashes.* New York: G. P. Putnam's Sons.

Colditz, G. A., Stampfer, M. J., Willett, W. C., Hennekens, C. H., Rosner, B., & Speizer, F. E. (1990, November 28). Prospective study of estrogen replacement therapy and risk of breast cancer in postmenopausal women. *Journal of the American Medical Association, 264*(20), 2648-2653.

Cooke, D. J., & Greene, J. G. (1981). Types of life events in relation to symptoms at the climacterium. *Journal of Psychosomatic Research, 25,* 5-11.

Cowan, G., Warren, L. W., & Young, J. L. (1985). Medical perceptions of menopausal symptoms. *Psychology of Women Quarterly, 9*(1), 3-14.

Cutler, W. B., Garcia, C.-R., & Edwards, D. A. (1983). *Menopause: A guide for women and the men who love them.* New York: W. W. Norton.

Cutler, W. B., Garcia, C.-R., McCoy, N. (1987). Perimenopausal sexuality. *Archives of Sexual Behavior, 16,* 225-234.

Datan, N., Antonovsky, A., & Maoz, B. (1981). *A time to reap.* Baltimore: Johns Hopkins University Press.

Flint, M. (1982). Male and female menopause: A cultural put-on. In A. M. Voda, M. Dinnerstein, & S. R. O'Donnell (Eds.), *Changing perspectives on menopause* (pp. 363-375). Austin: University of Texas Press.

Gannon, L. R. (1985). *Menstrual disorders and menopause.* New York: Praeger.

Gill, J. (1982). Smoking, alcohol, and body mass relationships to early menopause: Implications for risk of cardiovascular disease. In A. M. Voda, M. Dinnerstein, & S. R. O'Donnell (Eds.), *Changing perspectives on menopause* (pp. 160-169). Austin: University of Texas Press.

Kiel, D. (1989). Postmenopausal estrogens and hip fracture. *Geriatric Medicine Today, 8*(2), 46-56.

Leiblum, S., Bachmann, G., Kemmann, E., Colburn, D., & Swartzman, L. (1983). Vaginal atrophy in the postmenopausal woman. *Journal of the American Medical Association, 249*(16), 2195-2198.

Lindquist, O. (1979). Menopausal age in relation to smoking. *Acta Medica Sca dinavica, 205,* 73-77.

Mansfield, P. K., & Voda, A. M. (1991). *From Edith Bunker to the 6 o'clock news: Ho middle-aged women learn about menopause.* Paper presented at the meeting of tl Society for Menstrual Cycle Research, Seattle, WA.

Maoz, B., Dowty, N., Antonovsky, A., & Wijsenbeek, H. (1970). Female attitudes menopause. *Social Psychiatry, 5*(1), 35-40.

Martin, E. (1987). *The woman in the body.* Boston: Beacon.

Masters, W. H., & Johnson, V. E. (1966). *Human sexual response.* Boston: Little, Brow

McCoy, N., Cutler, W., & Davidson, J. M. (1985). Relationship among sexual beha ior, hot flashes, and hormone levels in perimenopausal women. *Archives Sexual Behavior, 14*(5), 385-394.

McKinlay, S., & Jefferys, M. (1974). The menopausal syndrome. *British Journal Preventive and Social Medicine, 28*(2),108-115.

McKinlay, S. M., McKinlay, J. B., & Avis, N. E. (1989, Spring). The Massachuset women's health study: A longitudinal study of the health of mid-aged wome and the epidemiology of the menopause. *Psychology of Women Newsletter Division 35, American Psychological Association, 16*(2), 1, 3.

Morokoff, P. J. (1988). Sexuality in perimenopausal and postmenopausal wome *Psychology of Women Quarterly, 12,* 489-511.

National Women's Health Network. (1989, May/June). Government plans HR study. *National Women's Health Network News, 14*(3), 4.

Neugarten, B. L. (1973). A new look at menopause. In *Psychology Today* (Eds.), *T female experience* (pp. 39-44). New York: Ziff Davis.

Neugarten, B. L., Wood, V., Kraines, R. J., & Loomis, B. (1968). Women's attitud toward menopause. In B. L. Neugarten (Ed.), *Middle age and aging* (pp. 19 200). Chicago: University of Chicago Press.

Polit, D. F., & LaRocco, S. A. (1980). Social and psychological correlates of men pausal symptoms. *Psychosomatic Medicine, 42*(3), 335-345.

Reuben, D. (1969). *Everything you always wanted to know about sex.* New York: Davi McKay.

Sarrel, L. (1988, July/August). Sex and today's menopausal woman. *SIECUS Repo 16*(6), 6-8.

Severne, L. (1982). Psychosocial aspects of the menopause. In A. M. Voda, M. Di nerstein, & S. R. O'Donnell (Eds.), *Changing perspectives on menopause* (p 239-247). Austin: University of Texas Press.

Sherwin, B. B., & Gelfand, M. M. (1987). The role of androgen in the maintenance sexual functioning in oophorectomized women. *Psychosomatic Medicine, 4* 397-409.

Sherwin, B. B., Gelfand, M. M., & Brender, W. (1985). Androgen enhances sexu motivation in females: A prospective, crossover study of sex steroid admii istration in the surgical menopause. *Psychosomatic Medicine, 47,* 339-351.

Theisen, C. C., Mansfield, P. K., Voda, A. M., & Seery, B. (1991). *Predictors of attitud toward menopause among midlife women.* Paper presented at the meeting of tl Society for Menstrual Cycle Research, Seattle, WA.

Treloar, A. E. (1982). Predicting the close of menstrual life. In A. M. Voda, M. Di nerstein, and S. R. O'Donnell (Eds.), *Changing perspectives on menopause* (p 289-304). Austin: University of Texas Press.

Utian, W. H. (1980). *Menopause in modern perspective.* New York: Appleton-Century-Crofts.

van Keep, P. A., & Kellerhals, J. M. (1974). The impact of sociocultural factors on symptom formation. *Psychotherapy and Psychosomatics, 23*, 251-263.

Voda, A. M. (1982). Menopausal hot flash. In A. M. Voda, M. Dinnerstein, & S. R. O'Donnell (Eds.), *Changing perspectives on menopause* (pp. 136-159). Austin: University of Texas Press.

Voda, A. M. (1983). *Coping with the hot flash.* Pamphlet available from Ann M. Voda, Ph.D., Professor of Physiological Nursing, University of Utah College of Nursing, 25 South Medical Drive, Salt Lake City, UT 84112.

Voda, A. M., & Eliasson, M. (1983). Menopause: The closure of menstrual life. In S. Golub (Ed.), *Lifting the curse of menstruation* (pp. 137-156). New York: Haworth.

Walling, M., Anderson, B. L., & Johnson, S. R. (1990). Hormonal replacement therapy for postmenopausal women: A review of sexual outcomes and related gynecologic effects. *Archives of Sexual Behavior, 19*(2), 119-137.

Weideger, P. (1976). *Menstruation and menopause.* New York: Alfred A. Knopf.

Wilson, R. (1966). *Feminine forever.* New York: M. Evans.

Winokur, G., & Cadoret, R. (1975). The irrelevance of the menopause to depressive disease. In E. J. Sachar (Ed.), *Topics in Psychoendocrinology* (pp. 59-66). New York: Grune & Stratton.

Woods, N. F. (1982). Menopausal distress: A model for epidemiologic investigation. In A. M. Voda, M. Dinnerstein, & S. R. O'Donnell (Eds.), *Changing perspectives on menopause* (pp. 220-238). Austin: University of Texas Press.

10

Living With Periods—and Without Them:
Using Current Knowledge to
Help Ourselves and Counsel Others

What do all the facts and theories we have today about menarche, menstruation, and menopause mean for women and men and for the health-care professionals who provide advice? Can we use what we know about menstruation to make women more comfortable with this normal, natural, but often nuisance-ridden event? The answer is "Of course," but not without making some changes: changes in attitudes and increased awareness of what we do and do not know.

The purpose of this chapter is to highlight what we know and to offer those who counsel others an outline for counseling that can be fleshed out, as desired, with details from previous chapters and from other sources. There is some repetition here of material from earlier portions of this book, and references can be found in the earlier chapters.

Some health-care professionals think that because they themselves are comfortable talking about anatomy, physiology, and matters that pertain to sex, others are too. Not so. Particularly with regard to menstruation, negative attitudes and taboos remain with us. Although there is no truth to it at all, one-quarter of Americans think women look different when they menstruate; one-third believe that women should restrict their physical activities during menstruation; and almost everyone believes women are more emotional during menstruation. So long as we continue to treat menstruation as a subject not to be talked about and focus on the unpleasant experiences associated with it, myths and misinformation will prevail—even among well-educated people. When I sent this book out for review, one editor at a major publishing house sent back this response: "I shared this proposal with people here and the response was not enthusiastic. As much as I wish we were ready to be open about the subject, we aren't. Thanks for sending it. I learned a thing or two." Most of the male editors who reviewed the manuscript said far less.

We are becoming more candid in talking about other taboo topics, such as sex and money and death, so why not talk more openly about periods, too? The contradictory messages conveyed by our culture in literature and the media can be changed and reinterpreted. Menstruation can be dealt with more realistically, neither unduly glorified while ignoring the bothersome aspects, nor hidden away as something shameful that must be concealed at all cost. Some progress has been made. For example, there are commercials on television that describe products and discuss absorbency in sanitary napkins or tampons. And research has shown that Americans are overwhelmingly in favor of menstrual education in the schools. However, two-thirds of Americans still believe that menstruation should not be discussed in the office or socially, and more than one-third believe that even at home women should conceal the fact that they are menstruating.

Because of modesty, or societal injunctions, women themselves often contribute to maintaining the silence, but both women and men can learn to be more open in discussing menstruation. Try this experiment: Start talking about periods in a group composed of both women and men just to see what happens. Ask how members of the group learned about periods. Compare it with learning about sexual intercourse. See who thinks that women sometimes use menstruation as an excuse for not doing something. Is the excuse considered legitimate? Pay particular attention to your own reactions to initiating the discussion as well as the responses of the others.

One of the many favorable outgrowths of the women's movement has been more openness in talking about women's health issues. (The finding that women with positive attitudes toward women's rights have more positive attitudes toward menstruation is encouraging too;

Golub & Donnolo, 1980). But to whom do women usually turn for information about menstruation? In my experience, both as a nurse and as a psychologist, women are most likely to ask another woman. They seek out health-care professionals who are women: nurses, physicians, psychologists, and health educators. I know women who have seen a male psychotherapist for years and talked about their deepest fears, yet they have never told him when they were having menstrual pain or that the reason they were avoiding sex this week was that their breasts were too tender to be touched. Gender alone does not guarantee that someone will or will not be receptive to discussion of intimate matters, but as with most things, shared experience makes a difference. It is easier to talk about periods with someone who has had them.

What You Need to Know
and What to Tell Girls at Puberty

The onset of periods, called menarche, is a meaningful event in every woman's life. The body changes associated with puberty affect a girl's psychological and social development, and, conversely, the girl's life experiences influence the physical changes that are occurring as well. Menarche is a stressful time for some girls, less so for others. But we can do a great deal to help girls through this tumultuous phase.

Ideally, girls should learn about menstruation before they have their first period. Although menarche can occur as early as age 8 or as late as age 16, on the average it occurs at about 12 years. Generally, it does not come as a big surprise—at least it shouldn't. It is usually preceded by a growth spurt, breast development, an increase in body hair, and changes in body proportions. The physical transformation from girl to woman takes about four years. Although the body changes gradually during puberty, girls often perceive themselves differently soon after they get their first menstrual period. Changes in body image are among the most dramatic reactions to menarche.

Several factors play a role in determining when and how quickly pubertal development progresses. Heredity is one of them: Identical twin sisters reach menarche within a couple of months of each other. There is also a well-documented link between nutrition and fertility: malnutrition retards growth and delays menarche; heavier girls menstruate at younger ages. Exercise, particularly intensive training such as that seen in ballet dancers and athletes, will delay menarche. But that is not necessarily bad: A weight gain will generally lead to the onset of menstruation.

Girls' reactions to menarche are about one-third negative or fearful, about one-half positive or pleased, and about one-fifth ambivalent. Mixed feelings are common, with girls feeling both "happy and embarrassed" or "excited but scared."

Early-maturing girls, especially those experiencing menarche in sixth grade or before, have a harder time. Unlike boys who are eager for their growth spurt and physical signs of maturity, girls would prefer to mature at the same time as everyone else.

After menarche girls are treated differently by their parents and their peers. They are allowed to act older: wear makeup, shave their legs, date, and do with less sleep. There is also some evidence that girls who begin to menstruate early are more likely to date, pet, and begin premarital coitus sooner than their later-maturing peers.

In spite of educational programs in the schools, misconceptions and negative attitudes about menstruation are very common among early adolescent girls and boys. Parents frequently find themselves tongue-tied when they try to talk about puberty. However, parents are an important and often untapped resource for menstrual education. Sometimes, all parents need is a little help. Two pamphlets written by Peggy Stubbs (1990a, 1990b) are a particularly good resource. *Body Talk for Parents of Girls* is designed to help parents talk to their children about menstruation. A companion pamphlet for the girls themselves is called *Body Talk for Girls Growing Up.*[1] Stubbs suggests some opening lines for starting a conversation, for example, Mom might say, "A friend told me her daughter who is about your age got her first period. It made me start thinking about the physical changes that girls experience as they grow up, and talking with you about them." Or, daughter might ask, "I want to know about getting your period, about why it happens and what it feels like. Can you tell me about it, or get me some books to read?" Suggested readings for both parents and their daughters are included, with special encouragement to the girls to use the library.

Much of the information in Stubbs' pamphlets derives from the ongoing work of a team of researchers, led by Elissa Koff and Jill Rierdan (1990), who are involved in a long-term study at the Wellesley

College Center for Research on Women on adolescent girls' development. When the Wellesley team asked girls who had recently gotten their first periods what they would say if they were going to prepare other, younger girls for their first menstruation, the girls emphasized three points:

1. Information about menstruation should focus on normality, girls need not be embarrassed or worried.
2. Girls should be given the facts about how and why it happens, how long it lasts, how much blood is lost, and about the possibility of cramps.
3. Girls should be given information about menstrual hygiene products and how to use them.

The pamphlet for girls goes one very commendable step beyond the basics. It says that some questions can't be answered. Girls and women have different experiences with menstruation, and no one description applies to everyone. Having periods takes some getting used to and that's alright. Ideally, girls have an ongoing relationship with someone they can talk to about their experiences with menstruation as they happen—ideally, we all do.

Menstruation:
Normal Variations and Possible Problems

Older girls and women have many of the same questions as the premenarcheal girls. "My period comes every 21 days. Am I normal?" "On my second day, sometimes I have to change my pad every two hours. Am I normal?" "My friend's periods last for only three days; mine goes on for a week. Am I normal?" "When I went to college my periods stopped for months. Am I normal?"

Women's knowledge of menstrual life still is generally inadequate and negatively biased. In a recent study of college women's conceptions and misconceptions of the menstrual cycle, 30% of the women sampled could not answer correctly the questions: "What is the cause of menstruation?" and "What is ovulation?" Similarly, one-third reported that they did not know how hormones fluctuate across the cycle. Questions about physical, emotional, and cognitive changes associated with menstruation, ovulation, and menopause elicited a litany of negative responses (Koff, Rierdan, & Stubbs, 1990). There is a clear need for menstrual education—not just for preadolescent girls.

Here are some facts. Although most people think that a normal menstrual cycle is regular and 28 days long, irregularity is common. Most women have cycles that are 25 to 31 days long and, typically, they vary from month to month. Variability is greatest among 15- to 19-year-olds and lowest among 25- to 39-year-olds. About half of women bleed between three and four days; 35% bleed between five and six days.

Menstrual fluid is not pure blood. It is a combination of blood from the lining of the uterus, endometrial cells, and mucus from the cervix and vagina. When women compare it with other blood, they describe menstrual blood as darker in color, thicker in texture, and having a mild but distinctive odor.

Average monthly menstrual blood loss is about one to two fluid ounces, heavier at the start and becoming less as the period proceeds. Women are not good judges of the amount of their menstrual blood loss. Very heavy bleeding may be defined as the need to change a pad or tampon every one to two hours. Very light bleeding may be defined as the need to change once a day.

Almost every body system is affected by changes during the menstrual cycle. These include temperature, cervical mucus, blood pressure, pulse rate, and the amount of urine excreted. Food intake varies: More calories (mostly carbohydrates) are consumed in the latter part of the cycle. A premenstrual weight gain of one to five pounds occurs in about one-third of women. Alcohol tolerance changes at different times of the month. Women hold their liquor best during menstruation and manifest highest blood-alcohol levels when premenstrual. Men do not show cyclical variations in alcohol absorption. All the senses appear to be more acute around the time of ovulation. Women are more sensitive to faint lights and certain odors at this time. And the premenstrual and menstrual phases of the cycle have been linked with increased vulnerability to certain illnesses and allergic reactions. Migraine headaches, for example, frequently occur in the perimenstrual phase of the cycle.

Stress may trigger the early onset of menstruation or cause a missed period. Regular cycles tend to be associated with lower levels of anxiety and life stress. Stress can also affect menstrual cycle length and symptoms.

Exercise is beneficial and often effective in alleviating menstrual symptoms. Some women experience a change in cycle length or amount of blood loss when beginning an exercise program. This is not a cause for concern. However, 7% to 10% of women who engage in frequent vigorous physical activity do lose their menstrual periods. To restore a normal hormonal milieu, they may choose to decrease their exercise, increase their weight, or take oral contraceptives.

There are some women who never experience menstrual pain, perhaps 10%, but most women have painful menstrual periods at least occasionally, some time in their lives. Few consult a physician about it.

Dysmenorrhea generally begins in the early teens and becomes most severe in the late teens and early twenties. Both age and childbirth alter menstrual cramps. There is a decline in both the incidence and severity of menstrual pain after age 25 or 30.

Contrary to the beliefs of many, dysmenorrhea is NOT in a woman's head. No link has been found between attitudes or personality and symptoms. Rather, a 50% to 70% incidence of menstrual symptoms has been found among women all over the world.

Menstrual pain typically starts between 2 and 12 hours before the onset of flow and lasts about 24 to 36 hours. It is generally agreed that dysmenorrhea is somehow related to ovulation and only occurs in ovulatory cycles. In women who suffer from dysmenorrhea, uterine activity is abnormal: Contractions are stronger and more frequent. These women also have higher levels of prostaglandins in their menstrual fluid. (Prostaglandins are hormonelike substances that cause muscle contractions and control the dilation and constriction of blood vessels that are also related to the pain.) Oral contraceptives or one of the prostaglandin synthetase-inhibiting drugs (for example, ibuprofen, which is commonly known as Motrin or Advil) are the treatments of choice for severe primary dysmenorrhea.

Secondary dysmenorrhea is caused by some kind of pelvic pathology, such as infection, tumor, or endometriosis and is discussed more fully in Chapter 7.

Like menstrual cramps, premenstrual symptoms are common and include cramps, backache, bloating, tension, irritability, and changes in eating behavior, among others. A majority of women have some premenstrual symptoms at one time or another. However, only about 5% of women have symptoms so severe that they interfere with work or interpersonal relationships. Symptoms do seem to be related to age, increasing in the late twenties and peaking in the midthirties.

Identifying just what constitutes illness here is tricky. What we think of as premenstrual syndrome (PMS) is more than just having the usual symptoms. However, defining exactly what PMS is has been fraught with controversy, with researchers and clinicians divided about whether or not such a syndrome exists and if so, what criteria are necessary to make the diagnosis. The diagnostic criteria currently in use are contained in an Appendix of the American Psychiatric Association's DSM-III-R (American Psychiatric Association, 1987). Rather than using the popular term—PMS—the disorder is called Late Luteal Phase Dysphoric Disorder, thus using a cycle-phase designation that refers to what is actually happening physiologically and hormonally. For a diagnosis of Late Luteal Phase Dysphoric Disorder to be made, symptoms of "marked affective lability," "persistent and marked anger or irritability," "marked anxiety," or "markedly depressed mood" must be present during the luteal phase and last no longer than a few days after the onset of menstruation. The criteria are confirmed by daily self-ratings during at least two symptomatic cycles. These are very stringent criteria and generally demonstrate that most women have mild to moderate premenstrual symptoms and not a medical disorder.

The cause or causes of PMS (or Late Luteal Phase Dysphoric Disorder) are not known. Current theories focus on hormones or brain chemistry and neurotransmitters. For some women, PMS began shortly after pregnancy; there is a higher incidence among nonusers of oral contraceptives and among women who stop taking birth control pills.

As noted in Chapter 8, there is no panacea for PMS. Progesterone, a controversial treatment highly touted by some clinicians and regarded with great skepticism by others, has been found to be ineffective. In a well-designed placebo-controlled, double-blind crossover study of 168 women receiving progesterone in doses of 400 mg and 800 mg or a placebo, progesterone was found to be no more effective than the placebo treatment (Freeman, Rickels, Sondheimer, & Polansky, 1990).

A surprising number of women thought to have PMS have been found to have an underlying psychiatric disorder. Women with symptoms of depression or anxiety may experience a premenstrual worsening of their symptoms. Two-thirds of women with a history of depression experience a significant premenstrual mood change (Harrison, Rabkin, & Endicott, 1985), but the primary or core disorder may be a depression that may respond to antidepressants and/or psychotherapy (Stone, Pearlstein, & Brown, 1991).

Where does that leave us? A treatment regimen comprised of dietary change, exercise, stress-reducing techniques, supportive psychotherapy, and medications as needed for water retention, anxiety, depression, and pain is often effective for premenstrual symptoms. In addition, keeping a daily record of symptoms and moods for two or three months sometimes leads to an awareness that symptoms occur at varying times of the month and may help focus attention on other disturbing things in women's lives, such as work or marital problems, that are not cycle related. Appropriate attribution can reduce fear and anxiety and may lead to effective problem solving as well.

Premenstrual symptoms are a political issue as well as a medical one. The symptoms that most concern women are depression, anxiety and irritability. These do not jibe with our stereotypic image of the ideal woman: nice, kind, caring. Some women, and the men in their lives, label the feelings they have premenstrually as signs of illness, providing an excuse for behaving in ways that are unacceptable at other times. The *Newsletter of the Society for Menstrual Cycle Research* had a cartoon that rings true. Two women are talking

> "I told him I felt like I was doing everything—the cooking, driving, child care—plus, of course, my own work. I thought he should help more.
>
> "What did he say?
>
> "He wanted to know if my period was coming."

Obviously, the down side of using premenstrual symptoms as an explanation for women's behavior is that it denies our right to be legitimately angry and explains away our complaints as just being "that time of the month" rather than taking what we have to say seriously. On a broader, societal level, some believe that PMS has become a media event because labeling someone as irrational and blaming it on menstrual cyclicity keeps women in their place.

The body strives for homeostasis but tolerates some variation: There is a range for what is normal, and changes occur over the course of a day as well as over the menstrual cycle. Women generally accept changes in their skin or weight with relative equanimity. But the mood changes—which not all women experience—bother some women a lot. How to explain the contradictory mood research findings? My best judgment at this time is that positive moods are heightened in the ovulatory phase of the cycle (women describe themselves as "warm" and "peaceable" midcycle), and anxiety and depression increase during the luteal phase and the first two days of menstruation. However, for most (not all) women the magnitude of these mood changes is small. Life stress and even the day of the week may have more of an impact on mood than menstrual-cycle phase. It is interesting that in one study a comparison group of males described a more stable existence, but they reported less positive moods and fewer pleasant activities than the females. So, maybe the ups are worth the downs.

What effect do mood changes have on behavior? Primatologists in Africa have found that in the days just before the onset of menstruation, female baboons seek solitude, spending more time in the trees, and initiating fewer social contacts than usual. So there appears to be a certain "menstrual quietude," which seems to exist in women, too. Women are less likely to initiate conversation or volunteer to participate in a psychological experiment during the premenstrual or menstrual phase of the cycle. Research shows that daily reports of women's sexual activity fit this same pattern. Researchers report postmenstrual and midcycle highs in sexual activity.

However, women's variability does not affect productivity. Although 35% of Americans believe that women's ability to think is impaired by menstruation, and 26% believe women cannot function as well at work when they menstruate, actual tests of women at different phases of the cycle, using all sorts of complex measures, almost always show no cycle-phase effects. This tendency to see menstruation as debilitating and the expectation that it will have an adverse impact on women's lives and activities persist in spite of more than 75 years of research demonstrating no impairment!

Menopause as a Rite of Passage

Most women will live a third or more of their lives after menopause. Yet menopause is frequently anticipated by women with ambivalence. On the one hand, there is relief at getting rid of the nuisance aspects of menstruation; on the other, there is concern about growing old, getting fat, and getting hot flashes, among other things.

Many women wonder when menopause will occur for them. Contrary to popular beliefs, there is no relationship between age at menarche and age at menopause. The mean age is 50.5 years, with a normal range from 41 to 59 years. Early menopause is associated, among other things, with smoking, and even with having smoked in the past. Menopause is later in heavier women and taller women, as well as in women who are currently married as opposed to those who are widowed, divorced, or unmarried.

An interesting relationship has been found between age at menopause and cycle length. In a recently concluded long-term study from the National Institute of Environmental Health Sciences in North Carolina, women who had shorter cycles (averaging less than 26 days when they were between 20 and 35 years old) reached menopause an average of 1.4 years earlier than women whose cycle length was 26 to 32 days, and 2.2 years sooner than women with cycles averaging 33 days or more. Moreover, the more children a woman had, the later her menopause. Women who had five or more children reached menopause about one year later than those who had never had children (Hodge, 1990). One can speculate that menopause is delayed if ova are conserved by a long cycle or pregnancies.

When asked what the worst thing about menopause was, various studies found the largest number of women saying, "Not knowing what to expect." Despite the worries of women about losing their minds during menopause, studies over the last 20 years have consistently shown no differences in depressive symptoms between women of all age groups and women during menopause. However, menopausal changes do occur—in women's bodies and in their lives.

Does menopause represent a loss? For some it does, for others perhaps not. Certainly the menopausal years represent a time of change. There are some losses. Children leave home; parents and other older relatives become ill or die; some women are widowed. Confronted with no longer looking young—a major disadvantage for women in our culture—the menopausal woman must come to grips with a new body image. But there are also gains. There is more time for self: for work or for play. There is an opportunity to develop or renew intimate relationships with one's spouse or other friends, especially if children are no longer around making demands. The feelings accompanying these life changes are not caused by menopause. Rather, menopause, with or without its discomforts, is part of this transitional period.

Responses to menopause are shaped in part by the cultures in which women grow up. Research shows that feelings of well-being are greatest when there is a good fit between what women expect their lives to be like and what actually happens. For example, modern women enjoy the opportunities to seek satisfaction outside the home, while the traditional woman's life provides her with a central role in the household and the comfort of the familiar. It is women caught in a time of rapid cultural change—women who do not feel that they belong in either niche—who seem to have most difficulty adapting to menopause.

In the United States, the impact of menopause is affected by socioeconomic status and vocation. More advantaged women have fewer problems, and work provides an additional, favorable influence. In the lower socioeconomic group, housewives appear to have more symptoms than women with jobs, but those women who are employed experience more stress than their more advantaged peers. Nonetheless, in postmenopause, regardless of socioeconomic status, having a job seems to add to a woman's satisfaction with life.

How does the menopause manifest itself? The first signs of approaching menopause are hot flashes and changes in menstrual bleeding. Frequency and duration of periods may become irregular: some women experience shorter cycles, others longer cycles, and some a short cycle followed by a longer one. Bleeding patterns may change, with amount of flow diminishing or increasing. Unpredictability is the rule. However, persistent bleeding or any unexplained bleeding that occurs six months after the apparent cessation of periods is cause for concern. Postmenopausal bleeding may be a sign of uterine pathology requiring treatment and should be reported to a physician.

By the time they are near menopause, most women have heard about hot flashes, even if they have not yet experienced any. They are the most common symptom experienced by menopausal women—about 75% of women have them. A hot flash is a sudden sensation of intense heat, sometimes followed by a flushing of the skin and profuse sweating. Some women experience a variety of other unpleasant body sensations along with the hot flash, including: palpitations, lightheadedness, feelings of suffocation, and nausea. Most hot flashes last about three minutes. They usually start in the head or neck and spread down. They may be mild, moderate, or severe, and there is a wide variation in the number of hot flashes experienced. Sometimes there appears to be a trigger, such as spicy food, coffee, tea, alcohol, heat, and stress. A recent laboratory study offers additional confirmation that stress does indeed increase the frequency of hot flashes (Swartzman, Edelberg, & Kemmann, 1990). As with dysmenorrhea, hot flashes are real, physiological events—they are not merely in the head. The difference between women who complain about hot flashes and those who do not has nothing to do with stoicism, it has to do with the severity of the hot flashes.

Other physical changes associated with menopause include a loss of skin thickness and moisture, increased sensitivity to the sun, decrease in the density of scalp and body hair follicles, and, perhaps most troublesome, thinning of the lining of the vagina and urinary tract. The vaginal changes accompanying menopause may lead to more frequent vaginal infections. A change in vaginal Ph contributes to the problem. During the reproductive years the vaginal Ph is acidic, which discourages growth of most of the harmful bacteria and fungi. When estrogen levels are low, the vagina becomes more alkaline and hence more prone to infection. Mild vinegar douches may be advisable to help restore the proper Ph balance, or a physician may recommend a medicated douche or medication to target a specific organism. If a woman has a vaginal infection, she should see a physician and have the organism identified, usually by culture, before treatment is begun (Nachtigall & Heilman, 1986). However, if the condition is recurrent, women often know what medication works for them.

The usual good hygiene advice applies in preventing vaginal and urinary infections: bathing, cotton underwear, urinating before and after intercourse, wiping from front to back after a bowel movement to prevent intestinal bacterial from migrating to the vagina or urethra, and using a condom when one's sexual partner is new or hygiene is uncertain. If there is vaginal dryness, using a sterile, water-soluble jelly, such as K-Y Jelly, for lubrication during intercourse prevents irritation. (Estrogen creams or Replens, a vaginal gel, may also be used to counter vaginal dryness.)

Hormone replacement therapy is a subject of controversy, and it is hard to get good advice. Many gynecologists advocate its use to prevent osteoporosis, a condition in which the bones lose calcium, become more porous and fragile, and have a greater likelihood of breaking. Most at risk for serious osteoporosis are thin, fair-skinned, small-boned women who have not had children, but it can occur in any woman. Smoking and heavy alcohol consumption add to the risk. However, there may be ways other than hormone replacement for minimizing osteoporosis, for example, adequate nutrition and weight-bearing exercises, such as walking, are excellent preventive measures.

Hormone replacement therapy will restore vaginal tissues to a less vulnerable state as well as alleviating hot flashes, night sweats, and vaginal thinning. However, as noted in Chapter 9, there are risks that must be weighed in making the decision to take hormones. To counter the increased risk of endometrial cancer that was found to occur when estrogen alone was given, it is common practice today to give both estrogen and progesterone in a pattern mimicking the natural menstrual cycle. This seems to work, but women with an intact uterus must be monitored closely. Other adverse reactions to the hormones include: breakthrough bleeding, premenstrual-like symptoms (breast tenderness, bloating), and headaches (including migraines). Women need to be aware of the possible side effects so that they can report symptoms to their doctor, should they occur. Sometimes simply changing the dosage of one or both of the hormones alleviates the problem. Also, some women experience an increase in blood pressure, so this, too, should be monitored.

The benefits of hormone replacement therapy include: avoiding serious osteoporosis with consequent reduced risk of fractures; relief of hot flashes; prevention of vaginal thinning; and possible reduction in the risk of heart disease. Risks include: a possible increase in the frequency of endometrial or breast cancer, and gall bladder problems. Also, there are some people who cannot take estrogens because of pre-existing medical conditions, namely, certain kinds of cancer, liver disease, high blood pressure, or blood clots associated with previous use of estrogen.

Generally, women do not perceive menopause as a disease or serious problem. In making their decisions regarding the use of hormone replacement therapy, most women, after getting professional advice, still need to weigh the benefits against possible barriers for them. Unfortunately, getting accurate information is not always easy, and women often depend upon women's magazines, where the reporting is sometimes good and sometimes not so good. For those interested in comprehensive coverage of this topic, the National

Women's Health Network publication, *Taking Hormones and Women's Health: Choices, Risks, Benefits*, presents a balanced appraisal of the risks and benefits involved in taking hormones. (National Women's Health Network, 1989). Obviously, there are still areas of uncertainty, and more information needs to be sought and gathered.

Where Do We Go From Here?

Menstrual cycle research has grown in quantity and quality over the last 20 years. There is an increased recognition of the need for prospective rather than retrospective research, more careful delineation of cycle phase, hormone measurement if possible, and the use of male comparison groups. But we still have a way to go. We need more qualitative as well as quantitative research, more longitudinal studies, greater attention to individual differences, and special efforts to include diverse populations of women as research subjects. Crucial in evaluating research results is the continued recognition of the fact that a statistically significant difference of small magnitude may have theoretical importance without having any clinically meaningful effect on an individual.

Topics of interest to researchers have changed. Earlier research, for the most part, utilized the medical model, concentrating on pathology, symptoms, and problems. While interest in alleviating discomfort remains important, attention is also being focused on other aspects of the menstrual experience, and different questions are being asked. For example, there is a push to find out what most women want to know, namely, "What is normal?"

Students often ask for research ideas, so there is a list in the Appendix that targets a few possibilities, many of them culled from free-associating and brain storming at Society for Menstrual Cycle Research meetings or from the undergraduate psychology of women and seminar courses I teach. Of course, some research requires sophisticated laboratory equipment, other research demands personnel for data collection and analysis, and all researchers need financial support. However, there are studies that can be done with minimal funds, even by undergraduates (see Appendix: Research Ideas).

The aim of this book is to present a broad overview of what is currently known about menstruation, including cultural, biological, and psychological advances in menstrual-cycle research and implications of this knowledge for women and men. The menstrual cycle—whether present or absent—influences women's bodies and behavior. An awareness of what is normal and shared by others is not only reassuring, but necessary, enabling women to foster their own health and well-being and to counter the ever-present claims that women are physically, emotionally, and intellectually handicapped during menstruation. In the past, menstruation was viewed as a pathological process because women were seen as different—that is, different from the male physicians and scientists investigating it. That is no longer true. As our attitudes toward women change, so does the meaning of menstruation.

Of course, we could take it a step further, turn a negative into a positive, and see periods as a source of strength. One of the new women comics, Elayne Boosler, does a PMS routine that is pro-woman. In Ms. Boosler's fantasy world, a woman president *with raging hormones* is a masterful power broker, capable of bullying a terrorist into giving up his demands. Imagine your president threatening, "Taking hostages on a day when I'm retaining water? This is going to go very badly for you" (Hopkins, 1990).

Note

1. Body Talk pamphlets may be ordered from the Publications Department, Center for Research on Women, Wellesley College, Wellesley, MA 02181. Two pamphlets (*For Girls Growing Up* and *For Parents of Girls*) cost $8.00. Two pamphlets (*For Boys Growing Up* and *For Parents of Boys*) are also available and cost $8.00.

References

American Psychiatric Association. (1987). *Diagnostic and statistical manual of mental disorders* (3rd rev. ed.). Washington, DC: American Psychiatric Association.

Freeman, E., Rickels, K., Sondheimer, S. J., & Polansky, M. (1990, July 18). Ineffectiveness of progesterone suppository treatment for premenstrual syndrome. *Journal of the American Medical Association, 264*, 349-353.

Golub, S., & Donnolo, E. (1980). *Attitudes toward menstruation: A comparison of mothers and daughters*. Unpublished manuscript.

Harrison, W. M., Rabkin, J. G., & Endicott, J. (1985). Psychiatric evaluation of premenstrual changes. *Psychosomatics, 26,* 789-799.

Hodge, M. (1990, July). Predicting menopause. *Longevity, 2*(9), 74.

Hopkins, E. (1990, September 16). Who's laughing now? Women. *The New York Times,* A37.

Koff, E., Rierdan, J., & Stubbs, M. L. (1990). Conceptions and misconceptions of the menstrual cycle. *Women & Health, 16*(3/4), 119-136.

Nachtigall, L., & Heilman, J. R. (1986). *Estrogen: The facts can change your life.* New York: Harper & Row.

National Women's Health Network. (1989). *Taking hormones and Women's health.* Available from the National Women's Health Network, 1325 G Street, N.W., Washington, D.C., 20005.

Stone, A. B., Pearlstein, T. B., & Brown, W. A. (1991). Fluoxetine in the treatment of late luteal phase dysphoric disorder. *Journal of Clinical Psychiatry, 52*(7), 290-293.

Stubbs, M. L. (1990a). *Body talk for parents of girls.* Wellesley, MA: Center for Research on Women.

Stubbs, M. L. (1990b). *Body talk for girls growing up.* Wellesley, MA: Center for Research on Women.

Swartzman, L. C., Edelberg, R., & Kemmann, E. (1990). Impact of stress on objectively recorded menopausal hot flushes and on flush report bias. *Health Psychology, 9*(5), 529-545.

Appendix:
Research Ideas

These research suggestions are loosely categorized as health-related, psychology and education, and basic research; some may already be "work in progress." Consider them scattered seeds rather than a presentation of tightly structured research plans. I hope some of them will grow.

Health-Related Research

DIET

There is some new evidence of a relationship between diet and mood and a need for research evaluating the efficacy of dietary change on premenstrual symptoms.

EXERCISE

What are the effects of different kinds of exercise programs, that is, aerobic and/or strength-conditioning, on: stress reduction, menstrual symptoms, hot flashes, and osteoporosis (in normally cycling, peri- and postmenopausal women, with and without hormone replacement therapy).

TAMPONS

Do women who use tampons experience more vaginal and/or urinary infections? Is there an effect on pap smears. Subjects should include both normally menstruating women, perimenopausal women, and postmenopausal women on hormone replacement therapy who are experiencing monthly bleeding. The effects of deodorant versus nondeodorant products should also be explored.

SYMPTOMS: LONGITUDINAL VIEW

Is there a relationship between early and later menstrual symptom severity? Are women who experience intense dysmenorrhea as teenagers more likely to experience severe premenstrual symptoms in their thirties and later, and are they more likely to have onerous menopausal symptoms.

DEPRESSION

Findings are reasonably consistent: Depressed women are more likely to experience premenstrual mood changes. Instead of targeting menstrual symptoms as the object of therapy, how about treating the depression? One possibility is using group or individual psychotherapy (with or without antidepressants) to increase marital and work satisfaction; then assess how effective treatment of the depression is in ameliorating symptoms of menstrual distress.

MENSTRUAL HEALTH EDUCATION

Develop and evaluate educational programs and support groups in schools and women's health centers. What coping mechanisms do women use? Look at the effect of knowledge and consequent changes in attitudes and behavior as well as symptoms. Assessing the incidence of urinary and vaginal infections requiring medical treatment before and after the educational programs would provide one objective measure of efficacy; the amount of analgesic medication taken for menstrual symptoms would be another. Also, what new coping skills are acquired? For example, knowing that many women experience water retention and weight gain as premenstrual symptoms may lead to dietary change (reducing salt intake) or simply greater acceptance of the symptom as something that is time-limited and not serious.

SEX AND MENSTRUAL SYMPTOMS

Some women report that orgasm ameliorates dysmenorrhea. Does regular sexual activity have any effect on menstrual and menopausal symptoms?

FERTILITY

Patterns of life-long sexual activity may affect fertility. In one study, a delayed age at first coitus was found in a group of infertile women (Cutler, Garcia, & Krieger, 1980). This study needs to be replicated: Do women who experience first coitus within seven years of menarche have fewer fertility problems?

SEX AND MENOPAUSE

How are sexual desire, arousal, and activity affected by menopause (natural or surgical)? Important: Note other sources of stress that commonly occur at the same time of life, such as the sequelae of aging, concurrent illness, retirement, loss of parents or spouse, changes in the nuclear family as children leave and focus on their own new families. Physical, psychological, and sociocultural factors are all likely to play a role here.

BLEEDING PATTERNS AND CYCLE LENGTH

Longitudinal study of changes in menstrual bleeding patterns—amount of bleeding and cycle length at different ages, that is, 20-29, 30-39, 40-49. What constitutes dysfunctional uterine bleeding?

SMOKING

What is the effect of smoking on menstrual symptoms? Do smokers have more severe dysmenorrhea or less severe premenstrual tension?

The same questions might be asked about the use of alcohol or other chemicals.

SPECIAL POPULATIONS

Explore the unique needs of blind, deaf, disabled, or hospitalized women, or women with chronic illness who may experience menstruation and menopause differently. There is a need for information to help women with diabetes, multiple sclerosis, thyroid disorders, and hypertension.

DRUG EFFICACY

Are there variations in drug efficacy during different phases of the cycle? Which drugs and when?

MEDICAL TREATMENT

How does menstrual-cycle phase influence women's responses to medication, surgery, radiation, and other medical treatments? In one study, avoiding breast-tumor removal during cycle Days 1-6 and 21-28 appeared to enhance the likelihood of patients being disease-free for five years by 27% (Myer, 1991). Can this be replicated? Does cycle-phase influence the efficacy of other treatments, such as chemotherapy, or even the success of oral surgery?

BLOOD DONORS

Yes, estrogen protects against heart disease, but does the bleeding episode play a role, too. Do regular blood donors have fewer heart attacks?

TEEN PREGNANCY

Adolescent pregnancy is fraught with risks to both mother and baby. Are early-maturing girls, whose psychological development may not be similarly advanced, at higher risk of getting pregnant? It seems obvious, but let's find out and perhaps target this group for special educational programs aimed at prevention.

Psychology and Education

INDIVIDUAL AND GROUP DIFFERENCES

There are religious and cultural differences in women's experiences with menstruation. Are there also regional, occupational, age-related, or other differences? Are marital status or the number and ages of children relevant? What about sexual preference? In order to establish what is "normal," it is important to find out how the experiences and beliefs of various subgroups differ.

QUALITATIVE RESEARCH

Case studies and interviews with open-ended questions and diaries, exploring the menstrual experience across a woman's lifetime. Posing questions such as: How did you learn about menstruation? What was your first period like? Did you celebrate in any way? What is the most positive or funny experience you have ever had with menstruation? Do you have any problems prior to or during your menstrual periods and if so, what do you do about them? Do they interfere with your everyday activities? What is your attitude toward sex during menstruation? Are your sexual feelings different around the time of your period? What do you want to know about menstruation or menopause?

MOOD, PERSONALITY, AND BEHAVIOR

How is family life (for example, as assessed by recording dinner-table conversations over a two- or three-month period) influenced by cycle-related mood and personality changes? Content analysis of recordings looking for changes in level of participation in conversation as well as expressions of affection, sexual interest, nurturing, laughter, playfulness, lability, aggression, and anger.

EMOTIONAL LABILITY

Are women more labile during the premenstrual (late luteal) phase of the cycle? Films or other mood induction techniques could be used to induce a mood change, with each woman serving as her own

control. (Once the methodology is worked out, this would be a
interesting question to explore with adolescent subjects.)

EXPECTATIONS REGARDING WORK
OR INTELLECTUAL PERFORMANCE

When asked, women consistently evaluate their performance dur
ing the premenstrual phase of the cycle or during menstruation a
less adequate than at other times of the month. Objective measure
show no such decrement. How can women's expectations of negativ
behavior be changed? Do courses in women's studies, such as th
psychology of women or women's health, effect such a change? Ar
personality variables, such as achievement motivation, relevant?

RESPONSES TO FRUSTRATION
AND IRRITABILITY

Women often say that irritability is one of their most bothersom
symptoms. Does it affect work performance? Instead of looking fc
cycle-related cognitive changes where meaningful differences hav
not been found, how about studying frustration tolerance as mea
sured by persistence at a task. If their symptoms are made salient, d
women try harder when experiencing premenstrual or menstrua
distress? (Replicate and build on Rodin's [1976] attribution research

SLEEP AND DREAMS

How are sleep and dreaming affected by the menstrual cycle
Record cycle phase, day of the week, important life events, drear
content, and associations. Note: color, action, anxiety, sex, aggressior
dependency, and achievement. A dream diary would be useful her

ATTITUDES

Do women's attitudes toward women and women's roles influenc
attitudes toward menstruation? What is the role of self-esteem? (Rep
licate and build on previous research [Golub & Donnolo, 1980].)

ASSERTIVENESS TRAINING

Evaluation of the effects of an assertiveness-training course on premenstrual symptoms, particularly anger, depression, and anxiety.

BLEEDING

How does amount of bleeding affect feelings and behavior? It is important to define light, moderate, and heavy bleeding in terms of number of tampons or napkins used. (Replicate and build on Paige's [1971] study.) How do young girls perceive menstrual flow, that is, what does it mean to them?

MENARCHE

What would constitute a positive rite of passage for girls at menarche?

MENARCHE AND FAMILY RELATIONSHIPS

What is the impact of menarche on mother-daughter, father-daughter, and sibling relationships? What changes are seen in amount of contact, sharing of feelings, joint or group activities? What is the effect of birth order, if any, or of parents' life stage? (This could build on the research reported by Ullman [1985].)

MENSTRUAL EDUCATION

What are the pros and cons of single-sex versus coed preparation for menstruation programs?

EDUCATION FOR MENOPAUSE

What do women want to know about menopause? Where do they get their information? How do they make decisions about hormone replacement therapy?

SURVEY OF POSTMENOPAUSAL WOMEN

What positive changes have you experienced in your life since menopause? Did you have any problems in going through meno pause? How long did the problems last? And, to confirm anecdotal information, are you aware of any changes in your sexual desire or responses to sexual stimulation?

MENOPAUSAL SYMPTOMS

Do women who have more symptoms have more difficulty talking about menopause? Explore feelings of shame and loss of control. To whom do women turn for support?

BODY IMAGE AND MENOPAUSE

Body image changes dramatically at menarche. Is there a change in body image at menopause as well? Does hormone replacement treatment have any effect? And is there a change in men's body image at the same age?

MENOPAUSE AND MARITAL STRESS

Does menopause cause marital stress, or does marital stress cause an earlier and more troublesome menopause? And how do you separate the menopausal factor from other concomitants of aging?

STRESS REDUCTION AND HOT FLASHES

Teach menopausal women stress-reduction and relaxation tech niques and assess the effect on the frequency and severity of their hot flashes.

Basic Research

NEUROENDOCRINOLOGY

Further identification of hormonal and neurohormonal cycle related changes. Look at individual differences, perhaps using hormone and neurotransmitter challenge studies, that is, give estrogen and monitor LH levels to assess neurotransmitter receptor function.

DIET AND NEUROTRANSMITTERS

Dietary effects on the brain and on levels of neurotransmitters. How are these effects influenced by the menstrual cycle?

INDIVIDUAL DIFFERENCES IN HORMONAL PATTERNS

Longitudinal studies looking at hormonal changes over a menstrual lifetime in the same women.

TAMPONS AND VAGINAL ANATOMY AND PHYSIOLOGY

Effects of tampons on vaginal tissue.

VAGINAL MICROBIOLOGY

Changes in vaginal microorganisms in different cycle phases and at different times of life. Are there menopausal changes?

BIOLOGICAL RHYTHMS

What are the interactive effects of circadian rhythms and the menstrual cycle?

MIGRAINE HEADACHES

What is the relationship between migraine headaches and hormone levels? How does one reconcile menstrual and menopausal migraine with premarin-induced migraine?

GENETIC FACTORS

Twin and family studies to explore similarities and differences in symptoms, bleeding patterns, and cycle length and variability.

HORMONES AND SEXUAL DESIRE

What roles do estrogen and testosterone play vis-à-vis sexual arousal? Is there a relationship in women between high estrogen and/or androgen levels and high energy/activity levels?

PHEROMONES

Further exploration of the effects of male pheromones on cycle length, fertility, and hot flashes.

HORMONE REPLACEMENT THERAPY

How can it be made safer? How can women at greater risk for the development of serious adverse reactions be identified? And what about alternatives—other drugs to ameliorate hot flashes?

OSTEOPOROSIS

Development and evaluation of new drugs (such as etidronate disodium, didronel) or therapeutic regimens for decreasing osteoporosis in postmenopausal women without the use of estrogen.

Product Improvement

Brainstorming can be a very effective technique. Witness the results of one session: At a Society for Menstrual Cycle Research workshop a group of researchers was asked, "How would you design a better tampon or sanitary napkin?" Participants said the product should be environmentally sound, convenient, comfortable, aesthetic, healthy, thin and superabsorbent, and available at a reasonable cost. Then they got creative and suggested: a pad shaped like a bicycle seat, sani-undies, different colors (to match your mood), designer boxes that could be left out rather than hidden away in a cabinet, and perhaps prizes or fortunes could be attached (Golub, 1991).

For more ideas see Barbara Sommer's paper, "Menstrual Cycle Research: Yesterday, Today and Tomorrow" (Sommer, 1981).

References

Cutler, W. B., Garcia, C.-R., & Krieger, A. M. (1980). Sporadic sexual behavior and menstrual cycle length in women. *Hormones and Behavior, 14*(1), 63-172.

Golub, S. (1991). "Trailblazing: New directions in menstrual cycle research." Workshop at the meeting of the Society for Menstrual Cycle Research, Seattle, WA.

Golub, S., & Donnolo, E. (1980). *Attitudes toward menstruation: A comparison of mothers and daughters*. Unpublished manuscript.

Myer, K. (1991, April 18). Surgery success tied to menses. *Medical Tribune*, 24.

Paige, K. E. (1971). "The curse": Possible antecedents of menstrual distress. In A. Harrison (Ed.), *Explorations in psychology*. Belmont, CA: Brooks/Cole.

Rodin, J. (1976). Menstruation, reattribution, and competence. *Journal of Personality and Social Psychology, 3*(3), 345-353.

Sommer, B. (1981). Menstrual cycle research: Yesterday, today and tomorrow. In P. Komnenich, M. McSweeney, J. A. Noack, & Sister N. Elder (Eds.), *The Menstrual Cycle* (Vol. 2, pp. 193-199). New York: Springer.

Ullman, K. (1985). *Impact of menarche on family relationships*. Paper presented at the meeting of the Society for Menstrual Cycle Research, Galveston, TX.

Index

268

About the Author

Sharon Golub is Professor of Psychology at the College of New Rochelle and Adjunct Professor of Psychiatry at New York Medical College. A Fellow of the American Psychological Association and the American Psychological Society, past-president of the Society for Menstrual Cycle Research, and former editor of *Women & Health*, she is recognized as an authority on the menstrual cycle.

She has written and presented papers on various aspects of menstruation to both lay and professional audiences, has served as media spokesperson on menstrual cycle related issues appearing on both radio and television, and she has been quoted in such publications as *The New York Times, The New York Times Magazine, Discover,* and *Glamour.*

Dr. Golub is editor of two books about menstruation, *Menarche* (which won the 1984 Distinguished Publication Award of the Association for Women in Psychology as well as an *American Journal of Nursing* Book of the Year Award) and *Lifting the Curse of Menstruation.* Also, she has edited three other books pertaining to women's health, contributed chapters for 11 books edited by others, and published 35 papers in professional journals.

In addition to her teaching and research, Dr. Golub is a licensed psychologist and maintains a private practice in Harrison, NY. She brings to her work on menstruation an unusual combination of scholarly expertise and clinical experience.